PENNSYLVANIA COLLEGE OF TECHNOLOGY LIBR

D1466888

Date Due

MAY 1 1 2004		
FEB 2 7 2006		
MAY 0 8 2006		
2007 8 0 MAY		
MAY 0 8 2007		
OCT 1 6 2007		

BRODART, CO.   Cat. No. 23-233-003   Printed in U.S.A.

Autism and Life
in the Community

AUTISM AND LIFE IN THE COMMUNITY

SUCCESSFUL INTERVENTIONS FOR BEHAVIORAL CHALLENGES

by

Marcia Datlow Smith, Ph.D.
*Community Services for
Autistic Adults and Children
Rockville, Maryland*

·P·A·U·L·H·
BROOKES
PUBLISHING CO.

Baltimore • London • Toronto • Sydney

LIBRARY

Pennsylvania College
of Technology

One College Avenue
Williamsport, PA 17701-5799

Paul H. Brookes Publishing Co.
P.O. Box 10624
Baltimore, Maryland 21285-0624

Copyright © 1990 by Paul H. Brookes Publishing Co., Inc.
All rights reserved.

Typeset by The Composing Room of Michigan, Grand Rapids, Michigan.
Manufactured in the United States of America by
St. Mary's Press, Hollywood, Maryland.

Work on which this book is based was in part funded by grants
#G008435019 and #G0088430115 from the U.S. Department of
Education. However, the opinions expressed herein do not necessarily
reflect the position or policy of the U.S. Department of Education.

Library of Congress Cataloging-in-Publication Data

Smith, Marcia Datlow, 1951–
    Autism and life in the community : successful interventions for
behavioral challenges / by Marcia Datlow Smith.
        p.   cm.
    :ludes bibliographical references.
    3N 1-55766-035-2
    Autism—Patients—Rehabilitation.   2. Behavior therapy.
    cial skills—Study and teaching.   I. Title.
    3.A88S65   1990
    39'8203—dc20   89-36954
                                                        CIP

RC
553
.A88
S65
1990

CONTENTS

Helen's Day
Evaluating Progress
Outcome

ACKNOWLEDGMENTS

First, I would like to thank the many people both with and without autism at Community Services for Autistic Adults and Children, in Rockville, Maryland, who shared their knowledge and provided the inspiration for this work. Special appreciation is due Patricia Juhrs, Jane Salzano, and Susan Goodman for their continuing support. Ronald Belcher, Susan Brown, and Doreen Coleman are acknowledged for the wisdom they shared through years of achieving community adjustment for people with severe autism. For faithfully keeping and providing years of data, I would like to thank Cathy Fowler, Erin Murphy, Karla Nabors, Colin Brown, Annalee Feldman, John Horne, Jan Miller; and thanks to Derek Berrian for graphing the data.

The following individuals deserve special praise for contributing to my understanding of autism: Sam, Marilyn, Brian, Danny, Frank, John, Arnold, Tim, Mary, Nadia, Charlie, Kenny, Lewis, Ellen, Geri, Donald, and Bill.

I would like to express appreciation to Dr. Donald Pumroy for the behavioral education that he provided, and to my parents, Lita and Gerald Datlow, for their general helpfulness.

A special debt of gratitude is due Paul Wehman for his encouragement and invaluable help with this book.

INTRODUCTION

Helen is a 23-year-old woman with autism and moderate mental retardation. She has lived in a state institution since age 3. She has good language skills, but her speech is not like the speech of the other patients. The words are right, but the rhythm is wrong. Helen's main problem is not her mental retardation, nor her unusual speech melody. Rather, it is her behavior. Helen has a variety of dramatic behaviors for which she is treated with high doses of medication. Helen screams, rips her clothes, destroys property, and scratches herself. Occasionally, she strikes out at others by kicking, scratching, and pulling hair. The staff at the institution do not hold much hope for Helen. Their goals for Helen are to keep her sedated.

Gregory is a 22-year-old man with autism who has no spoken language. He lives at home with his parents. Gregory has a number of peculiarities to which his parents have adjusted. Meals must follow a certain pattern and consist of a limited range of items, and furniture must be arranged in a prescribed manner. Gregory's parents have learned that if Gregory is twirling a piece of string or watching a certain television show, all concerned are better off if he is left alone. When Gregory experiences unexpected changes or demands, he goes into severe, high-intensity head banging.

Fortunately, Gregory's parents have helpful neighbors who are always available to provide emergency assistance should Gregory become upset. The local programs for people with mental retardation cannot handle Gregory. The only alternative is the state institution, several hours away. Gregory's parents are adamant about keeping him at home. They feel that caring for Gregory at home is as natural as caring for any of their other children. Their greatest fear, however, is what will become of Gregory after they are gone.

People with autism often have mental retardation. However, it is not their mental retardation that has kept them segregated from the mainstream of society. Many people with autism also have severe deficits in language and communication. Again, it is not the lack of speech or the unusual speech patterns that are responsible for the dearth of services.

What has kept women like Helen and men like Gregory out of the mainstream of society, and even out of the service delivery system for people with handicaps, is the dramatic behaviors that are associated with their autism. The intervention procedures that have been popular for people with autism do not make management of the syndrome appealing to even the most committed service providers.

The purpose of this book is to provide a comprehensive treatment of the topic of behavior management for people with autism. The process for assessing behavior problems and for developing intervention plans in integrated community settings is covered.

All of the strategies recommended in this book have been used with people with autism by this author over a 10-year period. These strategies have been used successfully with more than 70 people with autism who have achieved long-term adjustment to living and working in integrated community settings.

The strategies recommended by this author have proven useful in achieving community integrated adjustment for people with autism. Thus, the foundation for recommending procedures is empirical and clinical, not theoretical.

The strategies presented in this book were developed and used in the context of a community-integrated school and residential and vocational programs for individuals with autism. The residential program provided small group placement, two to four per house, with supervision. The vocational program, a supported employment program, placed individuals with autism in competitive employment in the community, in groups of two, under the supervision of job coaches.

The behavior management strategies were developed and implemented in these contexts. These strategies have been successful. However, the reader must be aware that they were successful within the framework of a program that provided meaningful, functional, integrated, work and living situations.

The cases and data presented in this book are based on actual cases. The names have been changed to provide confidentiality. The data were collected by group home counselors and job coaches. Reliability checks were conducted at least monthly by supervisors or trainers to ensure accurate implementation and precise data collection procedures.

This book is aimed at parents, teachers, supervisors, and direct care staff who are involved in the provision of care and services to people with autism. This book provides a basis for making decisions about behavioral intervention within the framework of functional, integrated programming. This book is written in a style that should be useful to families and direct care personnel. The data and procedures presented within these pages should also be of value to students, clinicians, and researchers.

Chapter One

AN OVERVIEW OF AUTISM

The learning difficulties and behavior problems that can be associated with autism provide unusual challenges to parents, teachers, and other caregivers who instruct children and adults with autism. Providing quality care and education to these people requires a great deal of commitment and expertise. Consequently, educational and living opportunities for people with autism have often been limited, and a tremendous effort has typically been needed in order to identify and procure such services. The purpose of this chapter is to provide an orientation to the definition of autism and an overview of service systems that are available to people with autism.

CHARACTERISTICS

Autism is a controversial term, and the diagnosis of the disorder has not been straightforward. A variety of definitions have emerged since Kanner first identified the syndrome in 1943. A review of the history of the definition, and the various forms it has taken, is of interest, but beyond the scope of this chapter.

The practitioner who is making a diagnostic determination of autism is referred to the *Diagnostic and Statistical Manual of Mental Disorders-III* (Revised), (*DSM-IIIR*) (Spitzer, 1987) published by the American Psychiatric Association, and the definition endorsed by the American Society for Autism. Elements of both of these definitions are covered to provide the reader with familiarity of the characteristics of autism. However, presence or absence of some of these symptoms alone does not necessarily suggest that an individual has autism. Therefore, this section should not be taken as a diagnostic scheme, but as an overview of characteristics that can be associated with autism.

Autism can vary in degree, as well as the extent to which the characteristics affect each individual. It is also important to note that many of the deficits associated with autism can be helped through education and training. Implications of education and training are provided.

Impairment in Social Relationships

Autism is characterized by an impaired ability to participate in social relationships and can result in significant deficits in the ability to make conventional friendships. People with autism often do not have the skills necessary to initiate social relationships. If these skills do exist, they often appear rote and awkward. When friendships are initiated, individuals with autism might experience problems maintaining reciprocal relationships. They often appear incapable of taking on the other person's perspective, they may lack empathy with the viewpoint and feelings of others, they might have difficulty providing comfort to others in a conventional way, or they might not seek comfort from others in normal ways. When feeling ill, tired, or hurt, an individual with autism might withdraw, engage in stereotypic behaviors, or even engage in self-injury or aggression.

Individuals with autism frequently do not engage in cooperative, reciprocal interactions with others. Children with autism might show no interest in playing games with other children. For example, fantasy play with other children, such as playing house, would be unusual for a child with autism.

People with autism often lack social conventions. Social behaviors that usually come naturally to people without autism, such as greeting others, inquiring about topics of interest to the other person, and providing offers of assistance, are often absent in people with autism. A person with autism might not readily initiate a conversation, and if he or she does, the conversation is likely to be self-centered with no regard for the interest level of the listener. A person with autism might even walk away in the midst of a conversation while the other person is still speaking.

Effects of Education and Training   Individuals with autism can be systematically taught skills that can improve their social functioning. They can learn how to initiate conversations, how to terminate conversations, how to express interest in others, and how to ask for assistance. Individuals with autism can also be taught reciprocal play and cooperative work skills. Although education and training cannot eliminate autism (awkwardness and a stiff quality might prevail), gains can be achieved in social functioning.

Impairment in Communication

Autism can be devastating to language development. Some people with autism develop no spoken language, and others have speech, but it is primarily either echolalic and repetitive or two- and three-word phrases. People with autism who have language might have peculiarities in grammar, volume, rate, rhythm, pitch, or intonation. They might speak in a flat tone, a high pitch, or very rapidly. Some people with autism have fluent speech, but have unusual content. Their speech might be marked by perseveration or stereotypic repetition of conversations they have heard.

Speech might also be devoid of meaningful understanding. This problem is dramatically evident during periods of behavioral crisis. A person with autism might engage in a tantrum while repeating, "I need to behave like a polite young man," or a person with autism might strike out while saying, "I shouldn't hit people." One young woman wet herself, held her wet garment in her hand, and said, "I didn't wet myself."

Social impairments might limit the usefulness of fluent speech in relationships. A person with autism might not have the ability to initiate or participate in conversations with others, or if they do converse, the conversations might consist of lengthy monologues with no regard for the interests of the listener or monologues that are on topics of narrow interest.

Nonverbal communication can also be affected. Eye contact might be absent or abnormal if present, and facial expressions might lack social convention. For example, an individual with autism might not smile upon initial social contact, might rarely smile under any circumstances, or, smiling might be perpetually present, even under adverse conditions.

Effects of Education and Training Gains in communication can be achieved despite the severity of the disorder. People with no speech can often be taught alternative forms of communication, such as sign or gesture. Although fluent communication in sign might not be achieved, some communication by gesture can often be a realistic goal.

Individuals with blatantly disruptive forms of communication, such as shrieking, yelling, hooting, and crying can often be taught alternate, more acceptable substitutes. Although it might not be possible or desirable to totally eliminate all forms of disruptive communication, some improvement can be possible. More fluent individuals can benefit from training in conversation skills. They can often make strides toward taking into account the needs of the listener. Gains might be slow, but over time improvements can be realized.

Perseveration on Interests and Activities

People with autism often have an unusually narrow range of interests. Both verbal and nonverbal individuals might engage in repetitive, stereotyped body movements such as hand flicking, spinning, or rocking. An individual with autism might spend hours engaging in such behaviors. Individuals with autism might also be consistently preoccupied with certain objects or parts of objects, or they might have strong attachments to particular objects to the exclusion of other objects and activities.

Perseverations might extend to food. An individual with autism might indicate a marked preference or dislike of certain foods. These responses, combined with dependence on routine, can make mealtime a challenge for even the most patient caregiver.

Individuals with autism who have better cognitive and language skills might perseverate on certain topics. An individual might remain absorbed with one or two topics, such as geography, music, sports, calendars, or modes of transportation. The individual might spend inordinate amounts of time researching the topic, talking about the topic, and performing calculations relevant to the topic. The same interest might be maintained over years.

Effects of Education and Training   Perseveration on self-stimulatory behaviors can be drastically reduced by individualized intervention plans. Often, these plans involve sweeping changes in the environment; however, such changes are often rewarded by significant reductions in self-stimulation and by replacement of more productive behaviors. Occasionally, the opportunity to engage in the behaviors of interest can be provided as a reward for a more constructive behavior.

Individuals with narrow interests in certain topics can often be taught to limit the time spent on such topics. Usually, it is not desirable to totally eliminate such interests, but rather to limit them in accordance with the demands of everyday life. People with autism can learn to put aside their interests for the sake of jobs and other activities of daily living.

Occasionally, it is possible for an individual with autism to find a job in which his or her interests are marketable. For example, one young man with severe autism was fascinated by tactile stimulation, and he often kept lint or other objects in his hands. He was successfully placed at a job that involved tearing unused bus coupons.

Dependence on Routine

Related to having a narrow range of interests, people with autism are often highly dependent on set routines. An individual with autism might insist on certain bedtime, mealtime, exiting, or greeting routines. Even small changes in the routine or in aspects of the environment can result in intense emotional reactions. Often, the serious behavior problems associated with autism, such as aggression, self-injury, or property destruction, occur as a result of unexpected changes in routine.

Effects of Education and Training   Education and training cannot necessarily change the preference for routine, however, training can alleviate some of the drastic reactions to change. Over time, education and training can decrease the reliance on rituals, increase flexibility, and increase the likelihood of more acceptable responses to unexpected changes.

Abnormal Responses to Sensory Stimulation

Autism is associated with unconventional reactions to sensory stimulation. Apparent disregard for some types of stimulation might be observed; for example, someone might speak, and there could be no sign of acknowledgment, or there might be a strong reaction to certain stimuli such as hypersensitivity to sound. The individual might have a fascination with certain types of stimulation including smells, visual events such as spinning objects, or sounds. Textures might also be highly appealing. An individual with autism might be fascinated by the feel of a piece of lint, and hours of enjoyment might be derived from watching a string twirl. Many of the repetitive behaviors associated with autism, such as rocking, finger flicking, and twirling, at least in part, serve the purpose of providing sensory stimulation.

Effects of Education and Training Sensory patterns associated with autism can be used constructively in teaching situations by using the preferred stimuli as a reward for desirable behaviors. Identifying sensory interests, and using preferred stimuli as reinforcers, is a valuable method of motivating individuals with autism.

Sensory patterns can be altered somewhat through training. Repetitive fixations on certain stimuli can be replaced by more acceptable behaviors through instructional and behavioral intervention plans. Individuals with autism can often be encouraged to limit their sensory obsessions in accordance with the demands of their schedules. Although it would be difficult to totally eliminate sensory abnormalities, it is possible to modify them. A productive area of intervention has been to replace unacceptable sources of sensory stimulation with more acceptable ones. For example, an individual who picks his or her skin in order to smear blood might give up skin picking when provided with lotion to smear instead.

Behavior Problems

A number of behavior problems are sometimes associated with autism. These problems can include tantrums (jumping, arm flapping, screaming), aggression, self-injury, and property destruction. Behavior problems associated with autism are often secondary to some of the other characteristics discussed. Deficits in communication often lead a person with autism to engage in undesirable behaviors as a form of communication. For example, an individual who has no language might head bang as a way of asking for help, or someone might use tantrumming as a way of communicating discomfort.

Deficits in social interaction skills certainly contribute to some of the severe behavior problems associated with autism. Lacking more conventional ways of engaging in social interaction, individuals with autism might learn to rely on more disturbing methods. Reliance on routine can also result in disturbing behaviors when the schedule is broken. Small changes in the routine can result in severe behavior problems in some individuals.

Abnormal responses to sensory stimuli might play a role in self-injury. Although self-injury can serve other purposes, in some cases it might actually serve the function of sensory stimulation, and perseveration on certain types of sensory stimulation is often perceived as a behavior problem. Without proper intervention, such perseverations can be counterproductive to learning and adapting.

Effects of Education and Training Behavior problems associated with autism can be significantly reduced through education and training, and more acceptable behaviors can be taught to replace the inappropriate ones. Significant strides have been made in the management of these behavior problems. The focus of this book is on the methods and strategies for managing these problems.

Mental Retardation and Learning Disabilities

Approximately three-quarters of people with autism also have some degree of mental retardation, however, the remainder of the population can have average to above-average intelligence. Whether mental retardation is present or not, autism itself can be considered a severe learning disability. People with autism often do not learn at the same rates or by the same methods as people without autism.

Effects of Education and Training People with autism can benefit greatly from education and training despite the severity of retardation and the extent of learning disabilities. However, people with autism often need specialized methods of instruction that take into account their sensory needs, communication deficits, and behavior problems. Well designed educational and training efforts can result in the acquisition of a variety of functional skills for working, living, and learning in integrated community settings.

Ability to Perform Special Skills

Not all characteristics of autism are deficits for the individual. Some individuals with autism have very specific, very amazing skills. These individuals have demonstrated superior skills in such areas as mathematics, calculations involving the calendar, rote memory, meteorology, navigation, geography, and music. These abilities often exist concurrently with some of the more severe deficits associated with the syndrome.

INCIDENCE AND CAUSES OF AUTISM

The number of people with autism varies depending on the diagnostic criteria used. *DSM-IIIR* estimates that approximately four to five people out of every 10,000 have autism. Others consider 15 out of every 10,000 to be a more realistic figure if milder cases are also considered. One undisputed statistic is that autism is more common in males than females.

Autism, once thought to result from poor parenting, is now recognized as a disorder with a physiological basis. Although the exact nature of the physical dysfunction is not known, it is now considered to be a neurological disorder. It is also possible that there is more than one cause. Currently, maternal rubella, anoxia at birth, and untreated phenylketonuria have been associated with autism. Genetic factors might also play a role (e.g., the Fragile-X syndrome has been associated with autism).

Although similarities exist among some people with autism, there are also vast differences in terms of exact combinations of symptoms and degree of symptoms. It is possible that autism is actually not one disorder with one etiology, but a group of similar disorders that can result from any of several etiologies.

HISTORY OF SERVICE SYSTEMS

The history of service systems for individuals with autism can be covered well in few words: Services have typically been limited and segregated. Historically, most people with autism lived either at home with relatives or in large institutions for people with mental retardation or mental illness.

Educational services for people with autism have also been limited and segregated. A typical scenario involved the parents sending the child to school, and as the behavior problems became apparent, the child would be expelled. If parents were persistent, placement in special schools was provided by the school systems, or if the parents were wealthy, the family might pay for such special schooling. However, prior to federal laws mandating education regardless of handicap, it was not unheard of for people with severe autism to go unserved by the educational system. When students with autism were served, it was typically in schools especially for people with severe handicaps. In many cases, children were sent to schools out of their neighborhood or even out of their home state.

The lack of services for people with autism may have been in part due to the overwhelming nature of the disorder. The severe behavior problems associated with autism defied traditional methods of child rearing, and the apparent psychological problems that this disorder created were not readily improved by traditional psychological services.

In the 1960s, interest in autism grew, due in part to behavior modification research that demonstrated that people with autism could learn. The very disturbing behavior problems associated with autism became amenable to change. Emerging instructional methods were able to cope with the severe learning problems that the disorder could cause; however, the translation of this knowledge to the daily lives of people with autism has been slow.

In 1974, federal legislation mandated a free public education to all children, regardless of handicap (PL 94-142). Public laws that provided for education for those with handicaps combined with the emerging behavioral and instructional technology resulting in an expansion of services to people with autism. Children with autism were afforded educational placements, and although these placements were mostly segregated, services were at least provided.

Over the past 15 years, individuals with autism have experienced some increased availability of services. Improved residential and vocational services have allowed for a very slow emergence from institutional placements.

EDUCATIONAL SERVICES

The potential for serving children with autism to date has not been fully realized. There is a wide gap between possibilities as demonstrated through model projects and the reality of services as currently provided.

The Possibilities

Emergence of children from segregated, one-to-one instructional situations to integrated, larger group situations has been demonstrated through systematic application of behavior management strategies coupled with systematic instructional procedures (Koegel, Rincover, & Egel, 1982).

Students with mild autism have been integrated successfully into regular education classrooms or special education classrooms within regular schools. Students with severe autism have also been provided with educational services that are based in regular schools. Functional curricula for students with severe autism include learning to use public transportation, to obtain services and goods in the community, and to work in integrated jobs with the help of teacher support.

The Reality

Functional, community based curricula and integrated educational systems have for the most part been limited to model demonstration projects or to a few communities nationwide that have made a commitment to integrated education for persons with severe handicaps.

Educational services for people with autism remain primarily segregated. Many school districts continue to resist mainstreaming and functional training of students with autism. Pockets of integration have developed in which people with autism have been provided with mainstreamed, supported educational opportunities. The challenge at this time is not so much to expand the technology, but to expand the opportunities to apply the technology.

LIVING SITUATIONS

Integrated community living opportunities for people with autism have grown very slowly since the late 1970s. Some people with autism have been included in group home arrangements for people with other handicaps; however, if these individuals have behavior problems, such as tantrums, aggression, or self-injury, they are often placed back with their family or in a large institutional setting.

The Possibilities

A few group homes have been established that specialize in autism. These programs provide behavior management and support services that can meet the needs of people with autism. Successful community integration has been demonstrated in those programs that have provided adequate support services.

People with autism can realize enormous benefits from living in homes or apartments with sufficient support from residential counselors, who are often needed to provide instruction and assistance in the activities of daily living. These counselors perform best when they receive general training in autism and specific training with the individuals for whom they are responsible. Even people with severe autism have adapted well to group home or apartment living in integrated community settings. Programs have emerged that meet the needs of this population by providing sufficient support services to achieve safe and productive integration.

Individuals with even the most severe autism have learned self-care skills, home-care skills, and have been able to participate in all activities of daily living. Individuals with severe autism, mental retardation, and no spoken language have enjoyed normal community leisure activities such as bowling, swimming, horseback riding, shopping, and eating in restaurants. Individuals with milder autism have learned how to wend their way through the community using public transportation, to do their banking, to do their shopping, and to participate in recreational activities in their communities. Some of these individuals who initially needed continuous supervision have learned to function independently, while others require some level of ongoing supervision.

The Reality

Since autism is a severe, pervasive disability, the overwhelming majority of people with autism need some type of supervised living situation. The methods exist to achieve community integration in living situations, and, gradually such residential programs for small groups of people, including those with autism, have emerged. Unfortunately, the majority of people with autism, unless living at home with their families, do not have the opportunity to enjoy such living arrangements. Instead, they continue to live in large, institutional placements.

VOCATIONAL SERVICES

Vocational services for people with autism have been severely limited until the 1980s. The behavior problems that some people with autism have are not tolerated in sheltered, vocational settings, so consequently, these people often are not served. Kanner, Rodriguez, and Ashenden (1972) found that only

10% of a sample of 96 children diagnosed as having autism at Johns Hopkins Hospital prior to 1953 were "sufficiently integrated into the texture of our society to be employable . . ." (p. 10).

The Possibilities

The 1980s have witnessed increased tolerance for people with autism in integrated settings; however, the most encouraging progress has been the demonstrated ability of these people to succeed directly in the job market. Work for individuals with autism has been sought in companies in the community. The goal is to find jobs that are compatible with the strengths and needs of the individual. Workers with autism are accompanied to work by a job coach and are paid by the companies for their work. Job coaches are hired by the service agency and trained to implement instructional and behavior programs at the industry sites. The job coach also teaches the worker specific work skills and social skills and assists with travel to and from work, with banking, and with other work-related skills.

Job coaches fade out from the worksite as the worker develops necessary skills for independence. In cases of severe autism, the support of a job coach might always be necessary, but in cases of mild autism, complete independence can be possible.

A psychologist, speech and language therapist, and other professionals are employed to design specific instructional programs, demonstrate programs, and train job coaches to implement the programs in the worksites. Worker progress is monitored by all involved professionals.

Upon entry into the supported employment program, individuals are placed in community worksites as soon as compatible placements are found. If the worker is unsuccessful in a particular job, then different work or a more compatible company is sought. Occasionally, it might take up to 2 years and a series of jobs to find a good match.

All individuals, regardless of their behavioral disorders, functioning levels, or previous experiences are placed and trained in nonsheltered sites among nonhandicapped workers. A continuum of support services is applied directly in the integrated workplace. The severity of the individual's disability is accommodated by provision of adequate supportive services including low staff ratios and additional professional services within the integrated, community workplace.

Supported employment programs that have been based on this model have achieved job success with this population. Employers and co-workers have been generally enthusiastic in welcoming people with autism into the work force. They have discovered that this population has able workers despite the presence of unusual behaviors.

The Reality

At this point in time the feasibility of people with autism working in integrated community settings has been demonstrated, and programs exist that can serve as models for new service providers. However, the majority of people with autism have not yet been afforded these opportunities. As with the educational and residential systems, opportunities need to catch up to technology.

SUPPORT SERVICES

Traditional methods of providing support services did not typically benefit people with autism. Problems with learning style, behavior, and generalization rendered traditional services somewhat powerless. However, the various disciplines have begun to usefully serve people with autism.

The Possibilities

The emergence of individuals with autism in the schools and in integrated community placements has been accompanied by a proliferation of services and technologies specific to their needs. Psychology, behavior management, speech/language, and occupational therapy are included in those disciplines that have begun to provide specialized services to individuals with autism.

Behavior management procedures have been designed that can be implemented by caregivers in integrated community settings. Speech/language training has made tremendous strides in meeting the communication and generalization needs of people with autism. The focus on function and integration in speech/language has resulted in impressive gains for both the field and the individuals served.

Less recognized specialties, such as occupational therapy, have provided valuable support services to individuals with autism. Again, the focus on practical function has enabled such specialties to assist in the adaptation of people with autism to the home and work setting. Psychiatrists and neurologists specializing in autism have successfully incorporated behavioral data into their medical decision making. Successful liaisons between the medical profession, psychology, and the service provider have resulted in individuals with autism making successful adaptations with generally decreasing levels of medication.

The Reality

The availability of support services that are adapted to meet the needs of people with autism is variable. Some people with autism have the benefit of these services; for the majority, however, a dearth of such services is probably the norm.

SUMMARY

People with autism have come out of the institutional closet. In 1970 an adult with autism probably would not have been seen in a local department store unless accompanied by a parent. In 1980 this same individual might have been seen in the department store, along with 10 other adults, who were severely handicapped, and their escort. In 1990, it is possible that the person who priced the items on the rack was a store employee who happened to have autism.

The emergence has been slow, but model programs have demonstrated that it can be successful. The technology has been generated, and slowly, people with autism are benefiting. However, to date, many people with this disorder continue to wait at home or in large institutions for these benefits to reach them.

REFERENCES

Kanner, L. (1943). Autistic disturbances of affective content. *Journal of Pediatrics, 25,* 211–217.

Kanner, L., Rodriguez, A., & Ashenden, B. (1972). How far can autistic children go in matters of social adaptation? *Journal of Autism and Childhood Schizophrenia, 2,* 9–33.

Koegel, R., Rincover, A., & Egel, A. (1982). *Educating and understanding autistic children.* San Diego, CA: College-Hill.

PL 42-142. (1974). Education for all Handicapped Children Act (EAHCA), 20 U.S.C. § 1401 et seq.

Spitzer, R. (1987). *Diagnostic and statistical manual of mental disorders III (Revised).* Washington, DC: American Psychiatric Association.

Chapter Two

MANAGING
BEHAVIORAL CHALLENGES

Autism is a pervasive developmental disorder with effects taking toll before a child reaches 2½ years of age. The effects of autism on an individual are numerous, but one of the more disturbing effects to the individual and the caregivers is the behavior problems. Individuals who are mildly affected by the disorder might experience severe difficulties in interpersonal relationships. Their social interactions might be awkward and lack spontaneity and warmth. Individuals with severe autism might display self-injury, aggression, property destruction, self-stimulation, and other abnormal or disturbing behaviors.

Initial attempts to deal with the behavior problems associated with autism were based on an illness model (Lovaas, 1979), but this model provided little hope for improvement. Autism was viewed as an illness with no cure or implications for treatment, and the individual was considered sick. Although autism has no cure, there is hope. The hope lies not in an eventual cure, but rather, in the intervention of the behaviors associated with autism. There is a history dating to the early 1960s of modifying the maladaptive behaviors of individuals with autism. Such modifications do not constitute a cure, however, the implications for integration into society and successful adjustment are enormous.

The purpose of this chapter is to provide a cursory survey of management strategies that have influenced the behavior of individuals with autism. The background and use of aversive and nonaversive strategies are traced, and the case is made that the difficult behaviors associated with autism can be successfully managed by a variety of procedures. The justification for avoiding the use of punishment procedures is presented.

EARLY HISTORY OF BEHAVIOR MODIFICATION

In 1949 one of the first studies of behavior modification with humans was published. Fuller (1949) used positive reinforcement on a ''vegetative human organism'' to increase the movement of the right arm by rewarding the subject with a sugar-milk solution. The interesting feature of this early study is that it used positive reinforcement to change behavior in a rather nonresponsive person.

Psychologists Using Their Own Children

In the 1950s and early 1960s, behavior modification was investigated by psychologists using their own children. In one classic study Williams (1959) eliminated bedtime tantrums in his 2-year-old son. He noted that after putting the child to bed, the child would cry, then the parents would go in and coddle him. Williams concluded that the function of the crying was to attract attention, so he put the behavior on extinction. Crying was no longer followed by rescue; instead the child was left to cry. The parents noted that bedtime crying very quickly disappeared. Several weeks later when an aunt came to visit, the child cried at bedtime. The aunt ran to the rescue, and the bedtime tantrums resumed. Williams concluded, ''It should be emphasized that the treatment in this case did not involve aversive punishment. All that was done was to remove the reinforcement'' (p. 269).

Pumroy and Pumroy (1965), both psychologists, reported on a toilet training study using their own child. With their son as a subject, the use of the toilet was reinforced with chocolate candies.

Early Gains Without Punishment

In the 1960s, psychologists began to systematically apply behavioral principles to people other than their own children. Children and adults in institutional settings became subjects of behavior modification investigations. From these very early studies, successful application of techniques was based on positive reinforcement.

Ferster and DeMyer (1961) published an early study on children with autism. The children were taught to key press by using rewards such as candy and toys. This early study demonstrated that children with autism could learn, given certain changes in the environment. With this knowledge, investigators quickly moved from the laboratory to the field. They also moved from the simple response of pressing a key to more compelling behaviors, such as aggression, self-injury, tantrums, and language.

Zimmerman and Zimmerman (1962) presented an early report of the successful treatment of tantrums. They reported on the use of behavior modification with two boys with emotional disturbance living in a residential treatment center. Zimmerman and Zimmerman used positive reinforcement of cooperative behavior and extinction of misbehavior to eliminate tantrums.

Harris, Wolf, and Baer (1964) studied the effects of adult social reinforcement on child behavior. They dealt with the problems of excessive crawling in a 3-year-old girl, prolonged crying episodes in a 4-year-old boy, isolated play in two other young children, and extreme passivity in a fifth child. After systematic observations of all five children, it was noted that they received a great deal of teacher attention for their undesirable behaviors. Treatment consisted of increased adult attention for desirable behaviors and no attention for the undesirable behaviors. Gains in desirable behaviors were reported in all five cases.

Bailey and Meyerson (1969) reported on the successful use of vibration as a reinforcer for lever pressing in a blind 6-year-old boy with mental retardation. The study concluded with the recommendation that further research be done on vibration and other tactile stimulation as possible reinforcers. This early investigation of vibration as a reinforcer is noteworthy, because recent work suggests that sensory stimulation can be an effective reinforcer for individuals with autism. In fact, Taylor and Chamove (1986) demonstrated the usefulness of vibration in the reduction of self-injury in an adult with autism.

In 1969, Osborne reported that free time could serve as a reinforcer in the management of classroom behavior. His results demonstrated that one activity could actually serve as a positive reinforcer for another activity. The Osborne study initiated numerous investigations into the use of activities as reinforcers.

Johnson and Frankel (1978) demonstrated that physical contact could function as a positive reinforcer for three young boys with diagnoses of mental retardation, brain damage, or autism. Their study demonstrated that physical contact could serve as the sole reinforcer in a behavior modification program. In another study, Hung (1978) reported that allowing a child with autism to engage in repetitive self-stimulation could actually serve as a reward for other more desirable behaviors.

Even the early behavior modification studies, then, demonstrated successful management of problem behaviors without the use of punishment. Positive reinforcement was effective in changing the behavior of humans, even a human, who, according to physicians, "had not learned anything in the 18 years of his life" (Fuller, 1949, p. 590). By the 1970s, important strategies based on the principle of positive reinforcement were demonstrated in research.

A variety of positive reinforcers proved effective in those early studies, including food, free time, physical contact, attention, vibration, and even the opportunity to engage in self-stimulation. A number of those studies were done with individuals with autism.

Other studies conducted over the past several years have demonstrated positive gains with individuals with autism without the use of punishment. The majority of this work has centered around the functional analysis. The functional analysis is a method for determining the purpose the misbehavior serves so that intervention can then focus on teaching alternate, more acceptable behaviors.

FUNCTIONAL ANALYSIS

Early studies, as well as early theorists, stressed the need for a functional analysis. The functional analysis is especially critical for persons with autism. The communication difficulties that are inherent in the disorder can make misbehavior a functional form of communication for people with autism. The key to the development of intervention strategies lies in an analysis of the purpose that the misbehavior serves. (Functional analysis is covered at length in Chapters Three and Four.)

Early Studies

Talkington, Hall, and Altman (1971) investigated aggression in individuals with retardation living in a public institution. They noted that individuals who had "no understandable communication" had higher rates of aggression than individuals who had understandable communication. They suggested that the aggression served the purpose of calling attention to some need that individuals without understandable communication could not otherwise communicate. Lovaas and Simmons (1969), in one of the early punishment studies, noted that unless the child is taught more appropriate behavior, more alarming behavior would develop to replace the misbehavior.

An early study of particular interest was published by Schaefer (1970). Schaefer shaped head banging in monkeys by using food reinforcers, and he reported that the monkeys could be taught to head bang in response to certain cues. The cue used was, "Poor boy, don't do that. You'll hurt yourself." The monkeys learned that when the experimenter made that statement, head banging would be rewarded with food. If the statement was not made, head banging would not be rewarded. So, if the experimenter opened the session by saying, "Poor boy, don't do that. You'll hurt yourself," the monkey would head bang, and if the cue was not given, the monkey did not head bang. Schaefer concluded, "It seems permissible and advisable to analyze each case of head banging among humans for the presence of control-stimuli that set the stage for, and the presence of reinforcers that sustain this behavior" (p. 116).

Use with Developmental Disabilities

Application of the functional analysis was discussed by Carr (1977). He reviewed several functions that self-injury, a behavior often associated with autism, might serve, and he noted that this behavior could serve many purposes including attaining social rewards, ending an unpleasant situation, and creating sensory stimulation. Carr concluded that effective intervention strategies are dependent on identifying the function of the self-injury for the individual. Carr's review had a significant impact on research on behavior problems associated with autism. A number of researchers subsequently provided data supporting the various functions that misbehavior could serve. Many of these either included individuals with autism or studied behaviors that are associated with autism.

Donnellan, Mirenda, Mesaros, and Fassbender (1984) presented a model for analyzing the functions of a behavior and basing intervention on the function. Intervention would follow directly from a functional analysis and would include teaching replacement communicative responses, teaching alternative behaviors, or manipulating antecedent conditions.

Gardner and Cole (1987) described an approach to behavioral assessment of aggression and other behavior problems. They suggested collecting data on the conditions under which the behavior occurs and developing hypotheses about the possible influence of the behavior. Then, based on the data and hypotheses, interventions can be developed.

Related Research with Developmental Disabilities

Studies now exist that show relationships between certain environmental events and misbehavior. Iwata, Dorsey, Slifer, Bauman, and Richman (1982) studied the functions of self-injury in nine children including several with autism. These researchers provided evidence that self-injury can serve different functions for different individuals. They concluded that identifying the variables that affect self-injury could lead to specific intervention recommendations.

Carr, Newsom, and Binkoff (1980) demonstrated that aggressive behavior served the purpose of allowing two children with autism to escape from tasks. Carr and Durand (1985) demonstrated that social attention can maintain self-injury, as can sensory consequences (Rincover & Devany, 1982).

Professional journals are now replete with data supporting the connection between environmental events and misbehavior, and data are now abundantly available on the functions or purposes that misbehavior can serve (LaVigna & Donnellan, 1986). In fact, Durand and Crimmins (1988) have developed an instrument designed to identify variables maintaining self-injurious behavior.

Functional Analysis and Autism

Research based on the functional analysis of behavior has provided good results in individuals with autism and/or with behaviors that are associated with autism. Carr and Durand (1985) achieved significant reductions in aggression, tantrums, and self-injury by teaching children, including a child with autism, more acceptable ways of soliciting attention or assistance.

Smith (1985) successfully managed aggression and self-injury in two men with autism. A functional analysis was completed for each man. The men were then taught more acceptable ways of obtaining food, gaining attention, and participating in desirable activities. A 5-year follow up revealed near-elimination of head banging in a young man with autism who had originally been head banging 95% of the 5-minute intervals in the day. Additionally, this young man became successfully employed in a supported work program where he earned more than minimum wage. Aggression was also reduced from multiple incidents per day to less than one per month in another young man by basing his intervention plan on a functional analysis.

Berkman and Meyer (1988) reduced self-injury in a 45-year-old man who had been institutionalized for the majority of his life. Reductions in severe self-injury were achieved by a comprehensive intervention plan that included a structured schedule of functional vocational and recreational activities, as well as instruction and communication training in integrated community settings. He, as well as Smith's subjects, became successful workers in supported employment programs. Willis and LaVigna (1988) reported on the significant reduction of self-injury in a 17-year-old boy with autism and with a profound hearing impairment. A multi-part intervention plan, based on a thorough environmental assessment and functional analysis, was devised. The intervention plan involved pervasive changes in the boy's living situation, instructional programming, and reinforcement contingencies.

The functional analysis might suggest that behavior is maintained by its sensory consequences. Strategies based on this function have proven useful with individuals with autism. Smith (1986) successfully managed pica in an adult with autism with reinforcement of behaviors incompatible with pica and provision of alternate sensory stimuli. Similarly, rectal digging by an adult with autism was significantly reduced through alternate sensory stimuli (Smith, 1985).

The usefulness of the interventions based on functional analysis is not limited to self-injury or aggression. Repp, Felce, and Barton (1988) reduced self-stimulation as well as head banging by basing intervention on the results of an informal functional analysis. When the function of the misbehavior was to obtain positive reinforcement, successful intervention consisted of ensuring that the misbehavior did not result in reinforcement. When the function of the misbehavior was to escape from a task, successful intervention involved compliance training and rewards for cooperation. When the function of the misbehavior was self-stimulation, successful intervention involved providing increased stimulation from the environment.

Durand and Carr (1987) achieved reductions in self-stimulatory behavior with an intervention plan that consisted of teaching the children to ask for assistance. Durand and Crimmins (1987) analyzed the function of psychotic speech in a young boy with autism. They determined that the psychotic speech served the purpose of escaping from difficult tasks, so they taught the boy to ask for help. As a result, psychotic speech was significantly reduced.

Donnellan and LaVigna (1986) reported on the successful intervention of the socially stigmatizing behavior of adolescents with autism in a public school setting. They reported significant decreases in self-stimulation (rocking) and inappropriate, repetitive questioning by a variety of nonaversive procedures, including teaching alternate responses and positive reinforcement for acceptable behavior.

PUNISHMENT

During the same period that positive reinforcement was being investigated with humans, punishment was being used. Many of the people on whom punishment was used had autism or behaviors that are frequently associated with autism.

Early Studies

Tate and Baroff (1966) suppressed self-injury in a 9-year-old blind boy with a diagnosis of psychosis. They first used withdrawal of physical contact to decrease self-injury, then did a second study that used electric shock to decrease self-injury.

In 1969, Lovaas and Simmons reported the successful use of shock to suppress self-injurious behavior in three children with mental retardation. They found that the self-injury could well have served the purpose of gaining adult attention and warned that if attention was not given for more acceptable behaviors, the children were likely to develop some equally disturbing behavior, such as feces smearing, in order to obtain attention.

The initial punishment studies with children with autism were published several years after Ferster and DeMyer (1961) demonstrated that the behavior of children with autism could be changed through positive reinforcement. They appeared almost concurrently with Schaefer's (1970) work demonstrating that self-injury could be functional, and that the environmental influences needed to be carefully examined. Punishment studies flourished despite the early calls supporting interventions based on function, warnings in the early punishment studies themselves, and the promise of positive reinforcement for the management of behaviors associated with autism. Since the 1970s, a variety of punishers have been used to suppress various behaviors associated with autism.

Early studies of punishment with individuals with autism or behavior problems associated with autism concentrated on the severe problems such as self-injury. However, punishment has also been used with a variety of other behaviors, including toileting, self-stimulation, rumination, and disruptive behaviors. Although electric shock was used initially in punishment studies, a variety of other punishers have since been investigated.

Variety of Punishers

Punishers have been categorized by their effect, and the variety is noteworthy. Numerous studies have been done using a variety of punishers, including auditory punishers, taste punishers, visual contingency punishers, and physical punishers (Axelrod & Apsche, 1983). Smell contingencies have been studied with aromatic ammonia being the most popular choice. Taste punishers have included pepper sauce, shaving cream, and lemon juice. Visual screening, by covering an individual's face or eyes, has also been used as a punisher. Research on many of these punishers continues.

Punishers causing physical discomfort have also been investigated. Physical discomfort punishers have included the use of cold baths, aversive tickling, forced running, and carrying heavy objects, as well as rubber band snaps, hair tugs, slaps, and water mist. Many of these punishers have been used on both children and adults with autism.

Punishment and Autism

Electric shock has been a popular procedure for people with autism. Risley (1968) used shock on a child with autism who climbed on furniture at home. Yeakel, Salisbury, Greer, and Marcus (1970) used a helmet that delivered shocks to a 14-year-old girl with autism each time she head banged. Romanczyk and Goren (1975) also used shock on an individual with autism who head banged.

Self-Injury and Aggression   Self-injury has been the subject of numerous punishment studies. Tanner and Zeiler (1975) used aromatic ammonia to reduce self-slapping in a young woman with autism. Neufeld and Fantuzzo (1984) used a helmet as a consequence for self-biting in a young child with autism.

Rojahn, McGonigle, Curcio, and Dixon (1987) modified pica, aggression, and self-injury in an adolescent boy with autism with water mist and aromatic ammonia. The water mist was sprayed in the boy's face or aromatic ammonia in capsule form was crushed directly under his nose following pica attempts. Altmeyer, Williams, and Sams (1985) used Tabasco sauce to treat self-injurious and aggressive biting in an adolescent girl with autism.

Luce, Delquadri, and Hall (1980) used forced exercise to manage aggression in a 7-year-old boy who was diagnosed as developmentally delayed with "autistic behaviors." Charlop, Burgio, Iwata, and Ivancic (1988) investigated the effects of varying punishers to manage aggression and property destruction in young children with autism. This study used overcorrection, time-out, verbal "no," and loud noise as punishers.

Self-Stimulation   Self-stimulation has received wide attention in the punishment literature. Koegel and Covert (1972) punished self-stimulation in two children with autism by verbal reprimands and slapping. Romanczyk (1977) punished self-stimulation, including rocking and twirling, in two individuals with autism by saying "no" and slapping them. Friman, Cook, and Finney (1984) used water mist, lemon juice, and vinegar with an individual with autism who engaged in hand touching.

Justifications for Punishment

Punishment is typically an unpleasant enterprise. By its very nature, it is unpleasant for the person being punished, and in many cases, it is probably just as unpleasant for the person doing the punishing. Nonetheless, punishment is widespread, and people with autism have been frequent targets of punishment procedures. The obvious question is, "Why?" Why use punishment on people with autism? The answer to that question must obviously come from the advocates of punishment. A number of justifications for the use of punishment follow.

The Ends Justify the Means   Advocates of punishment maintain that the research supports the efficacy of punishment. Since they feel it is effective, despite the unpleasant nature, they claim the ends justify the means.

It's the Only Game in Town   Punishment advocates maintain that punishment is necessary because there are no other alternatives.

Right to Treatment   Advocates of punishment claim that this is a moral issue. They maintain that people have the right to treatment. Punishment is considered to be a treatment by its advocates, so, they conclude that people have a right to be punished if it means that misbehavior will be modified.

Right to Treat   Many professionals maintain that the right to use punishment is a privilege conferred by their degree or license. This justification states that professionals have a right to choose the treatment. Again, since punishment is considered to be a treatment, they have a right to choose it.

Problems with Punishment

A review of the literature and clinical practices reveals two divergent fields going back to the 1960s or even the 1950s. There are studies that document the effects of positive reinforcement, positive programming, and the use of the functional analysis for modifying behavior in people with autism. Also dating back to the 1960s are studies of punishment of people with autism. Currently, there are a variety of procedures from which to choose. There are several compelling reasons for avoiding punishment and opting for the positive to manage the behavioral problems associated with autism. Several of these reasons follow.

Side Effects   Punishment can have side effects. Often, these side effects are unacceptable in integrated community settings. Newsom, Favell, and

Rincover (1983), in a review of the research on the undesirable side effects of punishment, pinpointed the following possible negative side effects: emotional responses, aggression, imitation of aggression, escape or avoidance, and suppression of behaviors other than the target behavior. It is worthwhile to examine how side effects of punishment can affect individuals with autism.

Emotional Responses People who are punished often react with a strong emotional response. They show signs of fear or of being upset, such as whining, crying, trembling, crouching, and attempts to escape or avoid the punishment. People with autism, in particular, are highly sensitive to even implied criticism. Outright criticism and punishment can create intense emotional outbursts in individuals with autism.

Aggression Aggression can be a side effect of punishment. When an individual is punished, aggression toward the person doing the punishing is a possible outcome. Again, individuals with autism are particularly prone to reacting to punishment with aggression. The risk of aggression as a side effect in adults with autism is of particular concern because of their size and strength.

Imitation People who are punished, even people with autism, might learn to punish others as they themselves have been punished. For example, a young man with autism might be punished with slaps for spitting. He might learn that slapping is the proper response when confronted with an annoying situation. The next time his roommate shrieks, he might slap him.

It is instructive to note the perseverative talk of people with autism. Lennie, a young man with autism who imitates others, would curse in a repetitive, rote fashion. Apparently he had learned this from an instructor. His new instructor gave a lot of praise, and subsequently, Lennie could be heard saying, "Good job, good job. Good work, boy."

Escape or Avoidance People who are punished often try to escape or avoid the person punishing them. This avoidance response is particularly strong if punishment is the primary method of management. Escape or avoidance tendencies can create problems in community settings since for many people with severe autism, staying close to their caregivers is a priority goal. Procedures that might result in running away, or otherwise escaping from the situation, can create unacceptable risks.

Overkill Punishment might very well reduce the frequency of the target behavior, however, it might also reduce the frequency of other behaviors as well. Those other behaviors might in fact be desirable. For example, if an individual is punished by reprimands for making annoying sounds, the annoying sounds might stop. However, other, more acceptable attempts at speech might stop as well.

Side effects may or may not occur in any given case. In segregated settings, such as schools or institutions, if side effects do occur, they can often be managed quickly and efficiently. Additional staff can rush in to contain the aggression, tantrum, or other side effects. The great danger of side effects lies in integrated community settings where such behavior is unacceptable. The fictitious case of Burt, presented in two scenarios, provides an example.

Scenario One: Without Punishment

Burt has autism and occasionally he bites his own wrist. He goes with his residential counselor to a grocery store, and while waiting in line, he bites his wrist. The counselor directs him to put his hands on the cart, but nothing is said about the wrist biting. Burt persists for another minute or two, then puts his hands on the cart.

Scenario Two: With Punishment

Burt is in the grocery store line. He bites his wrist and then is punished with water mist to the face (or aromatic ammonia, or electric shock). He reacts by crying, then running away. The counselor must abandon the cart and run through the store trying to catch him. When the counselor finally catches Burt, Burt strikes him. Burt then crouches, trembling and crying, on the grocery store floor.

Maybe Burt learned from the water mist that he should not bite his wrist, but other lessons were learned as well. Burt learned to inflict discomfort on others when they annoy him, and he learned that his counselor was someone to avoid. The counselor learned that Burt was not so easy to take out of the group home and might think twice about another trip to the store. He might even think twice about continuing in his present line of employment. The customers learned that people with handicaps are dangerous, or they might have learned that people who take care of people with handicaps are dangerous. The store manager learned that it might not be a good idea to allow Burt back in the grocery store.

Effectiveness   The case for the effectiveness of punishment is dependent on the research literature. Proponents of punishment state that it is tried and true, and their proof is the published research. Researchers and practitioners now note important deficiencies in the studies. These deficiencies are important because they impose severe limitations on the usefulness of the research for practitioners.

Generalization   Guess, Helmstetter, Turnbull, and Knowlton (1987) in a review of 61 studies using punishment procedures, noted that one major problem with the punishment literature is the lack of information on generalization. Many studies do not report information on generalization, and those that do address generalization often note that the suppression of the behavior did not generalize to situations outside the punishment situation.

Generalization is a critical issue when one considers that many punishment studies occurred during time-limited experimental sessions. The experimenter works with the individual for short sessions (sometimes as short as 15 minutes) and must draw results and conclusions from those short sessions. Many studies noted no carryover of gains outside of the experimental session. The limitations are obvious. Parents, teachers, job coaches, and other caregivers are responsible for their charges with autism around the clock, not just for 15-minute sessions. Procedures are needed that have been demonstrated safe and effective at all times, not just for short intervals.

Long-Term Use   Many studies make no mention of side effects, and it is important to note that the critical issue might be the duration of time that punishment is used. Punishment studies are limited in terms of length of intervention. A study might cover several weeks or even several months, however, people with autism require care and programming for years. Data on the effect of years of punishment are not available. The effects and side effects of the long-term use of punishment are unknown, and without such information, clients, practitioners, and advocates cannot be adequately informed of the risks.

Experimental Design   Guess et al. (1987) reported that less than 25% of the 61 studies evaluated had adequate experimental design.

Where Are the Failures?   A critical question about the punishment research is: How many times was punishment tried and found to be ineffective? Journals often have a tendency to publish studies that show impressive results. For example, Experimenter 1 tries shock to reduce head banging. For the 3 weeks of his study, he finds dramatic reductions in head banging. He might even have an elegant experimental design that gives credence to his findings, so he sends his paper to a journal, and because of the design and the great reductions found, his paper is published.

Now consider Experimenter 2 (and 3 and 4 and 5, etc.). This experimenter tries shock, lemon juice, Tabasco sauce, or aromatic ammonia and finds no effect. He might even have an elegant experimental design, but the individual continued to head bang despite the punishment. In most cases, this experimenter would probably not even submit his paper for publication, and if he did, the chances of publication are probably slim. Therefore, for every one study that purports to demonstrate that punishment is effective, one must ask: In how many other studies has punishment been tried and failed? The answer to this question is not available. Nonetheless, it could be critical.

Role of Functional Analysis   Another difficulty with punishment is that it fails to profit from a functional analysis. Even the earliest researchers in behavior modification and autism stressed the need to determine the environmental influences on the behavior. The need for functional analysis has been clearly stressed since the late 1960s. Once the functions are identified, the environment can be modified, and the individual can be taught alternative behaviors. Punishment short-circuits this process completely.

Risk of Ritualization   If an individual touches a hot stove, it is unlikely he or she will touch a stove again, but hot stoves cannot be used as punishers. Consequences that can be used as punishers are milder than hot stoves and run the risk of becoming part of a ritual for an individual with autism. For example, clinical observations of attempts at mild punishment revealed initial decreases in the target behavior. However, after a few weeks, the behavior increased to original levels when the individuals with autism came to incorporate the consequence into their routine. They would misbehave, then voluntarily submit to the consequence. Other individuals with autism have been observed engaging in a misbehavior, then giving themselves lengthy reprimands and lectures; or they follow their initial misbehavior with self-injury, in a sense, their own self-inflicted punishment ritual.

Risk of Backfire A more dangerous possibility is that the event that is designed as a punisher actually serves as a reward. People with autism often have unusual preferences. Some prefer to be yelled at, reprimanded, or physically removed from the room rather than do the task at hand. Events that typically are intended as punishers often backfire and actually reward the misbehavior. The users of punishment in applied settings can often find themselves in a no-win situation. If the punishment is effective, it might create undesirable side effects, if not, it can become part of the ritual, or worse, yet, the reward.

Lack of Practicality in Public Settings People with autism are now moving out of institutions and institutional settings. The punishment research has been conducted primarily in segregated settings, such as schools or institutions. The use of punishment does not easily translate from a segregated setting to an integrated one. It is one matter to use water mist, Tabasco sauce, or electric shock on an individual in a segregated, private setting. First, the public does not see the punishment, second, if there is an aggressive reaction, help can be called to contain the individual, or he or she can be removed from the scene of the problem.

Punishment is quite another matter in integrated, public settings. It simply is not practical. A job coach at a department store can hardly take out a shock stick or water mist and wield it on the individual with autism. It looks questionable to the public, and the individual with autism might well be bigger than the job coach. People who are sprayed with water mist, even people with autism, might strike back, causing injury to the job coach. Additionally, the supports that are available in the segregated setting to deal with the side effects (aggression, screaming, running) are not as easily available in the department store, restaurant, or shopping mall.

If John bangs his head in a department store, it is far better for his job coach to simply prevent injury than to spray him, shock him, or douse him with Tabasco sauce. If Carole has a problem with spitting while on the job at the library, the spitting can be eliminated quickly enough by rewarding other behaviors and not rewarding the spitting. The job coach does not need to risk full-scale tantrums by putting shaving cream in her mouth each time she spits.

The Only Game in Town? Proponents of punishment declare that for many serious behavior problems associated with autism, punishment is the only means of control. Fortunately, this is not the case. Greater numbers of researchers, scientist-practitioners, and clinicians are reporting impressive gains without the use of punishment.

Since nonpunitive methods are available to manage head banging, aggression, property destruction, and other behavior problems in individuals with autism, there is no longer justification for methods that cause discomfort. This book is devoted to providing information on a variety of strategies that have successfully reduced severe behavior problems in individuals with autism over a 9-year period.

SUMMARY

Punishment has prevailed as a procedure of choice for people with autism. Punishment has several disadvantages, primarily the side effects and the lack of practicality in community settings. Despite the popularity of punishment, researchers and practitioners have diligently investigated nonpunitive approaches to the problems of autism, and clinicians and researchers now have a variety of other procedures from which to choose.

REFERENCES

Altmeyer, B., Williams, D., & Sams, V. (1985). Treatment of severe self-injurious and aggressive biting. *Journal of Behavior Therapy and Experimental Psychiatry, 16*(2), 159–167.

Axelrod, S., & Apsche, J. (Eds.). (1983). *The effects of punishment on human behavior.* New York: Academic Press.

Bailey, J., & Meyerson, L. (1969). Vibration as a reinforcer with a profoundly retarded child. *Journal of Applied Behavior Analysis, 2,* 135–137.

Berkman, K., & Meyer, L. (1988). Alternative strategies and multiple outcomes in the remediation of severe self-injury: Going "all out" nonaversively. *Journal of The Association for Persons with Severe Handicaps, 13*(2), 76–86.

Carr, E.G. (1977). The motivation of self-injurious behavior: A review of some hypothesis. *Psychological Bulletin, 84* (4), 800–816.

Carr, E., & Durand, V. (1985). Reducing behavior problems through functional communication training. *Journal of Applied Behavior Analysis, 18,* 111–126.

Carr, E., Newsom, C., & Binkoff, J. (198^). Escape as a factor in the aggressive behavior of two retarded children. *Journal of Applied Behavior Analysis, 13*(1), 101–118.

Charlop, M., Burgio, L., Iwata, B., & Ivancic, M. (1988). Stimulus variation as a means of enhancing punishment effects. *Journal of Applied Behavior Analysis, 21,* 89–95.

Donnellan, A., & LaVigna, G. (1986). Nonaversive control of socially stigmatizing behaviors. *Pointer, 30*(4), 25–31.

Donnellan, A., Mirenda, P., Mesaros, R., & Fassbender, L. (1984). Analyzing the communicative functions of aberrant behavior. *Journal of The Association for Persons with Severe Handicaps, 9,* 201–212.

Durand, V.M., & Carr, E.G. (1987). Social influences on "self-stimulatory" behavior: Analysis and treatment application. *Journal of Applied Behavior Analysis, 20,* 118–132.

Durand, V.M., & Crimmins, D. (1987). Assessment and treatment of psychotic speech in an autistic child. *Journal of Autism and Developmental Disorders, 17*(1), 17–27.

Durand, V.M., & Crimmins, D. (1988). Identifying the variables maintaining self-injurious behavior. *Journal of Autism and Developmental Disorders, 18*(1), 99–117.

Ferster, C.B., & DeMyer, M.K. (1961). A method for the experimental analysis of the behavior of autistic children. *American Journal of Orthopsychiatry, 32,* 89–98.

Friman, P., Cook, J.W., & Finney, J. (1984). Effects of punishment procedures on the self-stimulatory behavior of an autistic child. *Analysis and Intervention in Developmental Disability, 4,* 39–46.

Fuller, P.R. (1949). Operant conditioning of a vegetative human organism. *American Journal of Psychology, 62,* 587–590.

Gardner, W., & Cole, C. (1987). Managing aggressive behavior: A behavioral diagnostic approach. *Psychiatric Aspects of Mental Retardation Reviews, 6*(5), 21–25.

Guess, D., Helmstetter, E., Turnbull, H., & Knowlton, S. (1987). *Use of aversive procedures with persons who are disabled: An historical review and critical analysis.* Seattle: The Association for Persons with Severe Handicaps.

Harris, F., Wolf, M., & Baer, D. (1964). Effects of adult social reinforcement on child behavior. *Young Children, 20*(1), 8–17.

Hung, D.W. (1978). Using self-stimulation as reinforcement for autistic children. *Journal of Autism and Developmental Disorders, 8,* 355–366.

Iwata, B., Dorsey, M., Slifer, K., Bauman, K., & Richman, G. (1982). Toward a functional analysis of self-injury. *Analysis and Intervention in Developmental Disabilities, 2,* 3–20.

Johnson, C., & Frankel, A. (1978). The use of physical contact as a positive reinforcer. *Behavior Therapy, 9*(5), 969–970.

Koegel, R., & Covert, A. (1972). The relationship of self-stimulation to learning in autistic children. *Journal of Applied Behavior Analysis, 5,* 381–387.

LaVigna, G., & Donnellan, A. (1986). *Alternatives to punishment: Solving behavior problems with non-aversive strategies.* New York: Irvington Publishers.

Lovaas, O.I. (1979). Contrasting illness and behavioral models for the treatment of autistic children: A historical perspective. *Journal of Autism and Developmental Disorders, 9*(4), 315–323.

Lovaas, I., & Simmons, J. (1969). Manipulation of self-destruction in retarded children. *Journal of Applied Behavior Analysis, 2,* 143–157.

Luce, S., Delquadri, J., & Hall, R. (1980). Contingent exercise: A mild but powerful procedure for suppressing inappropriate verbal and aggressive behavior. *Journal of Applied Behavior Analysis, 13,* 583–594.

Neufeld, A., & Fantuzzo, J. (1984). Contingent application of a protective device to treat the severe self-biting behavior of a disturbed autistic child. *Journal of Behavior Therapy and Experimental Psychiatry, 15*(1), 79–83.

Newsom, C., Favell, J., & Rincover, A. (1983). The side effects of punishment. In S. Axelrod & J. Apsche (Eds.), *The effects of punishment on human behavior* (pp. 285–316). New York: Academic Press.

Osborne, J.G. (1969). Free time as a reinforcer in the management of classroom behavior. *Journal of Applied Behavior Analysis, 2,* 113–118.

Pumroy, D., & Pumroy, S. (1965). Systematic observation and reinforcement technique in toilet training. *Psychological Reports, 16,* 467–471.

Repp, A., Felce, D., & Barton, L. (1988). Basing the treatment of stereotypic and self-injurious behaviors on hypotheses of their causes. *Journal of Applied Behavior Analysis, 21,* 281–289.

Rincover, A., & Devany, J. (1982). The application of sensory extinction procedures to self-injury. *Analysis and Intervention in Developmental Disabilities, 2,* 67–81.

Risley, T. (1968). The effects and side effects of punishing the autistic behaviors of a deviant child. *Journal of Applied Behavior Analysis, 1,* 21–34.

Rojahn, J., McGonigle, J., Curcio, C., & Dixon, M. (1987). Suppression of pica by water mist and aromatic ammonia. *Behavior Modification, 11*(1), 65–74.

Romanczyk, R. (1977). Intermittent punishment of self-stimulation effectiveness during application and extinction. *Journal of Consulting and Clinical Psychology, 45,* 53–60.

Romanczyk, R., & Goren, E. (1975). Severe self-injurious behavior: The problem of clinical control. *Journal of Consulting and Clinical Psychology, 43,* 730–739.

Schaefer, H.H. (1970). Self-injurious behavior: Shaping head banging in monkeys. *Journal of Applied Behavior Analysis, 3,* 111–116.

Smith, M. (1985). Managing the aggressive and self-injurious behavior of adults disabled by autism in the community. *Journal of The Association for Persons with Severe Handicaps, 10,* 228–232.

Smith, M. (1986). The use of alternate sensory stimuli in the community-based treatment of the self-stimulatory behavior of an adult disabled by autism. *Journal of Behavior Therapy and Experimental Psychiatry, 17,* 121–125.

Talkington, L., Hall, S., & Altman, R. (1971). Communication deficits and aggression in the mentally retarded. *American Journal of Mental Deficiency, 76*(2), 235–237.

Tanner, B., & Zeiler, M. (1975). Punishment of self-injurious behavior using aromatic ammonia as the aversive stimulus. *Journal of Applied Behavior Analysis, 8,* 53–57.

Tate, B. G., & Baroff, G. (1966). Aversive control of self-injurious behavior in a psychotic boy. *Behavior Research & Therapy, 4,* 281–287.

Taylor, C., & Chamove, A. (1986). Vibratory or visual stimulation reduces self-injury. *Australia & New Zealand Journal of Developmental Disabilities, 12*(4), 243–248.

Williams, C.D. (1959). The elimination of tantrum behavior by extinction procedures. *Journal of Abnormal Social Psychology, 59,* 269.

Willis, T., & LaVigna, G. (1988, May). *Non-aversive treatment of severe self-injury.* Paper presented to the annual convention of the Association for Behavior Analysis, Philadelphia, PA.

Yeakel, M., Salisbury, L., Greer, S., & Marcus, L. (1970). An appliance for autoinduced adverse control of self-injurious behavior. *Journal of Experimental Child Psychology, 10,* 159–169.

Zimmerman, E., & Zimmerman, J. (1962). The alteration of behavior in a special classroom situation. *Journal of the Experimental Analysis of Behavior, 5,* 59–60.

_____ *Chapter Three* _____

BEHAVIORAL ASSESSMENT

Education and psychology are fields that have hundreds, if not thousands, of standardized tests. These tests are designed to measure intelligence, personality, interests, vocational skills, academic skills, self-care skills, and/or language skills. With the variety of standardized tests available, if a person has a skill to measure, in all likelihood some kind of test has been developed to assess that skill.

Many professionals rely on standardized tests for a variety of reasons, and many tests are indeed valid for those purposes. However, there are some purposes for which standardized measures of achievement, intelligence, and interest are not needed and most likely are not valid. Achieving behavior change in individuals with autism is just such an area.

Behavioral adjustment of persons with autism does not rely on standardized tests, but that is not to say that adjustment does not rely on data. In fact, the process relies heavily on data, data collected during a behavioral assessment. A behavioral assessment is an evaluation, based on observations and analyses, of the interaction between the individual, the target behavior, and the environment. Behavioral assessment strategies are as individualized as the intervention plans themselves. They are the beginning of the behavior change process. The success or failure of the intervention strategy can very well depend on the integrity of the behavioral assessment on which it is based.

The purpose of this chapter is to discuss and illustrate the behavioral assessment process for use in solving the behavior problems of individuals with autism. In order to proceed, the reader needs no standardized tests, no norm charts, and no manuals of test interpretation. All that is needed is pencil and skill.

PURPOSES OF ASSESSMENT

Many unsuccessful attempts at behavior change are based on an incomplete assessment, an inaccurate assessment, or no assessment at all, and although a

29

good assessment does not guarantee a successful outcome, it certainly helps. There are several purposes that a good behavioral assessment serves.

How Big is the Problem?

Prior to planning an intervention, it is important to assess the severity of the problem. In other words, how big is the problem? The severity of the problem will dictate whether an intervention plan is needed, and, to a degree, the scope of the plan. Occasionally, caregivers will consider a behavior change plan for a particular behavior. After an initial assessment period, caregivers might agree that the problem was not as severe as originally thought, and they might decide not to proceed with a plan. An initial assessment, prior to developing a plan, helps prevent impulsive planning and unnecessary interventions.

Larry's case provides an example of this circumstance. Larry is a 35-year-old man with autism who works at a computer firm. His job coach complained that he was frequently off task. During the initial assessment period the job coach timed the duration of off-task intervals and discovered that Larry was never off task more than 2 consecutive minutes. The team agreed that his off-task behavior was not much different than that of his nonhandicapped co-workers, therefore, no intervention was needed.

Jim is a young man with autism who occasionally has difficulty adjusting to change. Jim started a new job in a restaurant under the supervision of a job coach. The job stipulates that Jim wear a hat that is part of a uniform, but he refuses to wear the hat. The psychologist was consulted and suggested a 1-week assessment procedure. By the end of the week, staff reported that Jim was cooperatively wearing his hat. No intervention was needed.

Not all problems need so little action. In fact, assessments can also reveal that much action is needed quickly. Initial behavioral assessments can often reveal that the problem is quite severe and even jeopardizes job or community placements. In those cases, a good assessment can alert all concerned that action is needed immediately. These assessments provide a quantitative, documented basis for any decisions that follow.

What Exactly is Going On?

A behavioral assessment provides critical information on more than just the severity of the behavior; it can help pinpoint exactly what the target behaviors should be. Luther occasionally screams at work, thus, screaming seemed to be the important target behavior. However, an assessment showed that Luther screams when presented with a difficult task, and it was suggested that a target behavior should be asking for help. As well as reducing screaming, staff needed to teach Luther to ask for help. A behavioral assessment can also tell under what circumstances the behavior occurs. For example, Luther usually only screams under certain conditions, that is, if a task is too hard. This information is key to solving the problem.

Kirk provides another good example. Kirk occasionally cries and destroys property. A behavioral assessment revealed that his worst behavior occurs during thunderstorms. The intervention plan then targeted thunderstorms as a time when Kirk needed increased supervision and behavioral strategies to help him deal with the weather.

What is the Purpose of the Behavior?

The behavioral assessment also provides information on how the behavior interacts with the environment. The behavioral assessment can lead to a functional analysis, the process of deciding what the purpose of the behavior is for the individual. It is assumed that the behavior has a purpose, and the assessment helps to pinpoint the purpose or purposes.

A functional analysis is done by looking closely at the conditions that are ongoing before and during the behavior. Such conditions might include weather, illness, hunger, thirst, little attention, increased attention, little to do, much to do, tasks that are easy, tasks that are hard, fights with peers, fights among peers, and even fights among staff. Functional analysis also looks at what events follow the behavior. Does the individual get what he wants? Does he get what he does not want? Do more staff come? Do all staff leave?

All of this information is helpful in deciding the purpose the behavior serves for the individual. The ability to determine the purpose or purposes of misbehavior can be critical to achieving long-lasting adjustment. A good behavioral assessment is critical for a complete functional analysis. (Functional analysis is discussed in more detail later in this chapter.)

How Effective is Intervention?

The behavioral assessment does not end when the intervention plan begins. Data collection continues throughout implementation of the intervention plan, and for individuals with severe autism, data collection might be an ongoing support throughout their lives. Behavioral assessments provide data that can be used to evaluate the effectiveness of the intervention program, and the data can also be used to evaluate the progress of the individual.

Ongoing behavioral assessment provides information that determines intervention decisions. Once the plan is developed, decisions are constantly evaluated and reevaluated. Frequency data provide information on whether the plan is successful. Behavioral assessment also provides a measure of the severity of the problem. In the case of skills, such assessment provides a baseline skill level (baseline is the level of behavior before intervention).

If the behavior is measured prior to intervention, and measurement continues during intervention, then staff can determine the effectiveness. If spitting occurs 45 times a day before intervention, and 5 times a day after 1 week of intervention, then one might conclude that the intervention plan is effective. However, if spitting does not change, or gets worse, over the course of 2 months of intervention, one might reasonably question the effectiveness of the intervention plan.

Continued data collection on the antecedents and consequences provides information on whether the plan is being followed. Furthermore, if new functions for the behavior develop, ongoing behavioral assessment can reveal such developments.

Good behavioral assessment helps ensure that decisions regarding the design and continued implementation of the intervention plan are based on objective data rather than on subjective opinion. Behavioral assessment provides a tool for evaluating the effectiveness of the intervention program and the individual's progress compared to baseline.

What's Next?

Decisions on goals for the coming year, job placements, supervision, and independence can all be made based on data acquired during behavioral assessments. Decisions on program change can be made based on objective measures, rather than on subjective impressions.

Who Cares?

Accountability to state, county, and local licensing boards as well as to accreditation organizations has made behavioral assessment almost mandatory. Although interactions between staff and individuals in group homes and job sites appear to be rather private, there are a myriad of organizations, families, and individuals who have a right to demand proof of progress, or at least attempts at progress. Behavioral assessment provides such proof by including precise documentation of pretreatment levels and levels throughout intervention. Evidence of progress can be clearly graphed for all to see, and if progress has not been made, then evidence exists to demonstrate that reasonable attempts were made to achieve goals and modify plans as needed.

CRITERIA FOR DATA COLLECTION

Data collection then, for several reasons, is an important component of any behavior change process, however, it presents unique challenges, particularly in integrated community settings.

The individuals who must collect data are the same people who serve as residential counselors, job coaches, and teachers. These people must provide supervision; they must teach, direct, and guide; they must run a home or oversee a job site; and they must manage any behavior problems that might occur. Along with these duties, caregivers are now required to collect data. These competing duties also exist if the data collector is the parent. It is essential to recognize the limits and priorities of caregivers when designing the data collection procedures.

Data collection procedures might also be limited by the job setting or the community setting in which the individual is living and working. Data collection procedures that are cumbersome might be difficult to implement, therefore, they should be designed with the individual's living and working environments in mind. Procedures for data collection should be developed and selected according to the following criteria:

1. The data can be collected by observing the participant on the job, at home, in restaurants, in stores, or in any other setting in which the target behavior may occur.
2. Caregivers can be trained in the data collection technique.
3. Caregivers can use the technique in addition to their training and supervision duties.
4. The data collection procedure is neither obtrusive nor intrusive, that is, it does not call attention to the individuals or the handicap.
5. The procedures do not interfere with the functioning of the work or home setting.
6. The data collection procedure is relevant to the target behavior being studied and will allow for evaluation of progress.

PINPOINT THE BEHAVIOR

The first step in the assessment process is to target behaviors in need of change. The behaviors targeted must be observable and measurable. It is natural at first to pinpoint behaviors that are undesirable, such as aggression, self-injury, screaming, wandering, or property destruction. It is best to target specific behaviors that are incompatible with undesirable behaviors, and then work to strengthen the desired behavior. Table 3.1 provides an example.

At this point the target behaviors are tentative and might change after the assessment phase. However, this first identification of target behaviors provides a starting point in the assessment process.

Table 3.1. Target behaviors that are incompatible with undesirable behaviors

Undesirable behaviors	Behaviors to target for strengthening
Aggression (hit, kick)	Keep hands and feet to self
Property destruction	Correct use of property
Wandering	Remain in assigned location
Screaming	Low voice volume
Clothes tearing	Maintain clothes in good condition
Wearing dirty clothes	Wear clean clothes
Spitting	Keep area dry

DATA COLLECTION METHODS

Once the behaviors are pinpointed, then methods for collecting data can be chosen. Many procedures for collecting data are available. Following is a description of strategies that have been helpful for assessment of individuals with autism.

Diary Approach

A diary involves observing the individual in the target setting and recording all events and interactions that are observed. A diary approach is cumbersome, but can provide valuable information about the setting and the individual's interactions with that setting. The details available from the diary can often provide the basis for functional analysis.

Structured Diary

A structured diary is similar to a diary but is not as complete. It limits the type of information recorded, and it provides a format for collecting that information. Typically in behavioral assessments, a structured diary involves recording a description of the events that preceded the target behavior (antecedents), the behavior itself, and the events that followed (consequences). An antecedent-behavior-consequences (ABC) form is shown in Figure 3.1.

Antecedents   Antecedents are those events or conditions that occur before the behavior. Who was there, what was going on, the time, the date, and what was said to the individual are all antecedents. Caregivers sometimes have trouble describing antecedents. People often expect the antecedents to be obvious causes of the outburst, and if there are no obvious causes, the caregiver might put "none" under antecedents.

The fact is that there are always antecedent conditions, that is, there is always something occurring. Even if the individual is sitting on the sofa quietly prior to the incident, an antecedent can be described. For example, the antecedent might be, "After dinner Ralph was told to sit on the sofa. Staff were still at the dinner table. Ralph sat about 15 minutes." Although there was no dramatic event that preceded Ralph breaking the window, it can be noted that it occurred after dinner and he was sitting on the sofa.

Another problem in recording is that caregivers focus exclusively on the target behaviors and fail to observe the events that take place prior to the incident. Figure 3.2 provides an example of how staff might complete an ABC form.

The problem with this record is that it does not describe the events that occurred before the behavior took place. Joan's crying can be considered part of the target behavior, along with scratching. Figure 3.3 describes the events that took place prior to her crying and scratching. Recorders must be careful

Date	Time incident began	Antecedents	Description of behavior	Consequences	Response

Figure 3.1. Sample ABC form. (Antecedents include what the individual was doing, what the counselor was doing, how long the activity had been taking place, and any other preceding events; description of behavior describes exactly what behavior(s) was exhibited; consequences are anything and everything that follows the behavior [what was said and done by anyone around]; response is what the individual did in response to the consequences.)

to describe the environmental events that preceded the behavior and not just the individual's reactions to those events.

Description of Behaviors The structured diary should include a description of the undesirable behaviors. Any milder signs that preceded the

Date	Time incident began	Antecedents	Description of behavior	Consequences	Response
1/6	2:30	Joan cried.	Joan scratched Anne.	Joan was told to sit down.	Joan did but she kept crying.

Figure 3.2. Sample completed ABC form.

Date	Time incident began	Antecedents	Description of behavior	Consequences	Response
1/6	2:30	Joan was cooking and Anne told her not to burn the meat.	Joan cried and scratched Anne.	Joan was told to sit down.	Joan did but she kept crying.

Figure 3.3. Sample ABC form illustrating observation of antecedents and consequences.

actual pinpointed behavior can also be included in this column. For example, in Figure 3.3., Joan's crying can be mentioned, but it should be mentioned as the behavior, not as the antecedent.

Consequences Consequences are details of what occurred after the behavior, including what was said to the individual, who said it, and whatever else occurred. Again, as with antecedents, recorders do not need to make judgments about which events are important. Any observable events and reactions should be recorded. It is also informative to add a final column for the individual's response. Figure 3.4 provides an example. The structured diary, like the dairy, can provide valuable information for the functional analysis. However, it must be completed in detail with judgments about what is and is not important left for later.

Description of Setting Events

Diaries or ABC forms should make some mention of setting events. These are the events that affect what behaviors will occur given certain antecedents. For example, on most days, Jim responds well to instructions and is cooperative. However, if it rains, he is more likely to become aggressive when given instructions. Rain, then, is the setting event that makes aggression more likely to result when instructions are given.

Gardner, Cole, Davidson, and Karan (1986) discussed the importance of setting events. Knowledge of setting events can answer the frequently asked question, "Why does this individual usually respond well to (antecedent), but sometimes does not?" Gardner and his-co-authors described several categories of setting events that should be considered, including physiological conditions and durational events.

Physiological Conditions Certain physiological states can have great impact on behavior. A person does not need to have autism to know that if he

Date	Time incident began	Antecedents	Description of behavior	Consequences	Response
11/12	10:00	Jim was asked to vacuum.	Jim hit staff.	Jim was told to vacuum.	Jim did.

Figure 3.4. Sample ABC noting response.

or she is hungry, and has not eaten all day, his or her temper may be short. Likewise, if a person is ill, he or she may not produce as well at work. Some people even claim that without their morning cup of coffee, they are of no use to anyone. Physiological conditions that might serve as setting events include being hungry, lacking sleep, too much caffeine, absence of caffeine, or the presence or absence of certain drugs. Illness and allergies are also important to consider.

Durational Events Gardner et al.'s article discusses durational events that serve as setting events. Durational events might refer to people. The presence of certain staff or relatives, or absence of certain persons, can serve as important setting events. For example, Henry is more likely to self-injure if his regular job coach is not the person who picks him up to go to work. Alfred is more likely to refuse to participate in his group home schedule on a Saturday if he expects his parents to come.

Durational events can also be absence of social interactions from others. For example, if no one talks to Joe all morning, and at noon he is asked to make his bed, then such a request might make Joe aggressive. If, however, people have been interacting with him all morning, he might be more likely to respond to requests cooperatively.

Research studies reviewed by Gardner et al. suggest that general environmental conditions can also serve as setting events. General working conditions, lack of space, lack of other activities, difficulty of tasks, and staff/client ratios can all be important setting events. Events that preceded the target behavior by several hours can also influence behavior. For example, arguments with staff, fights with peers, fights between other peers, or other disruptions in routine can influence behavior for hours to come. Where setting events can be identified, they should be recorded on daily logs, or directly on diary or ABC forms.

Tally Method

A tally involves counting the number of incidents of the behavior. For example, if the undesirable behavior is head banging, the number of times the individual bangs his or her head would be counted. If behaviors occur too often for ABC forms to be filled out for each occurrence, then frequency data might be used simply to provide information on how often the behavior occurs. Tallies, when accurate, provide an exact measure of how often a behavior occurs, however, there are several disadvantages to tallies.

At times it is difficult to keep accurate tallies of behaviors. This can be true if the behavior occurs at a high frequency. Some adults with autism display undesirable behaviors hundreds of times per day. Caregivers who are trying to teach these adults and implement their behavior programs might not have time to record every instance of the behavior. With high frequency behaviors, recording each instance of the behavior could disrupt good instructional and behavioral programming. Additionally, the tally method might require that the caregiver observe the individual continuously or an instance of the behavior might be missed. This is often not possible.

Time Block

A time block can be a reliable alternative to a tally. In this procedure, the observer records whether or not the behavior occurred in set periods of time, for example in 15-minute blocks. Using this method, staff would record whether or not the behavior occurred in each 15-minute block throughout the day and evening. Jim provides a good example of the use of a time block. Jim banged his head about 50 times per hour. Staff could not manage both Jim and a tally method of recording data. A good choice was a time block where the day was divided into 15-minute intervals of time. For each 15-minute interval, staff simply recorded a ''+'' if the head banging occurred and a ''−'' if it did not occur. Figure 3.5 presents an example of a time block data sheet.

The size of the interval should be large enough to allow for staff resources and small enough to be able to assess progress. For example, if a behavior occurs almost continuously, a 15-minute time block might be necessary. However, if a behavior occurs only a few times each hour, then a half-hour time block might be sufficient. Time blocks do not give as precise a measure as the tally, however, this method saves time. Time blocks can also be more reliable. For a tally to be accurate, every single instance of the behavior must be observed and counted, whereas time blocks require that the caregiver only note occurrence within each interval.

Duration

Duration measurements are used when length of time is a critical factor. For example, the duration of aggressive episodes might be recorded. Heavy reliance on duration data is not usually practical in integrated community settings or at the job site. Duration requires the observer to record the onset and ending of each incident of the target behavior. If the incidents are fairly long (i.e., over 5 minutes) then this recording can be done. However, if the incidents involve shorter time periods, then the actual act of timing can be very burdensome to staff.

Behaviors of short duration are typically difficult to time in integrated community settings. Staff are often too busy carrying out other responsibilities and usually do not have the luxury of timing events that are only several minutes in duration. In these cases, it is generally not worth the additional burden it places on staff time and other methods should be relied on.

Ratio of Responses to Opportunities

Some types of behaviors will have limited opportunity to occur, that is, the behavior is directly dependent on some environmental opportunity. For example, saying, ''thank you'' is directly dependent on being given something,

CLIENT:_____   WEEK:_____

DESIRED BEHAVIOR:_____

DIRECTIONS: Enter a + if desired behavior occurred during interval.
             Enter a − if it did not occur.

	DAY DATE	DAY DATE	DAY DATE	DAY DATE	DAY DATE	DAY DATE	DAY DATE
8:30 A – 9:00 A							
9:00 A – 9:30 A							
9:30 A – 10:00 A							
10:00 A – 10:30 A							
10:30 A – 11:00 A							
11:00 A – 11:30 A							
11:30 A – 12:00 N							
12:00 N – 12:30 P							
12:30 P – 1:00 P							
1:00 P – 1:30 P							
1:30 P – 2:00 P							
2:00 P – 2:30 P							
2:30 P – 3:00 P							
3:00 P – 3:30 P							
3:30 P – 4:00 P							

Figure 3.5. Sample time block data sheet.

giving customers accurate directions is directly dependent on a customer
asking for assistance, and responding acceptably to criticism is directly dependent on being criticized. For behaviors that are directly dependent on
environmental opportunities, a tally or time block alone might be deceiving.
The case of Sally provides a good example. Sally's job coach wanted to teach
her to ask for assistance any time a tool broke. The job coach was keeping a
tally of the number of times Sally asked for assistance, but this tally alone was
meaningless. If a 3 was recorded for the day, then it would indicate that Sally

asked for assistance three times. Without knowing how many times a tool broke, the three is meaningless. The tool might have broken 40 times, if so, asking for help on three of those occasions is not impressive. However, if the tool broke three times and Sally asked for help all three, then it appears she has the skill of asking for help.

Behaviors that are directly dependent on given opportunities can be assessed by examining the ratio of responses to opportunities. For example, if the target behavior is "response to correction," then the observer would record information on the type of response to each instance of correction. Then the total number of opportunities (i.e., instances of correction) would be divided into the number of acceptable responses. The quotient would be multiplied by 100% to result in a percentage of correct responses. This formula for computing percentage of correct responses is shown below.

$$\# \text{ of correct responses} \div \text{total number of opportunities} \times 100\% = \text{percent of correct responses}$$

Gary's case provides a good example of this procedure. Gary is a man with autism who works at a manufacturing firm. He has trouble sharing his workspace. If a co-worker should come to share his work table, Gary mumbles rudely under his breath and refuses to make room for the co-worker. To measure the percentage of correct responses, staff noted each time a co-worker came to share the workspace. Staff also recorded whether Gary politely made room or whether he refused to do so. A percentage of correct responses was then computed.

Figure 3.6 provides an example of a social skills data sheet that can be used to record correct and incorrect responses in both role play and actual situations. This type of data sheet can be used when role plays (see Chapter Six) are being done and data is of interest in both the role play and the actual situation.

Record Review

In some cases the severity of the behavior will dictate immediate implementation of an intervention plan. For example, Esther has a problem with biting and has severely bitten several staff. An intervention plan is needed quickly in order to prevent further staff injuries. In such cases a review of the records can be done in order to estimate a baseline measure of the behavior. Sometimes, antecedent and consequence information can also be found in the records.

Productivity

Measures of productivity are often computed from work that the individual has produced. For example, a worker in a bindery company may produce bound books. The number of books produced can be used to compute a

CLIENT:_____

OBJECTIVE:_____

_____

WORKSITE:_____

TASK:_____ _____

C = CORRECT AND INDEPENDENT
P = CORRECT WITH PROMPT
O = INCORRECT OR NO RESPONSE

RECORD ONLY <u>ONE</u> ROLE PLAY OR ACTUAL
SITUATION ON EACH LINE.

DATE	TIME	ROLE PLAY	ACTUAL SITUATION	COMMENTS	INITIALS

Figure 3.6. Sample social skills data sheet.

measure of productivity, this productivity measure can be computed to provide an hourly rate, and the individual's productivity can be compared with rates of nonhandicapped co-workers.

Productivity measures are often the measurement of choice when the focus is on off task or self-stimulatory behavior. For example, a job coach was concerned that Bart was off task too frequently. Measuring the duration of each time he went off task was awkward. Instead, staff took productivity data by counting the number of units of work he produced. Often in group homes and at job sites staff will complain about self-stimulation, such as flipping, spinning, and rocking. Again, rather then trying to measure the duration of such behaviors, focusing on productivity, such as number of dishes washed or number of towels folded can be easier and just as valid.

Permanent Products

Behaviors often create other products that can be counted, and this figure can be used to measure baseline levels as well as progress during intervention. For example, the products created through work (on-task behavior) can be counted and measured. Other products that can also be included in measuring systems are hospital bills, bills for damaged property, and other such records that result from incidents of aggression. Records such as these that document the effects of the aggressive, self-injurious, or destructive behavior can be used in conjunction with other measures.

Self-injury often results in bruises, scratches, or other marks left on the body. Sometimes it is easier to count such marks than to count the occurrence of the behavior. This is especially true in cases of self-abuse that are done privately. For example, Monica scratches her hands, but she does so in private. Staff do not actually see her scratching herself, but each morning and each evening they can check her hands for any new scratch marks. Destroyed property is another measure of aggression. Again, staff might not actually see the individual destroy the property, however, the results of such damage typically come to light, and can be counted. Even in cases where the behavior is observable, counts of the destroyed property can give valuable information on the severity of the problem.

Unfortunately, behaviors such as property destruction, bolting away, or screaming sometimes attract the attention of neighbors. Neighbors then occasionally lodge complaints, and these complaints can provide another measure of the target behavior.

Employment Status

A measure of behavioral adjustment for individuals in supported employment programs can be employment status. Employment status provides a measure of social validity that can transcend the numbers collected through tallies, time blocks, or any other behavioral measure. Employment status provides the ultimate measure of social validity. For example, Carl has occasional attacks of property destruction, screaming, and aggression. These behaviors are tracked on ABC forms. However, it is important to note that Carl has had the same job, despite these behaviors, for close to 3 years. His job retention provides a valid measure of the effectiveness of his behavioral program.

Time Sampling

Occasionally, data cannot be collected continuously throughout the day, and in such cases a sampling procedure can be used. Using sampling procedures, data are collected during designated periods of time using a variety of methods on the assumption that those data will provide representative information. For example, it might be determined that data will be collected on Tuesdays and Thursdays or only in the mornings. If a behavior occurs at a high frequency, then data might be collected on a time block format with a structured diary used on a sample basis. An example might be a case where spitting occurs many times per hour. Spitting then might be measured on a 15-minute time block basis, however, antecedent and consequence information is needed for functional analysis. There are too many incidents to record on structured diary forms, so a structured diary might be used for the first incident each hour, or kept for only the most severe incidents.

FUNCTIONAL ANALYSIS

Behaviors of persons with autism sometime appear irrational. Often, there is no obvious purpose; hitting, kicking, or head banging seem to appear out of the blue. Such behavior may occur with only slight provocation: The doctor's appointment has been cancelled, the parents are 30 minutes late to pick up their son or daughter from the group home, the mail arrives and the expected postcard does not come. The outbursts that follow these trivial events seem neither logical nor purposeful.

Behavior without a purpose poses at least two problems. If there is no purpose, then there can be no prediction. Without knowing under what circumstances the behavior might occur, no preparations can be made, and there can be no prevention. Second, behavior without a purpose provides little implication for intervention. If the purpose is unknown, then so must be the solution. Therefore, it is important to consider that behavior has a purpose so that predictions can be made, lists of cues can be compiled, possible reasons can be guessed, and then intervention strategies can be designed that can prevent the behavior from occurring. At the very least, these intervention strategies can prevent the possibility of injury should aggression or self-injury occur.

Assuming behavior has a purpose, then the implications for intervention are enormous. Once the purpose of behavior is determined, strategies can be designed that provide the individual with other ways of achieving his or her purposes. Alternatively, motivation can be provided for the individual to attain our purposes.

The functional analysis is a determination of what function the behavior serves for the individual. Nonverbal individuals will often use self-injury, property destruction, or aggression to serve the following functions: obtain attention, food, drink, change of activity, change of staff, change of scene, avoidance of task, social interaction. Verbal clients will often use undesirable behaviors as a way of establishing social interaction, avoiding task, obtaining attention, obtaining assistance, or changing activity.

The following question needs to be answered by functional analysis: "What functions do the behaviors serve for the individual?" (There may be more than one function for one behavior.) This information can be obtained from the diary or structured diary.

Antecedents

Information on antecedents can reveal the circumstances under which the behavior is likely to occur. The antecedents must be looked at closely and without bias. Just because an event appears to be innocent does not mean that it is not an antecedent to a problem behavior. Eddie provides a good illustration of this point. Eddie has severe autism and lives in a group home where he occasionally destroys property. He throws shoes, lamps, and other heavy objects, and typically he throws these objects at windows that usually break.

The ABC forms revealed that at least one-third of the incidents occurred after Eddie was finished with dinner and was told to sit on the sofa. While Eddie was sitting on the sofa, staff continued to eat. After about 15 minutes, Eddie would begin to destroy property. The antecedents seemed too innocent to staff, but innocent or not, the facts were clear: sitting on the sofa after dinner while staff still ate was an antecedent to property destruction. An intervention plan provided other activities for Eddie immediately after dinner, and decreases in misbehavior followed. Assessment of antecedents, then, involves listing all antecedents as revealed on ABC forms, and all such circumstances should be seriously considered as events that might set off the misbehavior, no matter how innocent they appear.

Setting Events

The functional analysis should include information on setting events. Behavior may serve certain purposes given certain setting events. When these setting events are identified, they should be considered in functional analysis. It is helpful to have a list of setting events, and the antecedents they influence, compiled for use during the planning of the intervention strategies.

Consequences

Consequences must be examined with the same attitude as antecedents and setting events. Information collected on consequences can reveal the individual's purpose for the behavior. Consequences that seem innocent may in fact make the behavior useful for the individual. When reviewing ABC forms, it is safe to assume that any consequences listed might in fact explain the purpose of the behavior. For example, individuals are frequently lectured or counseled after problem incidents, and such lecturing or counseling might in fact serve a rewarding purpose to the individual.

Individuals are often sent to their rooms after misbehavior. Escape from task may be just what they were looking for. In some cases individuals are "calmed down," and are provided with music, warm milk, reassuring talk, and other pleasant events after the misbehavior. If such events frequently follow the misbehavior, then these events might in fact be the purpose for the misbehavior. Caregivers must take an objective, unbiased look at all antecedents and consequences, and from this information a list of possible purposes must be developed.

Desirable Behavior: Does It Serve a Purpose?

So far, misbehavior has been discussed, but one problem with autism is that certain desirable behaviors do not occur. An adult with autism, although he or she is verbal, may neglect to say hello when a visitor enters, or an individual who is fully capable of doing the job or task may do it quickly and inadequately or not at all. Cases in which a desirable behavior is missing also requires a functional analysis. In those cases, the following question must be asked: "Why should the individual do the behavior I would like him or her to do?"

A functional analysis often reveals that there is no good reason for the individual to behave in a particular way. A job coach might want the individual to hang pants, and the worker with autism may even get a sizeable paycheck every 2 weeks for hanging pants. However, perhaps the individual cannot count, or possibly the individual does not understand money, or maybe every 2 weeks is too long to wait for a paycheck. A functional analysis might reveal that in fact the pants hanging serves no good function for the individual. An intervention plan would then have to provide a function for the desired behavior, in this case hanging pants.

The process of doing a functional analysis, is to find purposes of misbehavior, but a functional analysis also involves finding lack of purpose of desirable behavior. An intervention plan can be developed to use this information to teach new ways to achieve old goals. The plan might also need to provide purposes for behavior that so far had seemed useless to the individual.

SELECTING METHODS OF DATA COLLECTION

Data collection methods must serve two purposes. First, a measurement of occurrence or severity must be made, and second, data must be collected for a functional analysis. Selection of methods will depend on the setting and on staff resources. If staff are busy with instructional and behavioral programming, then data collection must be kept to a minimum, yet still provide a basis for assessment.

In a typical home, group home, or job setting, if the behavior occurs less than five times per day, caregivers can usually handle a structured diary. This method will provide information on the frequency of the behavior and also on the functions of the behavior. If the behavior occurs between 5 and 10 times per day, caregivers can usually take a tally, and structured diaries can be filled out on either a time sample basis or on a priority basis. A time sample might call for the first incident of the morning and the first incident of the afternoon being recorded on ABC forms, while a priority basis might specify that only the most severe incidents each hour be recorded on ABC forms. If the behavior occurs more than 10 times per day, then even a tally might be too cumbersome. A time block might be used to estimate frequency, and ABC forms can be completed on a time sample or priority basis.

Other data collection procedures, such as those discussed previously in this chapter, might be useful, depending on the nature of the pinpointed behavior. Staff should determine the method or combination of methods that are most appropriate for assessing the frequency and severity of the behavior.

SUMMARY

Individuals with autism might display a number of peculiar behaviors, however, even the most peculiar behaviors serve purposes for the individual. Before an intervention plan can be designed, a thorough assessment of the behavior and its purposes is necessary. Some measurement of the frequency of these behaviors is needed before and throughout intervention.

This chapter provides reasons for the use of behavioral assessment as an integral part of the behavior management plan. Criteria for selection of methods are provided to ensure practicality and usefulness. A number of data collection strategies are presented that can produce helpful information when designing intervention plans for adults with autism. The functional analysis and its role in behavioral assessment is discussed as well.

A good behavioral assessment does not guarantee a good intervention plan, neither does it guarantee positive results. Nonetheless, it serves as the foundation for the behavior intervention plan, and it provides the data from which success or failure can be determined.

REFERENCES

Gardner, W., Cole, C., Davidson, D., & Karan, O. (1986). Reducing aggression in individuals with developmental disabilities: An expanded stimulus control, assessment and intervention model. *Education and Training of the Mentally Retarded, 21,* 3–12.

Chapter Four

DESIGNING AN
INTERVENTION PLAN

Persons with autism can live and work in the community despite behavior problems such as self-injury, aggression, and property destruction. Placing the individual directly into integrated community settings can be a helpful step toward achieving adjustment. However, as many families and other caregivers can testify, such adjustment does not come automatically.

A shotgun approach, in which different strategies are pulled arbitrarily from the expert's hat, can often lead to disappointment. An approach that is not methodical and that ignores critical steps can result in placements being terminated, jobs being lost, and staff suffering from burn out.

The management of behavior problems requires a consistent approach to problem solving. This process includes pinpointing the behavior; assessing the problem behavior, the individual, and the environment, which includes completing a functional analysis of the behavior and setting goals; choosing strategies; writing the plan; training caregivers; reviewing progress; and troubleshooting. The purpose of this chapter is to describe the process for developing an intervention plan.

THE INTERVENTION TEAM

The composition of the intervention team will depend on at least two factors: the severity of the problem and the expertise of the caregivers. Caregivers with some expertise can conceivably plan interventions for some behavioral and social difficulties. In those cases, the caregiver may be the only team member. In many cases, the severity of the problem will require that an expert in behavior management and autism oversee the planning process. If there is such an expert, then he or she needs to work closely with the caregiver. If the caregiver is a parent, then the expert and the parent should progress through the intervention process together. The parent is the authority on the individual with autism, and the expert is the authority on behavior management of problems associated with autism. At each step of the process, the expert provides choices, the parent provides information, and together they develop an intervention plan.

If the caregiver is an agency, then the team might be larger than two. In the case of an agency, the direct care staff, such as the residential counselor or the job coach, together with their immediate supervisor, would work with the expert. The direct care staff are an essential part of the process since they have first hand experience with the behavior. They are also the ones who will be implementing the plan, and without their input, the intervention plan might be ineffective or impractical. The supervisor of the direct care staff would also play an active role and would need to provide the necessary support, supervision, and monitoring to the direct care staff if the plan is to be successfully implemented. The expert works directly with the direct care staff and the supervisor in order to plan data collection procedures and to choose intervention strategies based on those procedures. The expert then directs training of staff and provides follow-up evaluation and monitoring. Once the team is identified and assembled, the process can begin.

STEP ONE: PINPOINT THE BEHAVIOR

The first step of the approach to managing behavior problems is to pinpoint the behavior. A behavior might be pinpointed for change for any of several reasons. At the outset, caregivers should be clear about why the behavior is targeted for change. The behavior may have a negative impact on the individual or the surroundings, for example, screaming, spitting, property destruction, or even loud, rambling talking. Persons with these behaviors might find themselves out of a job or even out of a living situation because of the impact of such undesirable behaviors on others. Behaviors such as self-injury and aggression may present a danger to the individual or others. Any time a behavior presents a danger of injury, then that behavior should definitely be targeted for an intervention plan. The behavior may be one that needs to be decreased because it keeps the individual from "fitting in." Talking to oneself aloud is an example.

Often, the plan seeks to teach new behaviors. Individuals with autism frequently lack a variety of behaviors that allow or enhance interactions with other people in the community. Social skills, such as saying, "Please," "Excuse me," or "help me," are examples. Self-care skills, home care skills, and job skills are also examples. The behavior pinpointed must be described in specific, concrete terms. As discussed in Chapter Three, the targeted behavior must be observable and measurable.

STEP TWO: BEHAVIORAL ASSESSMENT

Data collection is the next step in the process to manage behavior problems. Data is collected in order to do a behavioral assessment, as described in Chapter Three, and is used to measure the frequency of the behavior and provide information needed for a functional analysis. The functional analysis provides insight into the purposes of the behavior. It can also point directly to necessary intervention strategies. Attempting to choose intervention strategies without a functional analysis is like building a house without a blueprint. It might get done, and it might even work, but it is a risky process of trial and error.

Chapter Three presented a variety of data collection procedures. Prior to choosing intervention strategies, data collection methods must be selected. Data should then be kept for a time-limited period in order to collect the necessary information on severity and function. This period is known as baseline and might last several days or several weeks, depending on the frequency and severity of the behavior. Behaviors that are threatening to people, property, or jobs might need immediate attention. Other behaviors might allow for the luxury of longer periods of baseline.

STEP THREE: SELECT STRATEGIES

Choosing strategies is the third step in the problem-solving process. Once the assessment is complete, the strategies that comprise the plan can be selected. A number of issues must be addressed at this point. The designing team must consider criteria for selection of strategies and then choose the most appropriate ones.

Criteria

Intervention plans must achieve goals for the individual and must also be reasonable and practical. The following criteria can be useful in selecting strategies:

1. The strategy involves no aversive or punishment procedures.
2. The strategy, or a variant of it, has been reported in literature as having been used successfully on a similar target behavior with a similar population. Aversive strategies, such as punishment procedures or time out would not be used in any case.
3. The strategy is based on learning theory and the assumption that new behaviors can be learned and misbehavior can be unlearned.
4. If the focus of the behavior management plan is a problem behavior, the plan includes a component that seeks to teach and strengthen a more acceptable behavior.

5. The procedure is portable if necessary. That is, if necessary, it is possible to use it at a worksite, in the group home, on a walk, in the car, or whenever necessary.

6. The plan can be implemented by direct care staff, such as job coaches and residential counselors, and family members. The plan is designed for implementation by caregivers for a number of reasons. First, since it is the caregivers who spend the most time with the individual, it makes the most sense for them to implement the plan. By virtue of the time they spend with the person, they are potentially more influential than an outside consultant who might only have 1 hour per week to spend in direct contact. Second, any given person's goals and intervention plans might include input from several professionals, such as a psychologist, language specialist, speech therapist, and occupational therapist. If each of these specialists had to provide treatment directly, then an individual could conceivably spend several hours per week in therapy sessions. The cost in terms of money and time would become prohibitive, and the individual receiving services would have little time left for job, recreation, and other activities of daily living. Finally, since the caregiver is most likely to be with the individual across many situations, then generalization can be built into the intervention plan.

7. The plan itself must be flexible and compatible with the individual's daily schedule.

8. The plan must be as unobtrusive as possible. Often, the handicapping conditions are enough to cause a particular individual to appear different and disabled in public. It is important to develop management plans that do not further identify these people as handicapped and do not interfere with the acceptance of the individual by the community.

Blueprint for Change

There are a variety of strategies to choose from, but strategies should not be selected haphazardly. It is not easy to make a collection of strategies work together for behavior change. The plan should follow a blueprint that designates what must be accomplished. The intervention plan will seek to do one or more of the following:

1. Eliminate antecedents and setting events that evoke misbehavior. Sometimes it is possible to simply alter antecedents or setting events. For example, if long periods of waiting are an antecedent to aggression, it might be possible to eliminate long waits; or if long periods without food is a setting event for self-injury, liberal snacks can be given to avoid possible harm. Sometimes, it is not possible to eliminate antecedents and setting events, however, when elimination can be accomplished easily, it should be considered as a possible intervention strategy.

2. Teach the individual a better way to achieve the function. The individual must learn new ways to fulfill the function of the undesired behavior. New learning would include ways to better handle those events that typically precede the problem behavior. If the individual screams for food, he or she must learn other ways to acquire it. If the individual's tantrums occur when in need of assistance, he or she must learn how to ask for help. Goals can be developed that specify target behaviors and help the individual meet his or her needs in more acceptable ways. For example: When a tool breaks, John will ask for assistance; while at work, Mary will speak in a low voice; at the worksite, Ralph will stay in his assigned area; when Richard has a change in plans, he will proceed to the next activity; when Albert makes an error, he will identify and correct the mistake. Once a functional analysis is done, the original behavior goals might be expanded. For example, jumping and screaming might have been pinpointed and a more positive set of goals, such as keeping feet on floor and working quietly, might have been set. The functional analysis might reveal that jumping and screaming occur when the individual is having difficulty with a task. It would then be necessary to teach him or her a new way to ask for assistance. Therefore, a new goal would be added: When having difficulty with a task, John will ask for assistance. The individual would then end up with three goals: John will keep his feet on the floor; John will work quietly; when having difficulty with a task, John will ask for assistance.

3. Give the person more frequent access to what he or she desires so that the undesirable behavior will not be necessary. For example, an individual who becomes aggressive when denied food might significantly reduce aggressive episodes if put on a liberal snack schedule or given free access to food.

4. Provide alternate sensory stimuli in cases of self-stimulation and self-injury. For example, a person who engages in skin picking might benefit from being given lotions to rub on the skin. Lotions would provide alternate, but more acceptable stimulation. A variety of alternate sources of tactile, olfactory, and auditory stimulation can be provided to replace self-stimulation or self-injury.

5. Provide motivation so that desired behaviors are more likely to occur. In cases of task avoidance, provide incentives for the individual to cooperate. Individuals who often throw tantrums or otherwise misbehave in order to avoid tasks may need schedules of positive reinforcement as motivation to engage in the task. Motivation might also be necessary to encourage meeting social skills goals.

6. Remove any possible rewards that may currently be encouraging the problem behavior.

7. Specify how the misbehavior should be handled so as to prevent injury and not inadvertently encourage the behavior.

STRATEGIES FOR BEHAVIOR CHANGE

There is not one-to-one correspondence between the general accomplishments described above and strategies to achieve those accomplishments. A variety of strategies are surveyed. When designing a plan, one or more of the following strategies might be useful. Any strategy chosen should fit reasonably into a blueprint for change. An important consideration is that all functions must be in some way addressed by one or more strategies, therefore, each strategy chosen should have some relationship to an identified function.

Supervision

Individuals with autism typically have a designated amount of supervision. For some people, this supervision is intermittent or even drop-in, and for others, supervision is continuous and may even be on a one-to-one or one-to-two staff/client ratio. Occasionally, an intervention plan may call for a change in supervision in order to prevent or manage certain situations. Difficult behaviors, such as aggression, self-injury, or property destruction often have identifiable antecedents or setting events. An intervention plan may call for increasing supervision when those events occur.

Alfred's case provides an example of use of supervision in an intervention plan. Alfred is normally fairly independent in his group home. During normal circumstances, he cares for himself and his home without incident; however, if there is a major change in his schedule he is at high risk for self-injury. Therefore, when major changes in his schedule occur, his supervision is temporarily increased.

Increased supervision may also be called for if the individual reliably shows certain signs that indicate serious problems may occur. As part of the assessment process, caregivers should compile a list of signs that the individual exhibits before the problem behavior. Then, the plan can call for increased supervision when those signs are exhibited. Marijean, a woman with autism, is an example. She lives in a group home with three other women with autism. Typically, she is under one-to-two staff/client ratio. However, occasionally she displays a package of behaviors that are precursors to aggression. This package includes crying, verbal threats, urinating on the carpet, and talking about past institutional placements. These precursors are good indications that extreme violence may occur, so when she exhibits these preaggressive behaviors, a back-up counselor is sent in to prevent injury and property destruction should she become violent.

If additional supervision is called for as an intervention strategy, the plan should be specific in several ways. The conditions under which the additional supervision is needed should be stated, exactly how additional supervisors should interact with the individual should be stated, and the criteria for removing the additional supervision should be included.

Physical Setting

Changes in the physical setting can occasionally be an important strategy. Certain aspects of the environment can be setting events or antecedents to misbehavior. Overcrowding, certain furniture arrangements, and other physical aspects of the setting might all contribute to difficulties in learning or behaving. Changes in the physical setting might be a useful strategy in prevention of behavior problems.

Occasionally, a person's behavior may require a change in physical setting, and this might actually mean a change in the job site. Supported employment is a good vocational option for persons with autism. One of its benefits is that it allows change for the sake of behavioral programming. If the physical aspects of the job site are antecedents to misbehavior, then the option exists to change job sites. Art's case shows the need for such a change. Art frequently paced and moved rapidly about. At his job site he was expected to work in one spot, at a table, all day long. His frequent roaming interfered with his production and was viewed as a behavior problem so a change in setting was recommended. Staff found Art a job in a stock room that required a certain amount of moving and pacing. At this new job, his roaming behavior was not considered a problem.

What They Want is What They Get

Misbehavior is often a means for the individual to acquire some item or activity. For example, a person might head bang in order to get attention, or bite staff who are preventing access to food. Simply providing what the individual wants, in liberal amounts, can do much to eliminate the behavior problem. In other words, caregivers examine the functions of the behavior and provide the individuals very easy access to what they want. Saul's plan provides an example. He had severe problems with biting. A functional analysis revealed that biting was often associated with trying to get food (e.g., Saul would grab a bunch of bananas and if staff tried to take them, Saul would bite staff). Saul's intervention plan called for a very frequent snack schedule. Saul could then learn that food was freely available, and that he did not have to bite people in order to get food.

Often, individuals with autism behave peculiarly in order to obtain certain sensory feedback. Leonard's arm banging seemed to be at least partly maintained by the sensory feedback it provided, so his intervention plan included a strategy of providing him what he seemed to want. At least every half-hour he was provided with a variety of tactile experiences, things he could touch and feel that hopefully would replace the need to bang his arms. He had a tactile box that contained a variety of objects to touch and handle, such as cotton balls, silks, and sponges. Back rubs and hands shakes were also frequently given.

Instructional and Social Skills Training

Individuals occasionally misbehave because a task is difficult. In those cases, one strategy is to reconsider how the task is taught, and a change in teaching methods may be needed. The intervention plan should then specify exactly how the task should be taught in order to minimize the likelihood of behavior problems.

Often, the function of the behavior is to achieve some reaction from others in the environment. People with autism may use verbal abuse or even physical abuse in order to communicate the needs for attention or help, or even to be left alone. It may then be necessary to teach the individual specific social skills and communication skills to replace the unacceptable behavior. Margo's case provides an example. Margo occasionally had tantrums at work, including foot stomping and arm shaking. A functional analysis suggested that the purpose of the behavior was to get help since antecedents were typically a difficult task or a jammed machine. One strategy in her intervention plan was to teach her how to ask for assistance. (Social skills training is discussed in greater detail in Chapter Six.)

Scheduling

Scheduling issues can be prime setting events or antecedents for a variety of problem behaviors. Lack of constructive activities can be a setting event for self-injury, aggression, or less severe behavior problems. Individuals with high-frequency self-stimulation are often in settings with little else going on.

If misbehavior is occurring in settings that provide few meaningful activities, then scheduling itself becomes an intervention strategy. This strategy can mean small changes in the environment in order to provide some additional activity. For example, Allan lived in a group home and participated in all self-care and home-care chores, thus he had a fairly busy schedule. However, there were periods as long as one-half an hour where he had nothing to do, so he would skin pick, creating large sores on his face. His schedule was rearranged to include more activities. Crafts, painting, and other enjoyable activities were interspersed among household and self-care chores.

Scheduling interventions might also mean sweeping changes in the environment. This is the case particularly with individuals who are placed in settings with little or no meaningful activity. Under these conditions, the person with autism might have high-frequency self-stimulation or self-injury.

The only effective strategy might be total restructuring of the person's day to include a variety of meaningful and functional activities.

People with autism are typically more than willing to participate in a variety of activities of daily living. Even people with severe autism can help cook, clean, set the table, do laundry, and participate in their self-care chores. When people with autism are in primarily custodial settings where everything is done for them, their schedules result in large gaps of empty time. Some individuals with autism fill this time with self-stimulation and self-injury. Therefore, in many cases filling out the schedule simply means including the individual in all activities of daily living. Ilene's case provides a good example of the need for more active scheduling. Ilene lived in a group home with three other people with handicaps and two residential counselors. Ilene frequently engaged in self-stimulation. Observation in the home revealed staff busily engaged in cooking, cleaning, and dinner preparation while Ilene was left to self-stimulate on the sofa. A part of Ilene's intervention plan was changing her schedule to include full participation in all activities of daily living. The importance of scheduling cannot be overemphasized. The most elegant reinforcement plan will fail if there is not a constructive, active schedule as its foundation.

Picture Schedules and Written Schedules

Misbehavior often serves the function of avoidance or escape, that is, the individual does not want to cooperate with the scheduled activity. Misbehavior can also serve the function of arranging a more preferred activity. For example, Mary learns that by hitting herself, she gets to go for a walk with her counselor, and Alfred learns that if he shrieks long enough, someone will finally relent and take him swimming.

Individuals who have difficulty cooperating with the schedule often benefit from a strategy that makes the designated activity very clear to them. For nonverbal individuals this can be achieved by a picture schedule. The individual is shown pictures of him- or herself engaged in the scheduled activities. The picture schedule is set up at the beginning of the day, and before and after each activity the individual is directed to look at the picture schedule. The person sees what is expected and also sees where favorite activities, such as meals and recreational activities, fall in relation to work and household tasks.

Written schedules can be used if the person reads. The day and evening schedules are put into written form and shown to the individual at the beginning of the day and between activities. In some cases, each activity can be written on an index card and each one can include the time the activity is to begin. The index cards can be arranged sequentially on a board. The individual with autism who has some reading skills can then be taught to use the index cards to initiate independently his or her scheduled activities.

Choice Making

Individuals who are given choices in their schedules may be more likely to cooperate. Nonverbal individuals can be given choices by being shown one or more pictures. The picture of the activity they choose is then inserted into the picture schedule. Individuals with verbal language can be given choices verbally. These choices can be given at the time the daily or weekly schedule is planned. Choices can also be given throughout the day. Individuals can help choose activities, chores, leisure events, and reinforcers. Choice making can be a small but critical strategy in encouraging behavioral adjustment.

Positive Reinforcement

A functional analysis might reveal that the desired behavior has no purpose for the individual. For example, a parent might want a son to shower regularly, however, showering serves no obvious function for the son. Group home staff might want Mark to wash the dishes, but dishwashing is a useless activity from Mark's point of view. Aggression, self-injury, and more severe problems also need to be viewed from this perspective. Staff might want Joseph to ask for food using signs rather than ask by biting, but signs might not be functional for Joseph.

If staff or parents want to build new or more acceptable behaviors, it might be necessary to provide reinforcement (i.e., rewards) for the acceptable behavior. Positive reinforcement, by definition, is a process for strengthening behavior. If caregivers want to strengthen a behavior, whether it is washing dishes, staying with the group on a walk, or keeping hands and feet to self, it might be necessary to use positive reinforcement. If positive reinforcement is to be used, certain decisions must be made. What the reinforcers are, how often they are given, and under what conditions they are given must be specified.

What Reinforcers to Use A variety of events or objects can serve as reinforcers. Favorite foods, drinks, activities or objects, attention, or certain sensory experiences, can all serve as positive reinforcers. A functional analysis often provides a list of events that serve as reinforcers for that individual. For example, if a functional analysis suggests that head banging serves the purpose of obtaining food, drink, attention, and new activities, then these very events can be used as reinforcers to strengthen more acceptable behavior. When choosing reinforcers, then, the first place to look is at the functions of the misbehavior. The list can be expanded from there.

Schedules of Reinforcement The schedule of reinforcement describes how often or under what conditions the rewards will be delivered. Several schedules have been useful in community settings with individuals with autism. Schedules must be easy to follow for caregivers and fit naturally into the ongoing activities of the individual's life.

Fixed Ratio   Fixed ratio schedules are useful for encouraging productivity. Under a fixed ratio schedule of reinforcement, reinforcers are delivered following completion of a set number of units of work. For example, Margie hangs pants at work. After each set of five pairs of pants, she is rewarded with a short break.

DRH   Sometimes caregivers want to encourage high rates of behavior, for example, working at a faster pace. A useful schedule then might be differential reinforcement of high rates of behavior (DRH). With a DRH schedule, the individual must produce at a certain minimum rate in order to earn a reward. For example, if Frank binds at least 50 books within a 1-hour period, he earns a reinforcer. (This procedure is described in more detail in Chapter Five.)

Variable Interval   Oftentimes counting the number of correct responses or the rate of behavior is not practical or is of little interest. Instead, a variety of good social behaviors may need to be strengthened throughout the day. In cases such as these, a variable interval schedule of reinforcement (VI) can be useful. On a VI schedule, target behaviors are rewarded at approximate intervals. The target behaviors can vary, the reinforcers can vary, and the time interval between reinforcers can vary, all within limits. Eric's case is an example of a VI schedule. Eric is nonverbal, and several times per day he hits others or himself. Functions of his behavior include getting food, drink, attention, and escape from tasks. His intervention plan included a VI 30-minute schedule. Under this schedule, about every 30 minutes Eric was given a reward for any of the following target behaviors: beginning a task, working on a task, completing a task, using materials correctly, and keeping hands in acceptable locations. Rewards were those items and events revealed by the functional analysis as pleasurable, including foods, drinks, attention, and favorite activities.

The variable interval schedule provides some flexibility for caregivers. Since the intervals are not exact, caregivers can look for good behavior within each interval to reward. Variable interval schedules work particularly well with nonverbal individuals. From their point of view, they go through their day and every so often something very good happens to them. Their cooperative behavior is strengthened, and their misbehavior becomes unnecessary.

Delays   A common mistake caregivers make with individuals with autism is to provide the reinforcer too soon after the misbehavior. Often, intervention plans call for reinforcers to be delivered immediately after the individual stops a misbehavior. This can often create big problems. If a reward is given too soon after a misbehavior, the reward might actually reinforce the misbehavior. The intervention plan should always specify a minimum amount of time that the individual must be cooperative in order to earn a reinforcer. Stated another way, the plan might specify a delay in the delivery of reinforcers should the misbehavior occur.

Janet's case provides an example of the use of a delay. Janet is a young woman with autism who occasionally head bangs. She bangs her head several times per hour. One part of her intervention plan calls for her to be given reinforcers about every 30 minutes for cooperative behavior. The plan also calls for a minimum delay of 15 minutes between head banging and a reward. In other words, Janet is to be given a reward about every 30 minutes when she is cooperative, but she cannot earn a reward within 15 minutes of head banging. If the reward is given within 15 minutes of head banging, it is possible that Janet would associate the reward with the misbehavior, and head banging might increase.

The length of the delay must be individualized. It should be long enough to prevent the individual from associating the delay with the misbehavior. However, the delay should not be so long that it is impossible for the individual to earn the reward. If an individual typically head bangs about every 15 minutes, the delay should probably only be 10 minutes. With a longer delay there is a risk of never earning the reward. However, if the individual only has tantrums twice per day, the delay could safely be 2 hours. For that individual, providing a reward within 10 minutes of a tantrum would be too close to the misbehavior since the individual can easily go 2 hours without a tantrum. The delay is not to be confused with the reinforcer interval. The reinforcer interval specifies about how often the reward should be given, and the delay puts a condition on the delivery of the reward. The following examples should clarify the distinction.

Martha is on a variable interval 15-minute schedule with a 5-minute delay should she head bang. This means that Martha is rewarded about every 15 minutes for target cooperative behaviors. However, staff need to make sure that the reward is not given within 5 minutes of head banging. For example, Martha might be rewarded for working quietly at 10:00A.M., and at 10:05A.M. she head bangs. Her next reward is due at about 10:15A.M. If her last head bang was at 10:05A.M. she can be rewarded at about 10:15A.M. for cooperative behavior since at least 5 minutes have elapsed since the head bang.

Jim is on a variable interval 2-hour schedule with a 30-minute delay should he hit someone, meaning that Jim is rewarded about every 2 hours for cooperative behavior. The job coach must be certain that the reward is not given within 30 minutes of aggression. Thus, Jim might be rewarded about 9:00A.M. for working quickly. His job coach is about to reward him again at 10:50A.M. However, at 10:50A.M. he hits his job coach, so the job coach needs to wait at least another 30 minutes before rewarding him. Jim can be rewarded for cooperative behavior at 11:20A.M.

Art is on a variable interval 3-day schedule with a 1-day delay for screaming. About every 2 days, Art goes on a special outing after work for cooperative behavior on the job. However, because of the delay, he is not to have a special outing on the day of a screaming incident. If Art is cooperative on Monday and screams on Wednesday, he would be eligible for a reward on Thursday or Friday, but not on Wednesday, the day of the incident.

Although the concept of the delay seems cumbersome, it is important. Without a reasonable delay, there is a risk of providing a reward too soon after the misbehavior. However, if the delay is too long, then it is possible that a reward would never be earned. Either possibility is counterproductive to behavior change.

Set Intervals   Reinforcers might also be scheduled at set time intervals. This type of schedule usually requires that the individual display certain behaviors for a set period of time. If the criteria are met, then the reward is given. For example, if John arrives at work on time every day for a week, he gets a special outing on Friday afternoon, or if Jeffrey stays in his assigned location all day, he can have a soda at the end of the day.

Checklists (Report Cards)   Checklists for rating behaviors can also serve as a schedule of reinforcement. With a checklist, or rating system, several desirable behaviors are presented in checklist form at set intervals. The individual can be rewarded with checks or points and praise for acceptable performance on the item. Tangible or activity rewards can be given if a minimum number of checks or points are earned. This system can also be called a report card. Alan's plan is an example of such a system. Each hour Alan is rated on the following behaviors: staying in an assigned location, completing assigned tasks, keeping hands and feet to self, and using property correctly. If Alan earns 85% of his checks, he can have his choice of a special snack or activity at the end of the day. If there are several behaviors on a report card, but one is particularly troublesome, then the plan can allow reinforcers for a minimum number of points and then stipulate that all of the points in a certain category must be earned. Alan, in the previous example, could be required to earn 85% of his points, including all of his points for keeping hands and feet to self, in order to earn his special activity.

Interestingly enough, some people with autism are motivated by points and feedback alone. In many cases, simply earning the points, and maybe graphing them, has been motivation enough for positive behavior change, and no tangible rewards have been necessary. If it is possible that the individual might be motivated by points alone, then it is best not to use a tangible reinforcer at first. If necessary, a tangible reinforcer can be added to the program later.

Considerations   Concrete reinforcers should only be used if necessary. If behaviors can be changed without the use of concrete reinforcers then they should not be used. Sometimes praise alone can work, and other times no reinforcer is necessary since many of the strategies may work without needing to resort to reinforcers. If reinforcers are necessary, then the schedule should be designed specifically for each individual. Rewards should be given as often as necessary, but as seldom as possible. Some individuals need to be rewarded every 15 minutes, others every hour, and some only every few days. The spacing of the rewards depends on the strength (frequency) of both the desired behaviors and the misbehavior.

Some people use formulas to compute reinforcement schedules, but rough rules of thumb might suffice. For example, if misbehavior happens several times an hour, then rewards may need to be given about every 15 minutes; if misbehavior occurs about once or twice an hour, then rewards may be needed about every 30 to 60 minutes; if misbehavior happens once or twice a day, a daily reinforcer might be sufficient, and if misbehavior occurs only once or twice a week, then a reinforcer may be provided every 1 to 2 days.

Concrete or activity reinforcers should typically be given with specific praise. That is, the individual should be told exactly why the reinforcer is being given. For example, "Mary, you washed the dishes so quickly. Have a cup of hot chocolate." Or, "Angela, I like the way you're keeping your hands on your work. Have a chip."

Self-Management Procedures

Several methods for teaching individuals with autism to manage their own behavior have been developed and appear to be effective. Some people with autism can be taught self-recording, self-reinforcing, self-scheduling, self-instruction, self-monitoring, and other self-management procedures, and these should be included whenever possible. (These procedures are covered in detail in Chapter Seven.)

Extinction

Since behaviors serve purposes, one way to eliminate misbehavior is to provide for those purposes in other ways. For example, if John hits himself for attention, he can learn that cooperation also results in attention, or he can learn that attention might even come free. However, he also must learn that hitting will not result in attention. If he does not learn this, then he still might continue to hit for attention, even if attention becomes available in other ways. To eliminate hitting, then it must no longer serve its purpose.

The process of destroying the relationship between the behavior and its function is called extinction. John's hitting must no longer pay off in attention. Over time John will stop hitting since it no longer serves the purpose. If attention is provided for other behavior, or for free, and hitting no longer results in attention, he is likely to give it up relatively quickly.

It is not always possible to know exactly what purpose the behavior serves. Functions can be guessed at based on the data, but these guesses might not be right, or they may not be complete. Since it can be difficult to determine exactly what is rewarding the misbehavior, the safest way of putting the behavior on extinction with individuals with autism is to provide no reaction at all. If staff are asking Margaret to sweep, and Margaret spits, staff should continue to have Margaret sweep. If staff are helping Paul dress, and he begins to bite his hand, the dressing procedure should continue. If Edgar throws his materials on the floor, the teacher should continue the lesson as if nothing happened. If life goes on exactly as usual, as if there were no misbehavior, then there is a good likelihood that the connection between the behavior and the reward will be severed.

In cases of behaviors that are dangerous to self or others, then obviously the individual cannot be allowed to continue. In those cases it may not be possible to have a perfect extinction procedure. Safety always comes first. If staff must physically prevent the person from hurting self or others, that prevention process may actually reinforce the behavior. However, this cannot be avoided since individuals with autism cannot be allowed to hurt themselves or others. If necessary, physical prevention by trained persons might be necessary to prevent injury, but as soon as the individual is willing to respond to verbal instructions, then the day should proceed in its scheduled manner with no mention of the misbehavior.

Extinction is never used alone. If a person has a history of misbehavior, functions of the behavior must be addressed. Extinction would occur as part of an intervention plan that addresses the functions as completely as possible. Since extinction is time consuming, the behavior may get worse before it gets better. The individual may give up on the original behavior and try some equally undesirable way of achieving the purpose. If a plan addresses functions, but allows the misbehavior to continue to result in a payoff, then the misbehavior might continue to thrive. An effective plan combines strategies that address functions as well as a strategy for extinction. Working together enhances the chances of effective behavior change.

Combining Strategies

An intervention plan might include several intervention strategies, or it might only consist of one strategy. In cases where the target behavior is not critical to safety or job success, it may be best to choose strategies sparingly and add more elements only if necessary. For example, an individual who has trouble sharing his work space might only need social skills training. If that is not sufficient, reinforcement procedures can be added later. However, for behaviors that have serious or dangerous effects, such as aggression or self-injury, or that are job threatening, such as screaming, it might be advisable to have a variety of strategies aimed at preventing the dangerous behavior, and promoting and rewarding acceptable alternatives.

For serious behavior problems, it is imperative that all functions be addressed in the intervention plan. Since different functions might need to be addressed by different strategies, the plan could have several components. Examples of multi-part intervention plans are provided throughout this book as case examples.

STEP FOUR: WRITING THE PLAN

Each set of data collection procedures and intervention strategies should be put in writing. This written intervention plan should contain each of the following parts:

1. Name of individual for whom plan is written
2. Date written
3. Author of plan and title (e.g., John Smith, Ph.D., Psychologist)
4. Brief history of the problem (if the behavior presents a danger to self or others, this fact should be mentioned at this point)
5. Results of the functional analysis, based on observations, data, and review of records
6. Goal(s) of the plan in behavioral terms
7. Description of the intervention strategies and the plans for implementation

    The description must be clear and specific, and all procedures should be expressed in language that is understandable to a lay person. Any technical jargon, such as "reinforcement," should be defined. If positive reinforcers are to be used, the plan should specify what the reinforcers are, how often they are to be delivered, what behaviors are to be reinforced, under what conditions the reinforcers are to be delivered, how they are to be delivered, and what should be said during delivery. The delay should also be specified. Praise might be an element of the program, and if so, directions should address how to give praise and how often. If training procedures are included, such as social skills training or training in self-control, self-disclosure, and decision making, the plan should describe exactly how these procedures are to be carried out, how often, where, and by whom. Behaviors that are dangerous must be prevented. Procedures should include preventative measures that can be taken. Changes in supervision, changes in setting, nonthreatening manner of communication, avoidance of a critical approach, and avoidance of power struggles all might be included as preventive measures. Each such measure should be described in the plan in detail. The plan must also describe how the behavior should be responded to. If the behavior presents a danger to self or others, the management of the behavior, should it occur, must be described in detail. This section should contain a statement requiring that a person trained in physical management of aggression or self-injury handle such situations. There should also be a warning stating that failure to follow the prescribed procedures by a person trained in physical management of aggression could result in injury to client or others.
8. Data collection to include how often and in what settings data are to be collected

STEP FIVE: TRAINING STAFF

Caregivers, whether family or direct care staff, should participate in the design of the intervention plan. Once the plan is developed, the caregivers need to be trained in its implementation. A well designed plan will not result in behavior change if it is not accurately implemented.

It is extremely helpful if caregivers receive initial, general training in the principles of behavior modification. This training can provide the background information necessary to allow them to participate in program design. It will also provide a basic understanding of the elements of the intervention plan. The introduction to behavior modification should include information on the following:

Definition of behavior modification
Behavior modification and autism
Pinpointing behaviors
Data collection procedures
Functional analysis
Principles of behavior
Reinforcement schedules
Designing intervention plans
Evaluating progress

Once caregivers are trained in the principles of behavior modification, they can be trained in the specifics of the individual intervention plan. Caregivers should be taught according to a formal training system that covers the following elements:

1. Exactly what the target behavior is
2. How to collect data on the target behavior
3. How to perform the strategy:
   a) What the strategy is
   b) Principles on which the strategy is based
   c) When and under what circumstances the strategy is to be used

Training caregivers to implement the strategies could be done according to the following schedule:

1. Caregivers are trained on all of the elements of the plan. This training can consist of verbal instructions, having the caregiver read the plan, demonstration, and role play.
2. Follow-up training is given in the target setting with the individual for whom the plan is developed. The trainer can demonstrate, observe the caregivers, and provide feedback and assistance as needed.
3. Once the caregiver demonstrates compliance with each step of the behavior program, then the program can be implemented.

4. Following initial training, the caregiver should be observed on a regular basis to ensure continued compliance with the intervention plan. The caregiver can be rated on compliance with each item on the intervention plan, and a percentage of items completed correctly can be computed.

STEP SIX: MONITORING AND EVALUATION OF PROGRESS

Data should continue to be collected and reviewed regularly. Should the individual fail to progress in a reasonable period of time, systematic changes in the intervention plan can be made.

STEP SEVEN: TROUBLESHOOTING

If behavior change does not occur, consider the following:

1. It may be too soon; change can take months.
2. The caregivers are not properly implementing the plan. The caregivers must be observed by a trainer who is competent to evaluate implementation of the plan. The caregivers should be rated on each step of the plan. That is, the trainer needs to note whether each step is completed correctly, and if necessary, the caregiver should be retrained.
3. Behavior is still being inadvertently reinforced. This can be determined through observation or by discussion with caregivers. If this is occurring, retraining might be necessary. It might be necessary to modify the plan to more clearly specify how to put the behavior on extinction.
4. The original functional analysis was incomplete. The behavior might still serve some function. These functions must be identified and addressed in the intervention plan. (This item is related to number three above.)
5. Reinforcing contingencies may need to be modified. Reinforcers might need to be more frequent, more varied, and so forth.

CONCLUSION

The design of an intervention plan can be a time-consuming process. Pinpointing behaviors, collecting data, determining functions, selecting strategies, training caregivers, and implementing the plan is a painstaking process. Skipping steps can be more troublesome. Without a systematic process for behavior change, one step forward can be followed by two steps backward. The approach must be systematic and thorough.

Many individuals with autism who need intervention plans have long histories of the problem behavior. Self-injury, aggression, property destruction, social skills deficits, and ritualistic behaviors may have been around for years, and so behavior change requires patience. Even without autism, behavior changes take time, as does learning. Unfortunately, autism does nothing to speed this process. But, people with autism can learn if strategies are well designed, if plans are complete, and if they are given time.

SUMMARY

The behavior problems that can be associated with autism can seem overwhelming. The long history of using punishment with people with autism might at first glance seem appealing. However, even the most severe behavior problems can be managed without punishment, given a systematic approach based on a functional analysis.

This chapter provides an overview on the process of behavior change. This process will certainly look familiar to readers with a background in behavior modification. The process itself is not new. The fact that it works should also not be surprising; neither should the fact that it has worked in integrated job and small group home settings with individuals with severe autism. Behavior modification is a powerful process, and just because a person has autism does not mean that he or she is immune to the principles of behavior.

This chapter provides a glimpse at the criteria for selecting intervention strategies and the variety of strategies available. An intervention plan is described as a compilation of strategies that together meet the functions of the misbehavior and provide motivation for learning more acceptable behaviors. The strategies alluded to in this chapter are described in detail throughout this book, and case examples provide in-depth information on how the strategies can work together for the good of the individual with autism.

Chapter Five

VOCATIONAL
SKILLS DEVELOPMENT

Autism is a severe disorder of behavior and communication. Fortunately, it is not a vocational disorder. People with autism can work, even those with severe autism, and they can hold a variety of jobs. In many cases they can work at the same rate as people without autism, and in some instances, they work even faster. Juhrs (1988) has reported on "101 Jobs for People with Autism." The variety of employers listed include printing companies, manufacturing firms, libraries, recycling companies, factories, and restaurants.

People with relatively mild autism can hold jobs that require reading, math, and complex fine motor skills. People with severe social skills deficits associated with autism can be taught to deal with the public. They can also hold jobs that are technologically complex and have little allowance for error. People with severe autism can work successfully in a variety of positions, including warehousing, pricing, stocking, recycling, printing, cleaning, and retail. A variety of jobs can be found that can capitalize on their strengths and that are not jeopardized by their weaknesses.

Many people with autism do need specialized instruction in order to learn their vocational tasks. The way they learn might be different from the way their co-workers without autism learn. They might also need some extra time.

The purpose of this chapter is to explore strategies for teaching adults with autism vocational skills directly in job settings. The strategies presented are suitable for use by paraprofessional job coaches. They are not inclusive of all existing teaching strategies, rather they were chosen because they are easily learned by paraprofessionals and can be readily implemented in non-sheltered competitive employment.

TYPES OF JOBS

People with autism have held a variety of jobs involving a range of tasks that vary in difficulty, complexity, and variety. Companies that have employed people with severe autism have included local governments, the federal government, manufacturing firms, printing companies, warehouses, greeting card companies, mailing services, department stores, hardware stores, clothing outlets, airlines, housewares stores, furniture refinishers, and laundries. Persons with autism have also been employed at a company that stocks vending machines, a firm that assembles computer cables, toy stores, restaurants, equipment rental companies, libraries, hospitals, electronic assembly firms, drug stores, waste removal firms, a business machine assembly firm, a venetian blind manufacturer, a lamination company, a book store, an automotive parts store, and an automotive accessories distributor (Juhrs & Smith, 1986).

People with autism are employed in these jobs through a supported employment program. Participating employers hire them and pay their wages. Job coaches, paid for by the supported employment agency, go to work with them. Typically, two people with autism go to work with one job coach. The job coach is responsible for teaching the worker with autism job skills and social skills necessary for the job. Individuals with higher levels of language skills and social skills can eventually work alone or under drop-in supervision from the job coach. Persons with severe autism, including mental retardation, serious behavior problems, and poor communication skills may need the job coach indefinitely. Job coaches learn the job, then teach the job to the worker with autism.

TARGET SKILLS

Since the possibilities for employment are endless, so is the list of possible target vocational skills. However, a partial list of jobs skills that have been mastered by persons with autism provides an idea of the scope of possibilities.

Manufacturing Skills

Workers with autism have mastered a variety of manufacturing skills. Several young men with autism, including an individual who has no speech, have learned how to assemble computer cables. This task involved measuring and cutting cable according to specifications, stripping the ends of each cable with a razor blade, attaching pins, placing pins according to a specified pattern, assembling a hood over the connection, labeling the cable, and testing the cable.

Workers with autism have learned to assemble venetian blinds, a task that includes assembling the material and cutting strips to specification, while a job in a business machine assembly firm requires the worker to rewire and reconnect circuits on computer circuit boards. Workers with autism have learned to make fuses for use in the marine industry. Their job tasks included cleaning plastic parts of excess plastic, assembling hardware with screws or bolts and nuts, wrapping copper lamp wire around a resistor, and soldering components together. Workers with autism have also manufactured parts for air conditioners and cable assemblies.

Printing Skills

Workers with autism have performed a variety of jobs in printing companies. Job tasks have included using an electric hole puncher to punch holes in stacks of printed manuals and covers, separating stacks of printed manuals, covering books, binding books, and packaging books for shipping. Printing jobs have also involved removing negatives from printing plates, and collating multi-page documents.

Library Tasks

Tasks in libraries have included sorting returned books by library of origin, sorting new books by destination, sorting reserved books, processing new books, printing posters, and setting the type for the printing press. One young man with autism who could not read was able to sort books by matching the letters on the spine of the book with the letters on the bins.

Order Filling Skills

Workers with autism have learned tasks necessary for filling orders in a variety of jobs. Electronics firms require workers to count electronic components, calibrate scales, package counted parts, label the package, and locate parts for a customer order. A clothing outlet hired workers with autism to fill mail orders for children's clothing. One worker with autism who would have difficulty learning to count and package tiny electronic parts does a good job packaging rubber dishware. A young man with autism who had very little speech and poor fine motor skills was able to learn to sort and package plastic eating utensils for an airline.

Stockroom Tasks

Stocking is a good field for persons with autism who have no speech and no formal academic skills. Stock work with clothes requires the worker to open boxes of clothes, hang clothes on racks, remove plastic from the clothing, and discard the plastic. Some jobs require the worker to place tags on the clothing. Stock jobs also involve unpacking merchandise, pricing merchandise, and loading and unloading merchandise from trucks. Some stock jobs require that the worker place items on shelves in a retail store.

Mailroom Tasks

Mailing jobs have required workers to collate, sort, insert materials into envelopes, label envelopes, and place envelopes into boxes.

Other Tasks

Workers with autism collectively have learned hundreds of individual tasks for a variety of jobs. Methods for training job skills are not nearly as varied as the job skills themselves. Several basic methods can suffice to teach a variety of skills to workers with autism.

PREPARING FOR TRAINING

Methods for training workers with autism proceed in an orderly sequence, up to a point. Then, choices can be made from a variety of strategies.

Step 1: Train the Job Coach

The first step in vocational training is to teach the job coach. The job coach needs to learn the task thoroughly before teaching the worker with autism. Several problems arise if the job coach or trainer is not thoroughly familiar with the task. A primary problem is that if the task is taught incorrectly to a worker with autism, it can be very difficult to reteach the task a new way since many people with autism have difficulty with change. To teach a task one way, then try to teach it another way can cause severe resistance in many cases. Another problem is that job coaches or trainers experience significant stress when they are not thoroughly familiar with the task. It is extremely difficult for a job coach to attempt to teach a task to an individual with autism while he or she is still learning the task.

The training sequence for a worker with autism has to be very carefully planned and followed. Such precision in teaching is not possible until the job coach learns the task first. The job coach or trainer is usually taught the task by the employer, a supervisor, or even another worker at the job site.

Step 2: Teach on the Job

There are several compelling reasons for teaching job skills to workers with autism directly in the job setting.

Cues Individuals with autism often attend to irrelevant cues in their environment. Such unpredictable attending behavior can make instruction difficult. When an individual with autism learns a task, it is not always apparent what cues are signaling the individual to proceed through the task. Often, the cues in the actual work setting are more pronounced than cues in training settings. The actual work setting typically has multiple cues regarding the work and work behavior. For example, in a department store stockroom, there are hundreds of pairs of pants to be hung, dozens of racks, and thousands of hangers. All the cues point to clothes hanging as the prominent task. Often in training settings, cues for many types of tasks are present. Such diversity of cues can make it more difficult for the worker with autism to focus on his or her own task.

Generalization   Generalization from one setting to another may be difficult. Teaching the tasks in the job environment ensures that cues that become important during training remain the same after training. Teaching directly on the job eliminates the need to generalize from cues in the training setting to cues in the work setting.

Precision   Teaching the task directly in the work setting allows for a high degree of precision. Even small differences between how the task is taught in one setting can create large problems when trying to make necessary changes in the new setting. Alex's case presents a good example of such a problem. Alex worked for a T-shirt manufacturer. He was originally taught to remove each T-shirt from a dryer, step back, shake the shirt, then put it in a box. He learned the task quickly and did the job well. Then, the dryer was moved closer to the wall. Alex could no longer step back without bumping into the wall and scuffing it. It became a major challenge to try to teach Alex to shake the shirt without taking a step back. Attempts to teach Alex a new method resulted in outbursts that were not tolerated by the employer. Alex was fired, and a new job had to be found for him. Although this might be an extreme example, it is important to take into account that some workers with autism might have a great deal of difficulty with even small changes in how a task is performed. Teaching directly in work settings reduces the need for reteaching.

Social Factors   Often training social behavior is more difficult than teaching vocational skills. When social behavior is a problem, it can interfere with the teaching of vocational skills. Workers with autism with severe behavior problems often have fewer problems on job sites than in segregated situations since job sites offer more well behaved models than segregated situations do. The co-workers are not only engaging in the required work, they are behaving in socially acceptable ways for that job site. The worker with autism has a greater chance of learning necessary social behaviors more quickly when surrounded by socially correct workers.

Step 3: Task Analysis

A task analysis is critical. The task must be broken up into its separate steps for training purposes. There are several important reasons for this. First, if the job is in competitive employment, doing a task analysis ensures that the job will be done according to the employer's expectations.

Second, when teaching people with autism, it is important to teach the steps in the same order each day. Teaching the task steps in one sequence on

Monday and in another sequence on Tuesday can be ineffective and frustrating. A task analysis allows the trainer to teach the task in a consistent sequence of steps.

Step 4: Prepare the Setting

Preparing the instructional setting is important. Materials, supplies, equipment, and work area should all be prepared prior to training. If obtaining the supplies or equipment is part of the job task, then they should be in their assigned place, ready for use.

This step is critical for people with autism who have problems with compliance or problems with communication. Telling a worker with autism who has little or no speech that it is time to learn how to sort, then having a wait of 10 minutes while the trainer looks for the materials, collects the materials, and organizes the materials can be confusing. When the worker is told that it is time to sort, sorting should begin.

INSTRUCTIONAL METHODS

Teaching vocational skills to workers with autism is not the most challenging aspect of the job experience. For many workers with autism, the challenge lies in social adjustment rather than vocational adjustment. Several strategies have proven useful in vocational skills development. These strategies are not impressive in either their originality or their complexity. They are simple and common to the field of education. They are strategies that job coaches have used directly in job settings to teach vocational skills to workers with autism.

Verbal Instruction

Verbal instruction is a key component in teaching vocational tasks. Unless an individual has no hearing, verbal instruction should be used. Even if an individual has no speech, verbal instruction can still be important. Receptive language is often much better than expressive language, so over time the individual may come to understand and follow the verbal instructions. Verbal instructions must be very specific. Vague descriptions of the task may evoke a wrong response or no response at all. Each and every step of the task needs to be described in detail. Similarly, verbal instructions should be kept very concrete. Abstract terms must be avoided as much as possible. Metaphors should also be avoided. Many workers with autism respond much better to concrete, realistic descriptions. Analogies and metaphors create misunderstanding.

Some workers with autism will only need verbal instruction. Following a specific verbal instruction, they will be able to do the task. If workers have this capability, then no other techniques are needed. However, many individuals with autism have difficulty learning new tasks with verbal instruction alone (incidentally, many people without autism also require more than verbal instruction to learn new tasks). They need other forms of instruction. In most cases, verbal instruction is necessary, but not sufficient for teaching new job skills.

Demonstration

Demonstration is almost always necessary when teaching new tasks. Most workers, with or without autism, benefit from demonstration of new tasks. Showing the worker how to do each step of the task, while giving specific verbal instructions, may be all that is needed to teach a new task. The number of demonstrations will of course vary from worker to worker. Some individuals may learn a task after one demonstration while others may need weeks of patient demonstrations, interspersed with practice.

Graduated Guidance

Some workers with autism will need more than verbal instruction and demonstration. They also might need physical assistance with doing the task. Graduated guidance might be the method of choice. It consists of giving the worker full manual assistance (hand over hand) with the task. As the worker becomes able to perform the motions, the manual guidance is gradually faded. Graduated guidance should be accompanied by verbal instruction. As the trainer provides the hand-over-hand assistance, he or she provides verbal descriptions of the steps of the task.

For example, graduated guidance should be used to teach Andrew to engage in tasks and activities. This is a process of initially leading Andrew's hands through the correct motions, then gradually fading out trainer assistance. Graduated guidance consists of the following steps:

1. *Full Guidance:* Trainer puts his or her hands over Andrew's and provides gentle guidance to get him to do the activity. When guiding Andrew's hands through the correct motion, he is told specifically what he is doing. For example, "That's right, Andrew, you're combing your hair."
2. *Partial Guidance:* As Andrew begins to cooperate with the full guidance, trainer can revert to partial guidance. Partial guidance consists of gently moving Andrew's hands through the correct motion by holding his hands by the trainer's thumb and forefinger. Again, specific verbal instruction is given during the process.
3. *Shadowing:* As Andrew begins to show more cooperation in his movement, the trainer can fade from partial guidance to shadowing. Shadowing consists of the trainer holding his or her hand several inches above Andrew's as he performs the correct motion. As Andrew continues to cooperate, the trainer can gradually move his or her hand away entirely.

Systems of Prompts

System of Least Prompts In many cases, trial and error will quickly reveal the most effective strategy to use with an individual. Some workers with autism learn best with demonstration, others with manual guidance. In some cases, a systematic strategy for increasing the level of assistance might be useful. A system of least prompts is a systematic method for increasing the amount of assistance necessary. Several systems of least prompts have been used and are reported to be effective in teaching skills to persons with severe handicaps. Doyle, Wolery, Ault, and Gast (1988) provided a thorough review of such strategies. A method of least prompts that has been effective with adults with autism is the prompt hierarchy. Smith and Belcher (1985) used this method with adults with autism who had several training sessions involving demonstration and manual guidance. Once the individuals could do the tasks with manual guidance and demonstration, the job coach reverted to the prompt hierarchy.

The prompt hierarchy provides for increasing levels of assistance for each step of the task. Six levels of assistance are provided as necessary. These levels are as follows:

1. Give the general instruction. If no response, then move to level two.
2. No help: Wait about 5–10 seconds for a response. If no response, then move to level three.
3. Nonspecific verbal cue: Say, "What's next?" and wait about 5–10 seconds for a response. If no response, then move to level four.
4. Specific verbal instruction: Give specific verbal instruction, breaking down the task into steps. Wait 5–10 seconds. If no correct response, then move to level five.
5. Gestural cue: Use a gesture and specific verbal instruction. Wait about 5–10 seconds. If no correct response, then move to level six.
6. Physical guidance. Gently provide physical guidance. Do not use physical guidance in a forceful way or in a manner that will create a power struggle or aggression.

Adults with autism have learned to perform a variety of self-care, home care, and vocational tasks with the use of the prompt hierarchy. The prompt hierarchy has several advantages when working with people with autism. It allows the individual time to respond with some degree of independence. A common problem among caregivers is the tendency to give too much assistance. Caregivers often hover over people with severe disabilities, anticipating their every need and shortcoming. Such hovering does not allow for independence. The prompt hierarchy teaches trainers to wait, and often, during that waiting period, the individual with autism will respond correctly. The prompt hierarchy has the secondary benefit of providing trainers with a method of redirecting off-task individuals back to task without unduly rewarding off-task behavior. Caregivers often use cajoling, reasoning, arguing, and terminating the session to achieve compliance. The prompt hierarchy minimizes attention to off-task behavior, and at the same time it provides cues for task completion.

The prompt hierarchy has one possible drawback that should be considered. Some individuals with autism might become prompt dependent. They learn to wait out the trainer through succeeding levels of prompts. In cases where the individual has a risk of becoming prompt dependent, a system of decreasing prompts might be best.

System of Decreasing Prompts   The prompt hierarchy calls for increasing levels of assistance. Another approach to instruction is the use of decreasing levels of assistance. In this approach, the individual is at first given high levels of assistance throughout the task. Gradually, levels of assistance are faded out. Graduated guidance is an example of decreasing prompts. Graduated guidance, discussed earlier, provides for full manual guidance, partial guidance, then shadowing, until there is no assistance. The individual is given a maximum prompt (full manual guidance) and this prompt is gradually faded.

A system of decreasing prompts can be designed to incorporate high levels of prompts that gradually decrease to no prompts. An example of such a system follows:

1. Full guidance and verbal instruction
2. Partial guidance and verbal instruction
3. Shadowing and verbal instruction
4. Demonstration and verbal instruction
5. Gesture and verbal instruction
6. Specific verbal instruction
7. Nonspecific verbal instruction
8. No help

The implementation of this system begins with training sessions in which the highest level of assistance is given. This level would be individualized. Some workers might need full guidance, others only demonstration. After several sessions with the highest level of assistance, an assessment session is held. During the assessment session, the individual is told to do the task and is observed. The trainer notes those steps that the individual cannot do independently. During the next several training sessions, as soon as the individual arrives at the troublesome step, the trainer immediately provides a high level of assistance. Gradually, the level of assistance provided can be faded. Training sessions are interspersed with assessment sessions. Performance during assessment sessions helps determine the level of assistance to give in subsequent training sessions.

Some Considerations Systems of prompts can obviously become quite elaborate. Decisions need to be made about increasing or decreasing prompts. Decisions then need to be made about what those prompts are to be and the amount of time that will separate prompts.

A major drawback to systems of prompts, either increasing or decreasing, is that many caregivers find them difficult to learn. Although some job coaches and residential counselors can learn these procedures in one or two training sessions, others take months to learn them. Furthermore, it is difficult to motivate staff to continue to use such systematic teaching procedures in field settings. Staff typically use the strategy immediately after training. However, follow ups several weeks later reveal that the staff typically revert to a less rigid method of instruction.

Many workers, even those with severe autism, do not need such rigid structure. Often, initial graduated guidance or demonstration is sufficient to teach the skill. Systems of increasing or decreasing prompts are useful when behavior problems are present that require a very structured way to divert the individual back to task. They are also useful when less formal systems have failed. Finally, these procedures are useful with staff who have little instructional training themselves. These procedures provide them with a structured approach to training that does not require a great deal of on-the-spot decision making.

Written Cues

Many adults with autism can read. Writing out the task instructions or writing certain cues can be a valuable instructional technique. Workers with autism can often do complex multi-step tasks. However, initially, retention might be a problem. If the individual skips steps or forgets the sequence, then when he or she is corrected a behavior problem can often result. Providing written cues can eliminate errors.

Milton's case is an example of the use of written cues. Milton has a job in a printing company. One of his tasks is to operate the binding machine. Milton often rushes through the steps, and as a result, he accidently combines steps. Combining the steps then causes the machine to jam. Verbal reminders make no impression. Milton was given a written list of the steps involved in operating the machine. Following each step is the word "STOP." Milton learned to stop briefly between steps. This slight stop prevents him from combining steps and jamming the machine.

Written lists have been used in a variety of work situations to teach individuals with autism the steps of their tasks. Written lists not only decrease errors, they also promote independence. Rather than relying on a job coach for instruction, the worker learns to rely on written instructions.

Adaptations

Occasionally a person with autism might have difficulty performing a task in the standard manner. However, it might be possible to make modifications that will make the task easier, and if the result is the same, employers usually do not mind such modifications. Making modifications to the equipment or the process should be considered as a part of the instructional process. In several cases, employers were so impressed by modifications made for workers with autism that the modifications were made for all workers.

ACCURACY

Some individuals with autism are exceedingly careful about their work. Their attention to detail and routine result in highly accurate performance. However, other individuals with autism might have problems achieving accurate performance. Inaccurate performance might signal a need for more instruction on the task itself. In these cases, an instructional procedure for teaching the skills would be necessary. The worker might need more verbal instruction, more demonstration, or even graduated guidance.

Some workers are capable of doing the task. They do not need further instruction on the task itself, but they may rush through a task, skip steps, combine steps, or be inattentive to the important parts of the task. In such cases, it might be necessary to design an intervention plan that targets accuracy. A checking and correcting errors plan has been useful with some workers with autism who had high error rates despite familiarity with the task. This plan teaches the individual to stop at designated parts of the task, check the work, and if necessary, correct any errors. It is conducted in a format similar to social skills training. It has the following components.

Instruction

The worker is told that it is important to find and correct any mistakes. The trainer explains that after completing a unit of work, the work must be checked for mistakes, and if any are found they need to be corrected. The trainer should stress that there is no problem with making a mistake, but that it is important to find the mistake and correct it.

Demonstration

The trainer demonstrates how to check work and correct errors. The trainer says to the worker, "Watch me." The trainer then takes a unit of work, completes it, and checks it for errors. If there is an error, the trainer will say, "Here, I've found a mistake. This mistake is not too bad. I can fix it. Now I will fix it." The trainer then corrects the error.

Practice

The trainer will then complete another unit of work and make an error. The trainer will ask the worker to check the work and correct the error. The worker is praised for finding and correcting the error. The trainer then asks the worker to complete a unit of work and then check and correct any errors.

This sequence of instruction, demonstration, and practice is carried out for different types of possible mistakes and solutions. Possible solutions need to be planned and taught to the worker. Possibilities might be: disposing of ruined material and selecting new material, undoing the mistake and beginning again, notifying the supervisor of a mistake. This procedure might be useful for individuals who have at least some verbal skills and who can participate in role play, training situations. It can help with individuals who normally become upset and agitated when errors occur. Since daily practices are held, the individual becomes desensitized to errors. Its primary benefit is in teaching workers to stop at designated intervals, check their work, and correct their errors.

PRODUCTIVITY

An important vocational goal for many workers with autism is to increase their level of productivity. Many workers with autism learn the task rather quickly, but maintain low levels of productivity. They might interrupt their work to stare into space, leave the work area, or engage in repetitive motor movements, such as finger flicking. There are a variety of strategies for increasing productivity.

Differential Reinforcement of High Rates of Behavior

Productivity can often be increased by a schedule of positive reinforcement known as differential reinforcement for high rates of behavior (DRH). This strategy involves having the instructor demonstrate to the worker how to do the task quickly, and explain that it is important to do the task quickly. Then, quick working is rewarded.

When the worker is observed working quickly, specific positive verbal feedback is given (e.g., "You're really sorting those books quickly."). At the end of predesignated intervals, the amount of work done is calculated and feedback is given to the worker. The amount done is recorded on a chart (by the worker if possible). If increases have occurred, the worker is praised. If necessary, rewards other than praise can be used, such as small amounts of money, free time, or snacks. The focus of this strategy is to catch the individual working quickly and provide positive feedback, rather than to catch the worker off task and provide a prompt to move back to task. The procedure also involves systematic feedback and rewards for increases in productivity.

Variable Interval Schedule of Reinforcement

Nonverbal individuals can be rewarded for working quickly with either praise or tangible rewards. Rewards are given on a variable interval schedule of reinforcement (described in Chapter Four), provided the worker is working quickly. Working quickly can be the only target behavior or one of several. Graphing would of course be omitted if the individual cannot read or interpret a graph.

Reinforcers can be given for working quickly as one of a list of target behaviors on a variable interval schedule. Each time a reinforcer is delivered, the individual is given specific praise, such as, "I like the way you're working quickly. Would you like some lemonade?" As an example, an individual might be on a variable interval 30-minute schedule of positive reinforcement for certain work behaviors. Reinforcers might be delivered about every 30 minutes for any of several behaviors such as working quickly, working quietly, working independently, or using work materials correctly.

Rating Systems

Individuals with autism who are verbal and possess some reading skills often respond well to rating systems. The worker is rated at designated intervals for certain target behaviors. The worker might rate him- or herself. Productivity goals can be included in such a system. Productivity ratings might be stated in any of the following ways: works quickly, completes assigned tasks, works steadily. Workers can be rated hourly, twice per day, once per day, or on any designated schedule that is convenient in the work setting and that is necessary for motivation. Successful ratings can earn the worker praise, tangible rewards, or activities.

Elmer's plan provides an example of such a system. Elmer had trouble with property destruction, screaming, and refusal to work. Productivity and social goals were addressed in part by a rating system. Each hour, Elmer was rated on the following behaviors: completes assigned task, works quietly, uses property correctly. If Elmer earned at least 85% of his points, including all of his points for correct use of property, he could go on a special outing on Friday after work.

Some Considerations for Increasing Productivity

Reinforcing high rates of production can be a positive and useful approach to increasing the productivity of workers with severe autism. This strategy can be applied by the trainer in either the work or training setting. Several cautions should be noted. First, reinforcers need to be chosen that have some value for the individual. In many cases, positive feedback alone might be sufficient to increase productivity. However, in some cases greater gains can be achieved by using stronger rewards. In all cases, the rewards should be items that are valued by the particular worker. For example, money might not be motivating for every individual with autism.

An important prerequisite to the use of this strategy is that the worker be capable of performing the skill. If the worker has not yet mastered the skill, then a program to increase speed could be interfering and frustrating, and could result in high error rates. The most important feature of programs that increase productivity is the emphasis on increases in rate and on working quickly. Brief pauses on the worker's part are ignored. If longer pauses occur, the worker is prompted to return to work with as few words as possible, such as, "What's next?" The great majority of trainer-worker interactions take place when the worker is on task and working at improved speeds. It is likely that long-winded efforts and continual, repeated prompting to get the worker on task could be counter productive.

CASE 1

Martin is a young man with autism with an IQ of 60 as measured by the Wechsler Adult Intelligence Scale—Revised (WAIS—R). Martin's symptoms of autism include severe language deficits and difficulty establishing relationships with others. At times he has incidents of minor self-injury and occasional clothes tearing. Martin is employed at a printing company where his job duties include separating books and covering books. Although Martin can perform his tasks, he works slowly with frequent pauses.

Procedures

A productivity program was implemented. The job coach explained to Martin that it was important to work quickly, and he was praised when he did so. At the end of set intervals each day, his work was counted and charted. Improvements were praised. The instructions to the job coach are as follows:

1. The production rate for a nonhandicapped worker should be calculated and recorded in a production notebook.
2. Each morning tell Martin that it is important to work as quickly as possible to be successful at work. Tell Martin that the supervisor will be impressed if the work is done quickly.
3. Before he begins each task, say, "Remember, it is important to work quickly."
4. During the day, Martin should be praised for working quickly (when he is). For example, he should be told, "You are covering those books quickly. That's great."
5. Each hour, the amount of work Martin completes should be recorded on a chart. He should be praised for improvements.

Results

Martin's production rate for separating books as compared with the rate of a nonhandicapped worker is shown in Figure 5.1. Martin's baseline rate was 60% the rate of a nonhandicapped worker and had been at that rate for 18 months. By month 3 of the productivity program, Martin's rate was 98% the rate of a nonhandicapped worker. A follow up 4 years later revealed that his productivity was equal to that of a nonhandicapped worker, indicating that Martin maintained his gains.

CASE 2

Arthur is a 24-year-old man with an IQ of 77 as measured by the WAIS—R. His symptoms of autism include abnormal speech rhythm, stereotypic behaviors, and occasional outbursts of verbal or physical aggression. He is employed at an electronics firm filling orders from "pick lists" and counting parts.

Procedures

Arthur was placed on a productivity program similar to Martin's. He was instructed to work quickly prior to each task and was praised throughout the

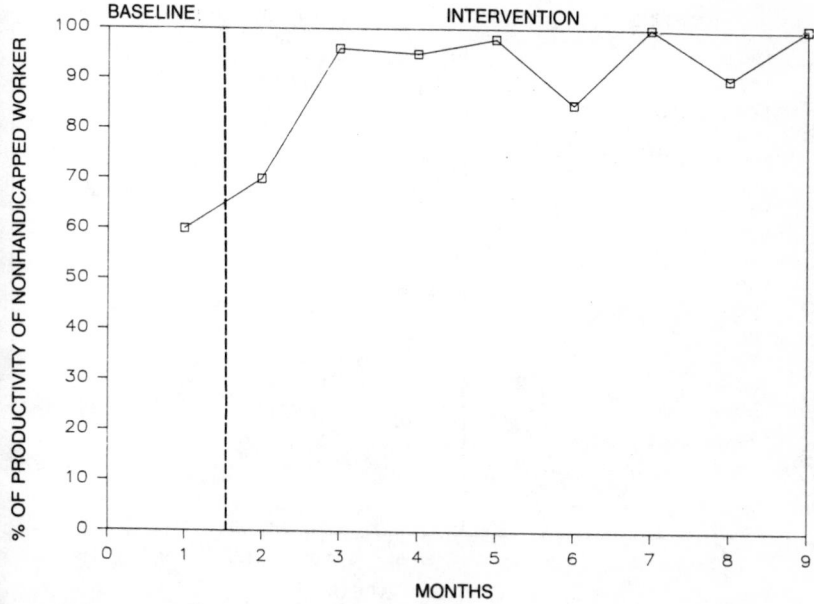

Figure 5.1. Martin's production rate compared to that of a nonhandicapped co-worker during baseline and intervention.

day for working quickly. Additionally, his rate for filling orders was charted, and he was complemented for improvement.

Results

Arthur's productivity rates were computed in the same manner as Martin's, and are shown in Figure 5.2 for filling orders from pick lists. Baseline data (rates prior to intervention) are shown for weeks 1 through 6 and intervention data for weeks 7 through 18. Arthur's rate increased from below 90% the rate of a nonhandicapped worker to well above the rate of nonhandicapped workers following the intervention plan. Arthur's rates for counting parts are shown in Table 5.1. His rates increased from 75% during the baseline month to 100% that of a nonhandicapped worker after intervention.

SUMMARY

Adults with autism are able to learn vocational skills. These skills are best learned in the work setting. A variety of procedures have proven useful for teaching vocational skills to adults with autism. The instructional plan needs to be individualized, taking into account the individual's learning style, strengths, and weaknesses. Elaborate instructional plans are not usually prac-

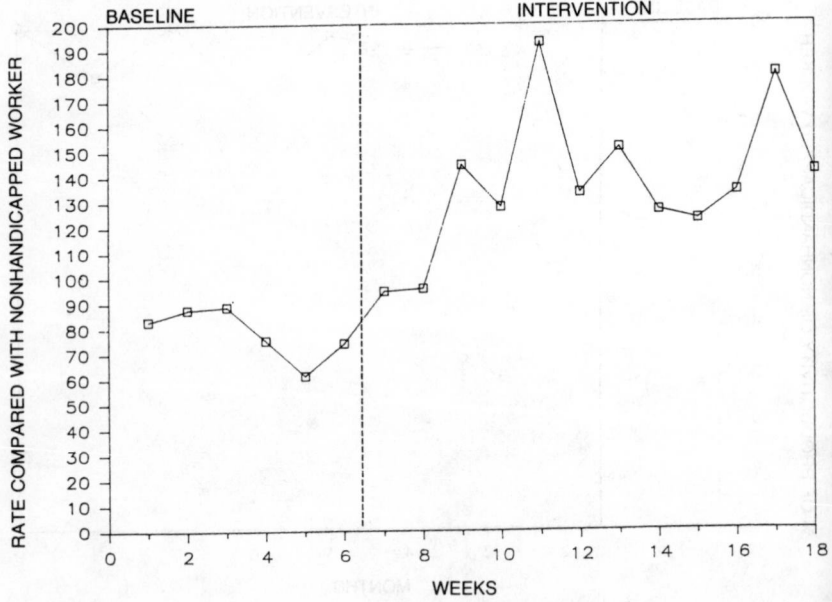

Figure 5.2. Arthur's production rate compared to that of a nonhandicapped co-worker during baseline and intervention.

Table 5.1. Arthur's rate of productivity as compared with nonhandicapped co-workers

Month	Arthur's rate of productivity
1 (Baseline)	75%
2	100%
3	102%
4	99%

tical; neither are they necessary. A step-by-step consistent method of teaching that provides sufficient instruction is usually enough to teach job skills to workers with autism. If the job is well chosen, and the job coach is prepared, even the most severely disabled individuals can become productive workers.

REFERENCES

Doyle, P.M., Wolery, M., Ault, M.J., & Gast, D.L. (1988). System of least prompts: A literature review of procedural parameters. *Journal of The Association for Persons with Severe Handicaps, 13*(1), 28–40.

Juhrs, P. (1988). *101 jobs for people with autism.* Presentation to the annual meeting of The Association for Persons with Severe Handicaps, Washington, DC.

Juhrs, P., & Smith, M. (1986). *Service demonstration model, secondary education, and transitional services for handicapped youth* (Final Report U.S. Department of Education Grant No. G008430115). Rockville, MD: Community Services for Autistic Adults and Children.

Smith, M., & Belcher, R. (1985). Teaching life skills to adults disabled by autism. *Journal of Autism and Developmental Disorders, 15,* 163–175.

Chapter Six

SOCIAL SKILLS DEVELOPMENT

People with autism often have difficulty fitting in. In fact, if they didn't, they would probably not be considered to have autism. People with autism often do not know how to get along with others. The will is there, but they just do not have the way.

Social skills refer to behaviors involved in relating to others. A major characteristic of autism is difficulty in relating to others. People with autism often have problems establishing relationships with others. When they do establish contact, they may have problems maintaining relationships in the conventional sense.

Although other behaviors associated with autism are more dramatic and obvious in their effects, such as aggression and self-injury, the importance of the social skills deficits cannot be overemphasized. In fact, Kanner, Rodriguez, and Ashenden in a 1972 publication of a long-term follow up of persons with autism, reported that social skills development was a critical factor in positive outcome. Schopler and Mesibov (1983) stressed the critical nature of this problem in their text on autism in adolescents and adults.

Adults with autism can live productively in group homes and with their families despite social skills deficits. Families and staff can learn to adjust to the idiosyncrasies of individuals with autism. This lack of social skills development becomes critical and cannot be hidden or glossed over when the person leaves the home to go to work, to go to a restaurant, to go shopping, or to take part in social activities such as bowling. Work is probably the area most critically affected by social skills deficits. Numerous studies of persons with developmental disabilities and mental retardation have suggested that a major reason for job failure is not job performance, but social incompetence.

Greenspan and Shoultz (1981) interviewed former employers and others to determine why adults with mental retardation lost their jobs. They concluded that social factors were at least as important as nonsocial factors in workers losing their jobs. Wehman et al. (1982) noted that problems in relating to co-workers and supervisors is a contributing factor to job loss. Salzberg, Lignugaris-Kraft, and McCuller (1988) reviewed studies done over a 35-year period on job loss in workers with mental retardation. They concluded that social competence, though not the only reason for job loss, is certainly a major reason in many cases.

Lack of social skills does play a part in long-term community adjustment as well as job success. However, severe deficits in social skills development need not rule out community integration or job success. In a study of 7 years of supported employment with persons with autism, Juhrs and Smith (1989) found that two-thirds of the individuals who have been described as withdrawn and isolated have been employed over three-quarters of the time they have been served in the supported employment program. Eighty percent of those individuals with ritualistic verbal behaviors have been employed over half of the time they have been in the program.

TEACH IN TARGET SETTINGS

Social skills are difficult for persons with autism to learn. Training in social skills must be carefully designed to make the learning process as simple as possible. One factor that makes learning easy is to teach the skills in the setting in which the individual must use them. Social skills are often taught to people with developmental disabilities in group or classroom settings. Most people can generalize such learning from the group or classroom to the real world, but people with autism have trouble making such transfers.

Belcher (1987) attempted to conduct assertiveness training with a group of adults with autism. Group sessions were held in a training room. The participants learned the correct responses in the training group and could give correct responses in role play situations within that group. Probes were made in community settings to determine whether these skills generalized. They did not.

People with autism often learn social skills in very specific situations with specific people. They will learn to say, "Hi" to their job coach, but they then must be taught to say, "Hi" to a co-worker. They learn to say, "Please" at the dinner table, but they must also be taught to say, "Please" at the work table.

A great advantage to teaching social skills in the target setting is that others in that setting are most likely using that same skill. In fact, the person with autism might be the only one who lacks the skill. The community is filled with people who talk, people who say "Please," "Thank-you," "Excuse me," "Hello," and "Good-bye." Watching other people display the skill might not be all that is needed, but it certainly cannot hurt, and, most likely it helps.

The target setting also contains any machines or materials needed in social skills training. For example, a worker with autism is expected to share his copy machine with other workers. Such sharing would be hard to teach anywhere else but at the copy machine. Role playing could be tried in the group home where one could pretend that the microwave is the copy machine, but try to explain that difference to the person with autism.

WHAT YOU TEACH IS WHAT YOU GET

Social skills can not typically be taught in packages. That is, it is difficult to teach a person with autism to be friendly. Friendly is too large a package. It is difficult to teach a person with autism to be polite, because politeness is also too broad a concept. It is difficult to teach a person with autism to be cooperative for the same reason. Skills must be taught in very small, specific units. It is difficult to teach the concept of friendliness. It is much easier however, to teach a person with autism to say, "Hello." It is difficult to teach the concept of politeness, but it is possible to teach someone with autism to say, "Excuse me." Although it is not easy to teach cooperation, it is manageable to teach a worker with autism to share the workspace.

Target goals for social skills strategies must be extremely specific. The training must specify exactly what the skill is and when it should be used. Failure to realize improvements in social skills is often due to failure to be specific when targeting skills to train.

Teaching social skills can be a time consuming process. It must be done skill by skill, place by place, person by person. The greatest chances for success occur when the training is done in the setting where the skills are needed and with the person to whom the skills must be directed. This is a small price to pay for adjustment.

TEACHING SOCIAL SKILLS

Target the Skill

Social skills must be defined in concrete terms, and should be taught in very small units. Defining the skill involves breaking down a larger concept and specifying exactly what part of that concept will be taught. There might well be an infinite number of social skills that need to be taught. However, certain skills are noted frequently for training in group home and work settings.

Social Amenities Adults with autism sometimes do not have social amenities. Phrases, such as "Please," "Thank-you," and "You're welcome" are simple, short, and can be easily targeted for social skills training.

Greetings A person with autism might walk into a room and not even acknowledge that others are there. Similarly, this individual might be sitting at home and not even think to greet an arriving visitor. Teaching the individual to say "Hello" and "Good-bye" is a start to teaching friendliness.

Eye Contact, Facing Speaker Avoidance of eye contact is a well known characteristic of autism. Some individuals with autism go a step farther and do not even orient their body toward the person speaking to them. Social skills training might need to specifically focus on eye contact and orienting.

Often, persons have more pressing needs, and work on eye contact may not be considered a priority. However, in at least one case in a supported employment program, an employer specifically complained that the worker with autism did not look at him when he spoke. When the behavior became job threatening, as in this case, it was made a priority for training.

Terminate Conversations Some adults with autism, even those who are fully verbal and have relatively high intelligence levels, need skills in terminating conversations. More than one conversation with an adult with autism has ended when the individual with autism simply walked away while the speaker was speaking. Target behaviors may need to include a more conventional way to end the conversation or waiting for the speaker to stop speaking before walking away.

Sharing Workspace Workplaces can sometimes be less flexible than a person with autism might like. Occasionally, changes in routine are called for that may seem intrusive to a worker with autism. One example is sharing the workspace. An individual with autism might have his or her own work area. At times, it may be necessary to share this area. The individual might need to be taught exactly what to say and do when a co-worker needs to share the workspace.

Welcoming Visitors Adults with autism often need very specific instructions about how to deal with visitors to their homes or worksites. One young man greeted female visitors by inviting them back to his bedroom. He needed to be specifically taught that female visitors should be greeted with an offer to sit on the sofa and have a soda.

Accepting Correction Difficulty accepting correction is not limited to people with autism. Many people have a hard time with this skill. However, people with autism often react more strongly, and in some cases may even respond with aggression, self-injury, or less severe behaviors such as mumbling to themselves or refusing to follow the instructions. Social skills training may need to focus on teaching the individual exactly what to say and do when given correction.

Speaking with Authority Figures Adults with autism sometimes have problems both at work and in the community because of the way they address, or fail to address, authority figures. Social skills training may need to specifically focus on how to respond to directions, questions, or suggestions from people in authority.

Conversational Skills Many individuals with autism can benefit from training in conversational skills. Conversational skills have many aspects. People with autism often need to be taught how to initiate conversations with others, what topics are acceptable, and how to respond to questions. Social skills programs that target conversational skills often need to be implemented for months or even years.

Social Skills in Stores Most people do not think of shopping in a grocery store or a drug store as a social experience. However, social skills are involved that are so automatic that people do not even consciously think of them. By observing a person with autism in a store, the social skills needed become quite clear.

Specific social skills that may need to be taught for shopping include: waiting in line, standing still in line until the person ahead moves forward, keeping one arm's distance from others in the store, keeping at least 1 foot of distance between the grocery cart and other shoppers, shopping silently unless asking for assistance, and walking with good posture with arms at side or on cart. Individuals with autism who are just learning to shop, or who have shopped under the supervision of staff and are becoming ready to shop independently, need to be carefully assessed regarding the shopping skills still needed. Social skills for shopping can then be taught during the supervised trips. For some individuals who can go out without supervision, training sessions can be done directly before the individual leaves the residence.

Assertive Responses People with autism can sometimes be easily taken advantage of. One young woman with autism was arriving at work quite distraught each morning. The problem was that a strange man had been sitting with her on the bus and putting his arm around her. She did not known how to respond. Social skills training was needed to teach her to say, ''Leave me alone.''

Answering Questions A person with autism may be placed in a job where customers occasionally approach and ask questions. Four separate adults with autism working in a supported employment program had similar problems when this occurred. When customers asked for assistance, a typical response was to either ignore them and walk away or mumble incoherently under the breath and then walk away. In one incident, a young woman with autism had a stocking job in a drug store. When putting items on the shelf, a customer asked her for directions. The young woman ignored her and walked away. The customer proceeded to follow her around the store, persistently asking the question.

Workers with autism who may have contact with customers might need social skills training in exactly how to respond when asked a question. In all four cases in the supported employment program, the workers were taught to look at the customer and say, ''Ask at the front.''

Target the Situation

Social skills often are needed in very specific situations. When defining the skill, it is important to identify the situation where the skill is needed. Many people with autism have the acceptable behaviors in their repertoires. However, they use them in too many situations or in the wrong situation. Individuals with autism need to learn more than just how to behave socially. They need to learn *when* to behave as well.

An example is the social skills involved in greeting others. Some people with autism know how to greet. They just do not know when to greet. One worker with autism was disrupting the worksite by greeting co-workers each time they passed him. Each co-worker might get greeted several times per hour. The frequent greeting behavior was distracting for the worker with autism as well as for co-workers. The worker with autism had to be taught to greet co-workers only the first time they walked by. Social skills training involved teaching the individual that the first time a co-worker walked by, he could say, "Hi." Thereafter, if the co-worker walked by, he was to continue working.

Conversational skills training must focus on when and with whom certain topics are acceptable. If an individual is taught to reveal problems, he or she must be taught exactly to whom to reveal these problems. If an individual is taught how to make small talk, he or she needs to be taught exactly what topics are acceptable with given groups of people. Social skills training, then, is grounded in targeting very specific skills and those situations in which the skills are to be used. Once the skills and situations are targeted, strategies can be chosen for training.

TRAINING STRATEGIES

Social Skills Training Package

A strategy that has been effective and practical for use with individuals with autism in job and other community settings is a conventional social skills training package. This package can be implemented directly in target settings and consists of the following components:

Instruction: The individual is instructed on the target social skill. Instructions are very specific and might even include the exact words to be used. For example, the individual is told that if a co-worker needs to share the work table, it is important to smile and say, "Have a seat."

Demonstration: The instructor demonstrates the social skill for the individual.

Role Play: The individual, in a role play situation, practices the skill as explained and demonstrated by the instructor.

Feedback: The instructor gives positive feedback on correct aspects of the role play and models again if necessary.

Rehearsal: The individual practices the behavior several more times in a role play situation.

Generalization: The individual is reminded that if the situation comes up during the day, he or she is to respond as practiced.

Positive Feedback: If the individual performs the desired behavior in the actual situation, positive feedback is given.

A sample of the instructions for social skills training that were provided to staff follows. This sample focuses on the social skill of greeting co-workers only once, but these instructions can be used for teaching many social skills.

Aaron's case provides an example of social skills training. Training is implemented to teach him to remain in his work area and work quietly as co-workers pass by. He can greet people with "Hello" the first time he sees them. After that, he must remain working quietly if they pass by him again.

1. Instruction: Aaron should be told that he can say "Hello" the first time he sees someone that day. After that, he must continue to work quietly if that co-worker passes by again.

2. Demonstration: The counselor will demonstrate this for Aaron. First, the counselor will have Aaron walk by, and he or she will look up, say "Hello" then return to work. The counselor will then say, "See Aaron, I said Hello then went right back to work. Now, let's pretend you're passing by again. Watch what I do." Aaron will be told to pass by the counselor again. This time, he or she will continue to work without saying anything to Aaron.

3. Role Play and Feedback: The counselor will have Aaron practice looking up, saying "Hello," and then going right back to work after the counselor passes by. The counselor will then say, "I'm going to go by again, and you show me what you should do." Aaron should then role play his responses. If he gives the correct response, he should be praised. If not, the instructor should demonstrate again.

4. Rehearsal: Repeat Step 3 two more times.

5. Generalization: Remind Aaron that during the day, if someone passes by, he can say "Hello," then he must go quietly back to work. Also remind him that if a person goes by him more than once, he needs to continue working quietly.

6. Positive Feedback: Aaron should be praised for responding correctly.

This training strategy is done on a routine basis, until the individual consistently demonstrates the desired social skill in actual situations. The number of practices per week should be determined ahead of time, as should the times of the practices. Behaviors may often need to be practiced once or twice per day. For example, if an individual needs to learn to share the workspace, and this situation comes up several times per week, it might be necessary to have training sessions daily. If an individual is being taught how to greet female visitors at his apartment, and if women only come to visit once or twice per month, training may only need to be done once per week.

Training Conversational Skills

Persons with severe autism have a variety of problems in conversing with others. One problem seen in some individuals is the tendency to initiate conversations with others by a barrage of questions delivered in a rote manner, such as, "Hi, my name is George. What's your name?" This question may then be followed by a series of other questions, such as, "Are you married? Why not? Do you have children? Why not?" This person does not take into account the needs or feelings of the listener.

Problems in conversational skills are also evident when individuals with autism engage in monologues on topics of interest only to themselves. Attempts at changing the topic to one of interest to the listener are usually unsuccessful. One young man with autism talked for about 50 consecutive minutes on a topic. The listener explained to him how he could have imparted the information in about two sentences. The man with autism replied, "I wouldn't know how to do that."

Conversational deficits can also be seen when observing the interactions between some individuals with autism and their housemates with autism. A visit to a group residence with two or three individuals with autism might reveal that the only conversations between housemates are requests or demands. Very little social interaction may be seen.

Small group training in initiating conversations and taking into account the needs of the listener can be helpful. The purpose of the group is to teach the participants to take into account the needs and interests of the listeners. A group can be composed of two to four participants with autism and a group leader. The group is best composed of other persons with whom it would be desirable for the individual to interact. For example, housemates with little social interaction could form a group. The group leader can be a paraprofessional such as a job coach, a teacher, or a residential counselor.

The group can meet once per week or two or three times per week. The group leader introduces a topic that would be acceptable for conversation among the group members. Topics such as weekend plans, evening plans, how the day went, favorite television shows, and vacation plans are examples. Current events can also be used. Group members are encouraged to ask each other questions about the day's topic. If a question or answer is not clear, the listener is encouraged by the leader to ask the speaker to speak up, speak more clearly, or whatever is needed to achieve understanding.

The group leader serves as a facilitator and avoids becoming the center of attention. The group leader does not make comments on what is said, other than to help group members seek clarification when necessary or to make appropriate responses. The group leader also provides positive feedback on participation. The instructions to leaders on running the group are as follows:

1. The group should be composed of two to four participants and a group leader (staff).
2. The leader introduces the training session by telling the participants that they will be learning how to show interest in other people.
3. First, the group members will be encouraged to greet each other by saying, "Hi." The leader can model this and then instruct the members to greet each other.
4. The first conversational category is introduced with an explanation of the topic. For example, "If you ask each other about work, this will show you are interested in each other. We will learn to ask each other about work."
5. The group members are called upon to ask each other a question about the topic (work). If necessary, participants are given suggested questions to ask. If no response or an off task comment occurs, the participant is prompted and/or the leader models a relevant question.
6. If a participant responds to a question with an off-topic comment, the leader says "(name) asked you about (topic). Tell him about (topic)."
7. The leader should be modeling, prompting, and praising two types of conversation: 1) asking of relevant questions and 2) on-topic responses. The leader should redirect the conversation, as necessary, back to the stated topic.
8. The leader's role is primarily one of facilitator of conversation among members. Efforts should be made to stimulate members to question and answer each other. The leader should not become the center of conversation. Redirection to other members can maintain the dialogue among members.
9. The leader should encourage members to give appropriate feedback and comments to each other, rather than such comments coming directly from the leader. For example, if Joe asks Mary how work went, and Mary replies that she was given a raise, the leader should not say, "Mary, that's great." Rather, if Joe sits there silently, the leader can say, "Joe, tell Mary that that's great."
10. As well as modeling, prompting, and praising conversation, the leader should also encourage attending behaviors. Group members can be praised for good posture, listening, making eye contact, and orienting toward the speaker.
11. Conversational topics include work, activities, plans, news, weather, TV shows, and pets. Each session should involve only one topic. Perseverative topics of narrow interest should be avoided since these topics do not show interest in others.

12. The participants should be praised for participating in the session, as well as for good and/or improved performance during sessions.

Chat Program

Some persons with autism are very talkative. Others are reluctant to speak and become annoyed when others ask them questions. While an adult with autism may carry on extended conversations with him- or herself, he or she may be reluctant to converse with others. For individuals who are reluctant to talk, a well as individuals who initiate conversations only in a rote, questioning manner, a strategy can be useful that models more acceptable ways of conversing. This strategy, dubbed the chat program, avoids questioning the individual. Persons who are reluctant to talk are put off by questions and persons who ask questions incessantly need to learn other ways of interacting.

The chat program is simply a strategy in which the caregiver (parent, job coach, house counselor), approaches the individual at specified time intervals, usually about once per hour, and takes the lead in initiating a conversation. The conversation is directed by the caregiver and avoids questions. Rather, the caregiver provides information on topics of general interest to the individual. Conversations might concern what the caregiver did that morning or that evening or comments on the weather, current events, news, upcoming events, or other topics in the individual's life. During the chat, the caregiver does not ask questions. The caregiver provides a short chat on the topic, then the conversation ends. The individual is encouraged to make a comment or participate. However, it is neither requested nor demanded.

The purpose of the chat program is to teach, by demonstration, how to make small talk without questioning. The avoidance of questioning puts those at ease who do not like to be questioned. For individuals who do too much questioning, the chat program provides them with frequent opportunities to learn by participating in other ways of making conversations. It may be that people with autism do so much questioning of others because people question them so often. The chat program provides a way out of that pattern.

The chat program is also useful as a way of providing frequent, undemanded attention. Occasionally, the bizarre or unusual conversations that are initiated by individuals with autism serve the function of obtaining attention. The chat program provides them with regular attention, and in doing so it helps meet the need for attention. Meeting the need for attention, then, helps reduce the more unacceptable attention-getting behaviors.

This procedure of structured conversation is recommended in order to provide the individual with the opportunity to talk with the caregiver about topics of general interest. The directions to caregivers on running the chat program are as follows:

1. The caregiver should have at least one conversation with the individual each hour. The caregiver should approach the individual and take the lead

in having a conversation on a pleasant or neutral topic, such as the weather, an event in the news, a funny or neutral occurrence at work or in the residence, good news about another caregiver or resident, or any other topics that may be of interest.

2. The caregiver should begin the conversation, engage in it for several minutes, then end the conversation. This conversation should be structured and fairly brief (several minutes), but long enough to provide the benefit of several minutes of pleasant interaction.
3. Before and after an outing or recreational activity, the caregiver should discuss the event with the individual in a positive, pleasant way. Again, the caregiver must take the lead in structuring the conversation.
4. The caregiver should take the lead in presenting information to the individual and avoid asking questions. If the caregiver takes the lead in providing information, then gradually the individual will learn how to approach others and provide them with information on pleasant topics.

Following are five examples of teaching specific social skills directly in integrated community settings.

CASE 1

Gerald was a 27-year-old male with autism who had an IQ of 61 and limited speech. He was employed in the bindery section of a printing company where he was supervised by a job coach. Gerald had difficulty following through in a conversation. When required to ask the supervisor a question, he asked the question, then walked away without waiting for a response.

Procedures

A social skills training package was used to train Gerald to wait for a response after asking a question. The social skills training was conducted daily with five rehearsals per session. The instructions for the job coach are as follows:

Goal: Gerald will wait for an answer from the supervisor when he asks a question.

1. The training should take place once in the morning and once in the afternoon.
2. Instruction: Gerald should be told that after asking the supervisor a question, he should wait for an answer before walking away.
3. Demonstration: The job coach will demonstrate this for Gerald. He will ask a question then wait for an answer before walking away.
4. Role Play and Feedback: The counselor will have Gerald practice waiting for a response. He will be praised when he waits for an answer before walking away.
5. Rehearsal: Repeat Step 4 two more times.

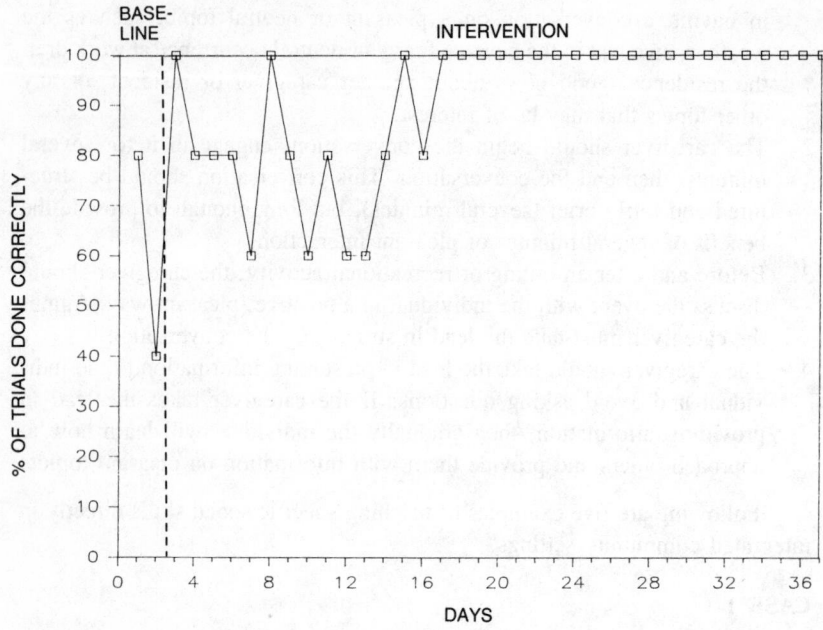

Figure 6.1. Percent of questions for which Gerald waited for an answer during baseline and social skills training.

6. Generalization: Remind Gerald that during the day, if he needs to ask the supervisor a question, he must wait for a response before walking away.
7. Positive Feedback: If Gerald does wait for a response from the supervisor, he should be praised.

Results

Prior to training, Gerald waited for an answer between 40% and 80% of the trails. During the other trials, he would walk away before the supervisor answered his question. As seen in Figure 6.1, progress was uneven for the first 2 weeks. It was determined that Gerald did not understand the word "wait." Training was restructured and instead of being told to wait, Gerald was told to look at the supervisor's eyes and stay still until the supervisor was done talking. Following this change in the program, Gerald learned the skill.

After 18 days of training, Gerald waited for a response in 100% of the trials. While waiting for a response, he would stay oriented toward the supervisor and maintain eye contact. Training sessions were faded and his waiting response generalized to actual situations.

CASE 2

Ben was a 23-year-old male with autism who had an IQ of 85. He was employed at a factory where he was supervised by a job coach. A problem arose at the job when it became necessary for Ben to share his workspace with a co-worker. If a co-worker attempted to sit near him, Ben scowled, mumbled to himself, and refused to make room at the table. His refusal to share and his interactions with co-workers put Ben's job in jeopardy.

Procedures

A social skills training package was implemented by Ben's counselor. Each morning, the social skills training sequence was implemented with a role play where a co-worker came to share the workspace. The counselor instructed Ben on how to handle the situation, modeled the correct behavior, and asked Ben to practice. The procedures written for staff are as follows:

Goal: Ben will cooperate with others by sharing his workspace when co-workers approach.

1. Training sessions should take place at the worksite each morning and each afternoon.
2. Instruction: Ben will be told that if somebody wants to work or put work at his table (point to space), then he will need to make room for him or her.
3. Demonstration: The job coach will demonstrate this for Ben. The job coach will say, "If I am working here, and (co-worker's name) comes by to put work down, I will move my work aside." The job coach demonstrates moving over and making room.
4. Role Play and Feedback: The job coach will ask, "What will you do if (co-worker's name) needs to work next to you?" The job coach will have Ben practice the correct response. He will praise Ben for moving over and making room or will give corrective feedback.
5. Rehearsal: The job coach will rehearse the situation with Ben in which the job coach needs to share Ben's workspace. Praise for correct response or corrective feedback will be given if necessary.
6. Generalization: Remind Ben that if during the day a co-worker needs to use his workspace, he must make room for him or her.
7. Positive Feedback: If the situation arises in which Ben needs to share the workspace, and if he readily moves over, praise should be given. If necessary, prompt him by reminding, "What do you need to do?" If necessary, refer to practice sessions.

Results

The routine implementation of the social skills training package was followed by rapid improvement on the targeted social skill. Within weeks of the initiation of training, Ben was cordially allowing co-workers to share his table space and training was terminated.

CASE 3

Teddy was a 23-year-old man with autism who had an IQ of 82. He was employed at a manufacturing firm. Co-workers had complained because Teddy asked them embarrassing questions such as, "Can I hug you?", "Will you kiss me?", and "How much money do you make?" Teddy's abrasive questioning was a real problem.

Procedures

A social skills training package was implemented by a job coach at work to teach Teddy correct greetings. Each morning Teddy was instructed to greet co-workers with, "Hi, how are you?" The procedures written for the job coach are as follows:

Goal: Teddy will greet co-workers with, "Hi, how are you?"

1. Social skills training for greeting others should take place each morning.
2. Instruction: Teddy should be told that he should say, "Hi, how are you?" the first time he sees someone that day. He should be told that is all he needs to say.
3. Demonstration: The job coach will demonstrate this for Teddy. First, he will have Teddy walk by and he will look up, say, "Hi, how are you?" then return to work. The job coach will say, "See Teddy, I said, 'Hi, how are you?' when you passed me."
4. Role Play and Feedback: The job coach will have Teddy role play the situation by saying, "Hi how are you?" as the job coach walks by. The job coach will praise correct response or give corrective feedback.
5. Rehearsal: Repeat step 4 two more times.
6. Generalization: Remind Teddy that during the day, if someone passes by, he should only say, "Hi, how are you?"
7. Positive Feedback: If Teddy is seen greeting others correctly, he should be complimented or praised. If he greets a staff person correctly, the staff person should enthusiastically greet him in turn. As staff pass by Teddy, they should be sure and say, "Hi" and wave as they go by. In this way, they can serve as models to Teddy on how to greet others.

Results

Prior to training, Teddy had no instances of acceptable greetings. By week 4 of training, all greetings were acceptable. That is, they consisted of Teddy saying, "Hi, how are you?" and returning to his task.

CASE 4

Alfred was a 32-year-old man with autism. He worked in a manufacturing firm with approximately 20 nonhandicapped co-workers and his job coach. The aisles in the work room were narrow. When walking through the corridors or aisles at work, Alfred walked directly into co-workers who were in his path.

Procedures

Using the social skills training package described, Alfred was taught to keep an arm's distance from people in his path and either wait for them to pass or say, "Excuse me," if he has to go around them. The instructions for the job coach are as follows:

Goal: Alfred will learn to keep an acceptable distance from others and will say, "Excuse me" if he needs to pass.

1. Social skills training should be done once daily at the worksite.
2. Instruction: Alfred will be told that when someone is in his way, he needs to walk around him or her by at least an arm's length or say, "Excuse me," and wait for him or her to move so that he can walk by.
3. Demonstration: The job coach will demonstrate this for Alfred. The job coach will have Alfred stand in the way. First, the job coach will demonstrate walking around Alfred, then he or she will demonstrate saying, "Excuse me," and then pass. The job coach will say that both are acceptable behaviors.
4. Role Play and Feedback: The job coach will then stand in Alfred's path and have him practice: 1) walking around and keeping an arm's length distance, and 2) saying, "Excuse me," and waiting for the job coach to move. Praise for correct responses or corrective feedback will be given if necessary.
5. Rehearsal: Repeat step 4 two more times.
6. Generalization: Alfred should be reminded that if someone is in his way he needs to go around by at least an arm's length, or say, "Excuse me," and wait for the person to move.
7. Positive Feedback: Alfred will be praised for any aspects of the procedure that he does correctly. If necessary, the job coach can provide another demonstration of the correct behavior. "Alfred, watch me again and notice how I keep at least an arm's length away." Praise should be given when Alfred does pass people correctly or says, "Excuse me," and waits to go by.

Results

Alfred successfully learned this skill by week 5 of training.

CASE 5

Ellis was a 20-year-old male with autism who worked in a retail store. Occasionally, while stocking the aisles, customers asked for directions. Ellis either did not answer or mumbled under his breath.

Procedures

Ellis was taught to say, "Ask at the front," when questioned by a customer with a standard social skills training package. The social skills training was implemented each morning at worksite. The instructions for implementation are as follows:

Goal: Ellis will respond to customer's questions by directing them to the front counter.

1. Social skills training should take place once per day, in the morning. This training should be done on the worksite by the job coach.
2. Instruction: Ellis should be told that if a customer asks him where something is, he should say, "Ask at that counter," and point toward the counter.
3. Demonstration: The job coach will demonstrate this for Ellis. First, he or she will have Ellis ask for directions. The job coach will respond by saying, "Ask at the counter," and point toward the counter.
4. Role Play and Feedback: The job coach will tell Ellis to role play the situation and will demonstrate how this is done. He or she will ask Ellis for directions, and if Ellis responds correctly, he should be praised. If he does not respond correctly, the job coach can repeat the explanation and role play again.
5. Rehearsal: Repeat step 4 two more times.
6. Generalization: Remind Ellis that during the day, if a customer asks for assistance, he needs to direct the customer to the counter. Specific situations related to customers asking for assistance should be practiced each day. For example, in one practice the job coach can ask where the Kleenex are. During another day's training he or she can ask where the pencils are.
7. Positive Feedback: If Ellis is approached by a customer during the day and responds correctly, he should be praised after the customer leaves the area. If he ignores the customer, the job coach should intervene and provide the directions to the customer.

Results

Prior to training, Ellis gave no correct answers to customers asking for assistance. In all cases he mumbled or ignored the customer. Following training, Ellis began to respond correctly to customers by saying, "Ask at the front."

SOME CONSIDERATIONS FOR SOCIAL SKILLS DEVELOPMENT

The development of social skills in some cases may not be a high priority. However, social skills training at the worksite might, in many cases, be essential for success on the job. Since persons with autism could have difficulty generalizing from one situation to another, it makes the most sense to do the training in the setting where the skills are needed. Therefore, work-related social skills should be taught at the job site. A second advantage to training social skills at the job site is that the planner is in a better position to determine those skills that need to be trained. For example, in Case 2, the problem of sharing space did not even become apparent until Ben had been working on the job.

An element of the social skills training package that is important is the routine, systematic nature of the training sessions. This approach does not involve waiting for the individual to produce a social error in order to provide an explanation of how the situation should be handled. Rather, once a social skill is targeted, sessions are held regularly, on a routine basis. This approach has the advantage of preparing the individual to better handle the situation when it does occur, thus preventing the recurrence of the problem.

The social skills training package discussed here also includes positive feedback to the individual when the social skills are demonstrated during the work day, outside of role play sessions. Although it is not clear how important feedback is, it seems conservative to include the positive feedback as a means of strengthening the newly developed social skills.

When designing a social skills training package, two considerations are important. First, the identification of the target skills can be critical to the success of the program. The target skill chosen must be relevant to the situation at hand and must be broken down into steps that the individual can learn. The case of Gerald provided an example of the need for specificity. When teaching Gerald to wait for an answer from a supervisor, the instructions included the term "wait." After several weeks passed with no improvement in waiting behavior, it became clear that he did not understand "wait." When told, "Keep your feet still on the floor and look into Mr. Jones' eyes until he stops talking," then Gerald learned the skill. Second, social skills training done at the worksite can conceivably either interfere with the work routine or call undue attention to the individual. Therefore, it is necessary to be discreet when conducting the training sessions, as well as to schedule the sessions so as not to interfere with production.

Social skills training at work requires a trainer to be at the job site in order to teach the skills. Since many persons with autism fail to maintain employment because of social problems, the provision of instructional support at the actual job site in order to teach job-related social skills might be viewed as a necessary component of successful job placement.

SUMMARY

Most people with autism, almost by definition, can benefit from training in social skills. As people with autism join the work force, social skills become critical. For individuals who live in institutions and are accepted in group homes, social skills are also critical. Often, social skills training has taken a back seat to the more dramatic behavior problems of self-injury and aggression. However, as self-injury and aggression decrease in frequency and severity, then it becomes possible to deal with social skills. Teaching social skills can itself be an intervention that helps eliminate more severe behavior problems.

Social skills training is comprised mainly of demonstrations and opportunities for practice. Conversation training and the chat program rely heavily on modeling and direct prompting. The social skills training package presented provides opportunities for both.

Acquisition of social skills can be very slow in individuals with autism. In some cases, the more dramatic problems of self-injury and aggression are more easily remediated than the severe social skills deficits that are evidenced by people with milder autism and no severe behavior problems. Social skills training is no cure for autism, however, it does provide a means of slow but steady growth in an area of functioning that has been devastated by the disorder.

REFERENCES

Belcher, R. (1987). *Assertive social skills training with autistic adults.* Unpublished master's thesis, American University, Washington, DC.

Greenspan, S., & Shoultz, B. (1981). Why mentally retarded people lost their jobs: Social competence as a factor in work adjustment. *Applied Research in Mental Retardation, 2,* 23–38.

Juhrs, R., & Smith, M. (1989). Community-based employment for persons with autism. In P. Wehman & J. Kregel (Eds.), *Supported employment for persons with disabilities* (pp. 163–175). New York: Human Sciences Press.

Kanner, L., Rodriguez, A., & Ashenden, B. (1972). How far can autistic children go in matters of social adaptation? *Journal of Autism and Childhood Schizophrenia, 9,* 9–33.

Salzberg, C., Lignugaris-Kraft, B., & McCuller, G. (1988). Reasons for job loss: A review of employment termination studies of mentally retarded workers. *Research in Developmental Disabilities, 9,* 153–170.

Schopler, E., & Mesibov, G. (1983). *Autism in adolescents and adults.* New York: Plenum Press.

Wehman, P., Hill, M., Goodall, P., Cleveland, P., Brooke, V., & Pentecoste, J.H. Jr. (1982). Job placement and follow-up of moderately and severely handicapped individuals after three years. *Journal of the Association for the Severely Handicapped, 7,* 5–16.

Chapter Seven

SELF-MANAGEMENT

Autism is a disorder that breeds dependence. Severe problems in communication, problems in getting along with others, problems in getting along with oneself, and problems with behavior all create dependence. People with autism often depend on others to provide for them, care for them, communicate for them, interpret for them, and support them in countless ways.

Many individuals with autism are dependent on others to not only control their environment, but also to control their very selves. Caregivers must often provide controls for aggression, self-injury, and property destruction. Learning self-management is one way that individuals with autism can begin to overcome the devastating effects of their handicap. The problems of self-injury, aggression, severe deficits in social skills, and other difficulties associated with autism become magnified when the individual is totally dependent on others for control. Self-management adds some degree of dignity to an otherwise very undignified disorder. Self-management allows the individual to manage him- or herself.

Self-management, then, is a critical goal for many individuals with autism. Self-management, defined here, means obtaining the skills involved to change one's own behavior and providing intervention for oneself. Self-management procedures are particularly useful for behaviors that occur in private, but that are detrimental to the individuals's welfare. For example, self-scratching often occurs out of view of others. Therefore, it is desirable to teach the individual to self-manage, that is, to stop scratching on his or her own, rather than to be dependent on others in order to stop. Clothes tearing is another example. Some individuals with severe autism rip their clothing. This destruction is often done in private.

Research on self-management with persons with severe handicaps is scarce. However, many self-management strategies have been investigated with persons with mild, moderate, or no handicaps and appear promising for persons with severe handicaps. One method is the use of picture cues to teach self-management skills. Connis (1979) taught adults with mental retardation

103

to self-record at work using picture cues. Sowers, Verdi, Bourbeau, and Sheehan (1985) taught adults with mental retardation to use picture cues and self-monitoring to independently initiate a series of work tasks. In fact, two of the adults in this study were able to initiate tasks independently at the end of the study after being shown a new series of pictures.

Self-monitoring is another valuable method in teaching self-management. It involves the individual monitoring his or her own performance, resulting in more independence at work. Ackerman and Shapiro (1984) reported that self-monitoring increased productivity in adults with mental retardation. Self-instruction has also been used to teach adults with handicaps to self-manage. Self-instruction is a technique in which a person tells him- or herself exactly what to do. Agran, Salzberg, and Stowitschek (1987) taught adults with severe handicaps, including autism, to ask for assistance at work by first self-instructing.

Self-evaluation has been explored as a method for encouraging self-management. It involves teaching the individual to evaluate his or her own behavior. Harvey, Karan, Bhargava, and Morehouse (1978) found that teaching adults with moderate mental retardation to make positive self-evaluations while using relaxation procedures could reduce aggression. Teaching individuals to deliver reinforcers to themselves is also another technique. Wehman, Schutz, Bates, Renzalia, and Karan (1978) used self-reinforcement to increase productivity rates in workers with both moderate and severe retardation.

Gardner, Cole, Berry, and Nowinski (1983) worked with two adults with moderate retardation and histories of aggression. They had success with a self-management program that included self-monitoring, self-evaluation, and self-reinforcement to reduce disruptive verbalizations that often preceded aggression. Gardner, Clees, and Cole (1983) also successfully helped a young man with moderate retardation to eliminate talking aloud to himself with a self-management program. Their program included self-monitoring, self-evaluation, self-consequation, and self-instruction. The purpose of this chapter is to explore a variety of procedures for use with adults with autism to promote self-management. Self-management is discussed in terms of reducing behavior problems as well as promoting behaviors that are necessary for better adjustment.

PINPOINT THE BEHAVIOR

As with any behavior change program, planning a self-management program begins with pinpointing observable behaviors. The behaviors targeted in a self-management program may be selected in one of two ways. First, the targets might be undesirable behaviors that are obviously causing difficulty for the individual or others. Self-injury, aggression, and property destruction are all examples of behaviors that might be targeted for a self-management program.

Second, behaviors for a self-management program might also be revealed through a functional analysis. A functional analysis of a misbehavior may reveal that it is serving a function for the individual that can be replaced with a self-management skill. For example, an individual might engage in self-injury in order to obtain assistance with a task. Teaching the individual to ask for assistance might then be the target of a self-management plan. Similarly, an individual might become aggressive when having difficulty with another person. Teaching the individual to verbalize the problem might replace the function that aggression serves. A self-management program that targets revealing problems might help reduce the need for aggression.

PINPOINT THE SETTING

An integral part of teaching self-management is to identify the antecedents or settings in which the self-management is needed. If the individual with autism is to be taught a new response, it must be taught in the context of the antecedents or setting events that normally are associated with the problem behavior.

SELECT THE STRATEGY

Following a behavioral assessment that pinpoints the behavior and setting, a self-management strategy can be selected. The strategy is chosen as part of a blueprint for change as described in Chapter Four. That is, the strategy is chosen as part of a systematic behavior change process. The remainder of this chapter is devoted to describing several strategies. The strategies described are useful with individuals with autism who have some spoken language skills.

ASKING FOR ASSISTANCE

It is not uncommon for self-injury or aggression at work to occur during a difficult task. The misbehavior may serve the purpose of escape or it could serve the function of getting help. Teaching the individual with autism to ask for assistance when having difficulty with a task might eliminate the need to misbehave, and if the individual gets the needed help, he or she might even eliminate the desire to escape.

Recognizing that assistance is needed and asking for such assistance are two skills that can be lacking in an adult with autism. When difficulties arise and an individual does not have an acceptable way to ask for assistance, behavior problems, such as tantrums, self-abuse, or property destruction may occur. For example, Elinor, a young woman with autism, typically threw her materials on the floor when she had difficulty with a task. George would flap his arms and scream when in need of assistance.

A standard social skills training package, as described in Chapter Six, can be used to teach individuals to ask for assistance. The first step consists of identifying situations that might present difficulty for the person. Daily, routine training sessions are conducted following identification of target situations. Each day, or as designated in the individual's intervention plan, a training session is held. During this session, the individual is instructed on the need to ask for assistance under specific circumstances. After a demonstration, the individual is asked to describe how the situation should be handled, and then he or she practices asking for assistance.

During the actual situations when assistance is needed, the individual is prompted, using a hierarchy of assistance to ask for help. First, the trainer waits several seconds to allow the individual time to ask for help unassisted. If he or she does not, then the counselor says, "What's next?" and waits 5 seconds. If there is still no correct response, the trainer prompts saying, "You need to ask for help with the broken tool."

Case 1

George has autism and an IQ of 65 as measured by the WAIS—R. George is in a supported employment program working at a printing company under the supervision of a job coach. George needs to be taught to ask for assistance if a tool breaks. Typically, if a tool breaks, George begins to flap his hands and, in some cases, jump up and down. Teaching him to ask for assistance would give him a more acceptable response.

Case 2

Elinor is a worker with autism, and her IQ, as measured by the WAIS—R, is 70. She participates in a supported employment program working at a manufacturing firm under the supervision of a job coach. When having difficulty with a task, Elinor throws her materials, scratches herself, or cries. She needs to be taught to ask for assistance when having difficulty with a task.

Procedures for Cases 1 and 2 George and Elinor were trained to ask for assistance using daily instructions and practices. The instructions for staff are as follows:

1. Instruction: The individual should be told, "If you need help with your work, you must ask for help. We will practice asking for help."
2. Demonstration: The instructor says, "Let's pretend I need help with my work. I would say, 'I need help with this.'" (A specific work related task where assistance might be needed can be demonstrated.) The job coach would then pretend to need help with a task and would demonstrate asking for assistance.

3. Role play: The instructor says, "Now let's pretend you need help with this task. What would you do?" Praise correct responses or assist with a correct response if necessary.
4. Rehearsal: Repeat step 3 twice.
5. Demonstration, role playing, and rehearsal should be done in later training sessions for other hypothetical situations where the individual might need help. If he or she asks for help, then he or she should be given assistance and praised for asking for help.

Results   Both George and Elinor learned to ask for assistance following daily training sessions. For George, this training was one component of a program designed to eliminate his tantrums at the worksite. In both cases, the incidence of aggressive and destructive behaviors declined significantly following training programs that included these routine sessions.

Some Considerations

The ability to ask for assistance is a skill that most nonhandicapped workers take for granted. For an adult with autism, asking for assistance is a skill that is often absent and that can be critical to job or community adjustment. Not only does the ability to ask for assistance allow the worker a higher degree of independence, it also prevents behavior problems that would be likely to occur when the worker with autism is in need of assistance but does not have the skills to acquire it appropriately.

The basic premise of the strategy presented here is simple. If, on a routine basis, under nonstressful conditions, the individual is taught to ask for assistance, then when assistance is needed, he or she will be able to ask for help. This routine training in the work or other target setting can be sufficient to teach individuals to ask for assistance under a variety of conditions. The daily, routine training sessions are central to the success of this strategy. If the trainer does not conduct routine sessions, but instead waits for the individual to actually need help before providing training, then several problems may arise. First, if the trainer does not intervene quickly enough, the individual might begin to demonstrate an undesirable behavior. For example, if George has difficulty with a task, and the counselor does not immediately recognize the difficulty, George would begin to scream, flap his arms, and jump up and down. A second drawback to waiting for the actual moment of difficulty to teach the skill is that at the time, because of the difficulty, the individual might be upset and not able to learn. So, for example, if George tends to become upset when his tool breaks, then at the time the tool breaks George may be too upset to learn that it is necessary to ask for assistance.

However, in both examples, if the individual has daily training on asking for assistance, then when the situation actually occurs, he or she is likely to draw on the training and respond correctly. If a prompt is needed, more than likely the individual will be able to provide the correct response if routine training sessions have been held. This training can be conducted quickly and in an unobtrusive manner at the job site if needed. To maximize success, it is important to pinpoint relevant situations to train, to provide positive feedback for participating in training, and to provide assistance and praise when the individual asks for help in actual situations.

A final consideration is worthy of mention. In both cases described here, the training on asking for assistance was one component of a comprehensive program to enable these individuals to achieve better vocational adjustment. When treating multiple behavior problems in vocational settings, this program may be a necessary, but inefficient approach to achieving vocational success. success.

SELF-DISCLOSURE TRAINING

Persons with autism are often reluctant, or do not know how, to disclose that they have a problem. It is not unusual for a person with severe autism with good verbal skills to misbehave when a problem arises instead of discussing it. A number of cases have been observed in which the individual has a problem, appears upset, is asked what is wrong, says everything is fine, then tears a shirt or throws a clock. Teaching verbal individuals with autism to disclose to others when they are having a problem can be a valuable strategy in decreasing severe behavior problems and teaching self-management.

For example, Jane, a 25-year-old woman who has autism, became upset because a substitute counselor in her group home did not clean his dishes. She became agitated, but when asked what the problem was, she replied, "Nothing." She then went to her room and scratched herself.

A number of adults with autism, even those with average intelligence as measured by standardized intelligence tests, have exhibited this same pattern of behavior. The person becomes upset, does not reveal the cause, and then becomes self-abusive, aggressive, and destructive. A critical skill for adults with autism, then, appears to be the ability to self-disclose, to verbalize problems or difficulties to the appropriate person, such as the parent, house counselor, or job coach.

A self-disclosure training program can teach the individual to make truthful self-disclosing statements to reveal needs and difficulties. This strategy is based on a social skills training package that includes the following components:

1. Instruction: The individual is instructed to tell the truth about problems.
2. Demonstration: The caregiver demonstrates by example, revealing a truthful self-disclosure. It should be noted that the hypothetical situations presented by the caregiver are relevant issues that have created problems for the individual in the past.

3. Role Play: The individual is prompted to role play a truthful self-disclosure from a given hypothetical, relevant problem by the counselor.

4. Feedback: The caregiver provides constructive feedback, primarily giving praise for successful attempts by the individual. If necessary, assistance is given.

5. Rehearsal: The individual is given two more opportunities to practice self-disclosure.

6. Generalization: The individual should be reminded that if at any time a problem arises, it is important to make truthful self-disclosures.

This strategy is similar to the standard social skills training package used to teach other social skills and to teach the individual to ask for assistance. The following case illustrates its use.

Case 3

Marty was a 24-year-old male with autism and with an IQ of 90 as measured by the WAIS—R. His verbal expression was good, but his willingness and ability to provide personal information on difficulties and problems was low. On those occasions when he had a problem, his reluctance or inability to disclose the problem often compounded matters. For example, when ill, medical care was delayed because he did not tell his mother or his group home counselors that he was not feeling well. When he broke his glasses, it took several weeks before his job coach found out. He was often late to work, and again, it took several weeks to discover that the reason was that he was having trouble finding his keys in the morning.

Procedures Marty was placed on a self-disclosure training program to encourage him to reveal personal difficulties and problems to his counselor. The instructions to staff are as follows.

1. Instruction: Marty should be told, "Marty if something is bothering you or if you have a problem or need help, you should tell me. We will practice asking for help with problems."

2. Demonstration: The counselor says, "Let's pretend I lost some money. I would say, 'I need help. I lost my money.'" The counselor actually role plays the situation and demonstrates how to disclose the problem.

3. Role Play and Feedback: The counselor says, "Now let's pretend you lost your money. What would you say?" Praise correct responses or assist with a correct response if necessary.

4. Rehearsal: Repeat step 3 twice. Demonstrations, role playing, and rehearsal should be done in later training sessions for other hypothetical problem situations.

5. Generalization: Marty should be reminded that if at any time he feels upset or has a problem, he should tell his job coach or group home counselor right away.

6. Generalization: If Marty appears to be having a problem at some point during the day or evening, and does not readily discuss it, the counselor can attempt to elicit self-disclosure by referring to the practice sessions, for example, "Remember our practice session, when you need something you must tell someone."

Each training session should involve only one hypothetical problem. Marty should not be pressured to come up with the examples. The counselor should provide the examples.

Results Marty responded very well to the self-disclosure training. After several weeks of training he began to initiate his own self-disclosures, and now he readily self-discloses about a variety of issues including roommate relationships, his health, relationships with counselors, feelings about his family, and difficulties at work. Following are several examples of appropriate self-disclosures made by Marty. It is important to note that prior to training these types of self-disclosures did not occur:

"Now that my roommate wakes up later than me, I am concerned about turning the light on in the morning because it might bother him."

"I am concerned about budgeting my money. Every day I seem to either lose or gain money. Maybe there is another way to keep track of that money."

"My stomach and head have been hurting."

"I would be upset if I goofed off at my job and people might say, 'He can't handle this job; he must go in a sheltered workshop.'"

Case 4

Lena is a young woman with an IQ of 65 as measured by the WAIS—R. Prior to self-disclosure training, she was unwilling or unable to discuss any problems. Instead, when experiencing difficulty she would become self-abusive, destructive, or would engage in bizarre, irrelevant verbalizations. When asked what was wrong she would reply, "Nothing is wrong. I'll be good. Everything is fine." Her standard answer was, "Everything is fine."

Procedures Self-disclosure training was done with Lena on a daily basis. (See procedures for Case 3, Marty.)

Results The self-disclosure training program resulted in Lena making appropriate and truthful self-disclosures to her counselors. The fear that seemed to be associated with discussing problems was no longer apparent. Relating difficulties to her counselors became an accepted part of her routine. Following are examples of Lena's self-disclosures:

"I had a very hard day and worried about (the job coach's) vacation."

"I was upset today because I didn't have enough money."

"I am feeling sad today because Cathy can't come and get me tomorrow."

Some Considerations

The self-disclosure training program was designed, and seems most suitable, for individuals who have expressive language skills, but who do not readily reveal problems or difficulties. This program, through regularly presented opportunities for demonstration and role play, seeks to teach individuals to make truthful, appropriate self-disclosures.

The use of the self-disclosure strategy requires well-trained caregivers. Since the caregivers are eliciting private information, it is important that they be trained to handle the information in a sensitive, confidential, and helpful manner. The purpose of this program is to teach individuals to disclose difficulties so that solutions can be found. The caregivers using this program must make every effort to treat the individual's concerns with respect and assist them in obtaining solutions. They must also keep in mind that the purpose of the training is to present hypothetical, relevant problems for practice. It is hoped that, when actual difficulties arise, the individual will more readily disclose them.

One difficulty that is common among novices is that they tend to pressure the individual to come forth with difficulties and self-disclosures during training sessions. This pressure is incompatible with the goals of the program. The goal of the program is to teach individuals to self-initiate self-disclosures as a form of self-management. The emphasis of the training session is to teach the individual that self-disclosure should be made *at the time the problem occurs*. The self-disclosure strategy can increase the quantity and variety of topics that individuals with autism will self-disclose. Use of this program has also been associated with decreases in self-abuse and aggression in verbal adults with autism.

It should be noted that this strategy alone may not be sufficient to stem self-abuse or aggression, but instead provides individuals with an alternate, nonviolent way of handling problems and a better means of self-control. In many cases, however, this strategy will be best used as part of a multi-part, comprehensive plan and should not always be expected to stand alone.

DECISION MAKING

Functional analyses occasionally reveal that inability to make decisions bears a relation to behavior problems. Targeting decision making as a goal can provide a valuable skill that can help provide a means of self-control for an individual with autism. Problems with decision making often take one of two forms. One, the individual with autism might have a problem with dependence on others for making decisions. Whenever a decision is called for, the person may need to ask another's advice. Or, two, decisions might be made too hastily and based on insufficient information.

Persons who can make their own choices in a satisfactory way can live more independently than those who rely on others or those who make hasty, ill-founded decisions. Decision making skills can provide people with more opportunity to exert control over their lives. Teaching decision making begins with breaking the process down into steps. Decision making can be divided into the following steps: 1) define the decision to be made, 2) gather information, 3) consider possible outcomes of each choice, 4) consider values (which of the possible outcomes is desirable), 5) make the choice, and 6) act on the choice.

During training sessions, the caregiver goes through the steps with the individual. Initially, the trainer explains the steps and demonstrates the use of each step by example. Then sample decisions are presented to the individual and the trainer assists in making choices according to the decision making process. Gradually, counselor assistance is faded out and the individual is encouraged to make decisions independently.

Case 5

Tony was a 25-year-old male with autism with a low-average IQ as measured by the WAIS—R. His verbal expression was excellent for a young man with autism. One problem area for him was his inability to make decisions. When a decision was called for, no matter how simple, Tony asked others to decide for him. He was reluctant to make choices about even the simplest matters, such as what to eat for dessert.

Procedures Tony was placed on a decision making program to teach him to make decisions independently by following a logical decision making process. The instructions to staff are as follows:

1. Define decision to be made.
2. Gather information.
3. Consider possible outcomes of each choice.
4. Consider values of the possible outcomes.
5. Select the choice.
6. Act on the choice.

The training should take place three times per week, and the counselor should explain to Tony that it is important to learn to make choices. The counselor should select a sample decision that is relevant to Tony. The trainer should demonstrate how to make a choice by going through the decision making process and explaining it to Tony. That is, he or she should explain for each step how it applies to the decision being made. He or she should also get Tony's input on each step.

Sample problem: Shall I go to my parents' house on Saturday or stay home?

1. Define decision: Where to go on Saturday?
2. Gather information: Find out what will be going on at the group home, what will be going on at parents' house, who will be involved, and so forth.
3. Consider possible outcomes of each choice: If I go to my parents', I can help with yard work and mow the lawn; or I might have to sit in my room while they have company. If I stay at the group home I can go bowling.
4. Consider my values: I would like to help my mother with yard work; I would also like to go bowling. I would not like to sit in my room while my mother has company.
5. Make the choice: I choose to stay at the group home on Saturday. Next week I will mow my mother's lawn one evening after work.

Proceed through the decision making steps in training sessions. Use decisions that are relevant to Tony. At first, the trainer may need to give many examples and assistance. Gradually, the trainer should fade out assistance and encourage Tony to provide the input. Initially, if Tony has difficulty, the trainer should make suggestions such as, "Well, you might consider . . ." or, "Well, you might want to find out . . ." Later in training, the trainer should be less directive in assistance (e.g., "What do you need to consider next?"). When Tony is confronted with a choice outside the training sessions, the trainer should assist him in following the decision making process to make a choice.

Results Tony gradually learned the decision making process. He began to apply this process to decisions that he had to make. A record was kept of the percent of decisions that he made completely independently following all the steps. Figure 7.1. shows the percent of decisions made independently each month for baseline month 1 and the subsequent 9 months.

During baseline, Tony independently made 65% of the decisions presented to him. Following an erratic course of progress, Tony eventually was able to make all decisions presented to him by following the decision making process. Decisions on which data were taken were sample decisions presented during role plays as well as actual decisions that came up during the month.

Some Considerations

First, it is important to realize that data collected are on those decisions that were presented to Tony during training. It is possible that Tony used the procedure for other decisions without even discussing it as such, but these instances could not be reliably measured. Second, training on decision making is a long-term process taking place over months or even years with persons who have autism. It is possible that if training were terminated, a pattern of dependence could re-emerge.

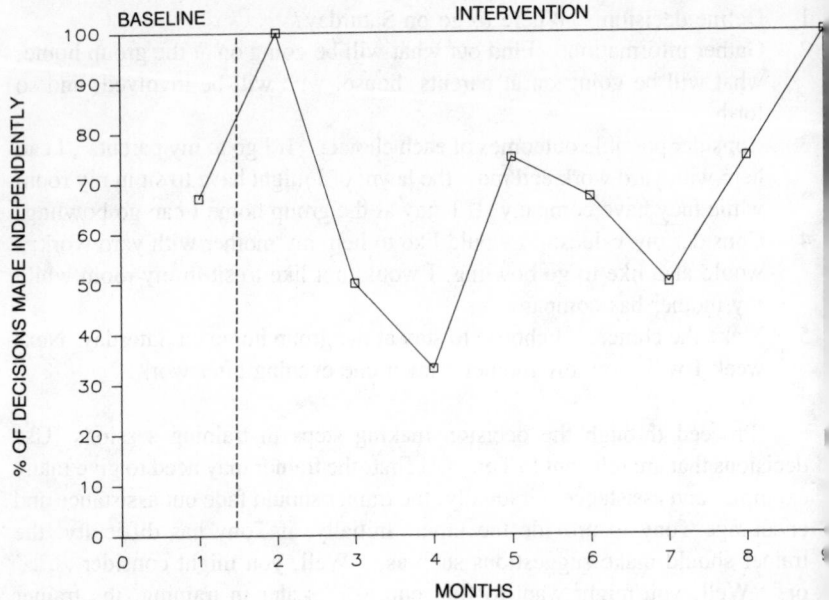

Figure 7.1. Percent of steps of the decisions that Tony made independently during baseline and intervention.

Decision making skills should be an important component of an individual's program. As people with autism become acclimated to living and working in the community, they must learn to make their own choices about how to spend their money, their time, and their energy.

SELF-EVALUATION

Teaching individuals with autism to evaluate their own behavior can be a valuable self-management strategy. This strategy involves developing a checklist specifying those behaviors that the individual is expected to have, then, at designated time periods, the individual rates him- or herself on those behaviors. Behaviors included on checklists can be task-related. With task-related checklists, the individual self-rates on critical aspects of the tasks. Case 6 provides an example of a young man who learned kitchen safety by self-evaluation on a kitchen safety checklist.

Self-evaluations can also be done with checklists that focus on social behaviors that are incompatible with problem behaviors. The behaviors should always be stated in positive terms. This procedure is actually a report card, as described in Chapter 4, with the individual rating him- or herself. Below are sample checklist items with definitions. Items and definitions need to be individualized.

Respects self: Individual keeps body in healthy condition with no self-injury.

Respects others: Individual keeps hands and feet to self. (This item can also be called: Hands and feet to self.)

Stays in assigned location: Individual stays in assigned location (area, room, building, whatever is applicable) with no instances of darting off.

Interesting conversation: Individual speaks about topics of common interest with no instances of bizarre talk (this can be specific for the individual).

Polite conversation: Individual speaks politely with no name calling or threats.

Completes assigned tasks: Individual completes assigned work either at home or on the job.

Rates self-accurately: On self-rating programs, it is often helpful to include an item for rating oneself accurately.

This list is not meant to be inclusive. It simply provides examples of items that can be included on behavioral checklists for self-rating. Checklists should be limited to six items. Too many items can be overwhelming for both the caregivers and the individual. Individuals can rate themselves hourly, at key points during the day, or once per day. The timing of the rating needs to be individualized. Individuals with several instances of problem behaviors each day may need hourly ratings. Individuals with several incidents per week may need two ratings per day. In cases where only sporadic behavioral problems exist, only one daily rating may be all that is necessary. Cases 7 and 8 provide examples of self-evaluations of social behaviors.

Case 6

Arnold is a young man with autism who lives under partial supervision. At time, he is alone in the apartment and has to cook his own dinner. Cooking is a dangerous activity for Arnold. He occasionally leaves the stove on after the meal is cooked; or he puts something on the stove, walks away, and forgets to go back. At times, he puts food in the oven with the wrapper still on, or he puts utensils in the oven.

Procedures A self-rating checklist was developed for Arnold to serve as a reminder of the safety guidelines. The instructions to staff are as follows:

1. Arnold should be given a checklist with the following items: put food in oven with wrappers off, make sure no utensils go in the oven, turn burners to the to the correct setting, remove food when the timer goes off, turn burners and oven off when finished cooking, put knives and utensils away when finished.

2. The counselor should have the checklist in an area in the kitchen that is convenient for Arnold. Arnold should take a copy of the checklist each

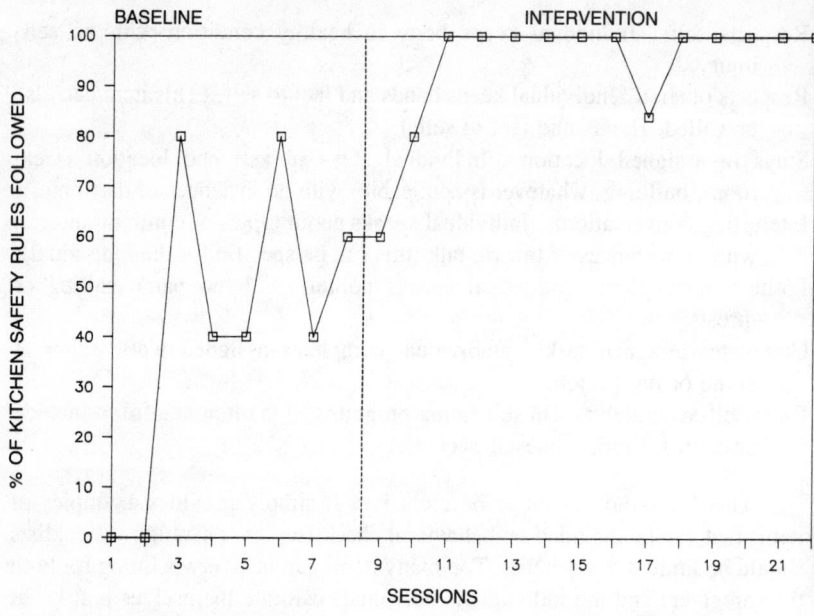

Figure 7.2. Percent of kitchen safety rules Arnold followed throughout baseline and training.

time he cooks. He should be told to read each item, and check it off after
he completes it.
3. At first, staff should go over the checklist with Arnold as he cooks to
make sure that he completes each item and checks it off. As Arnold
becomes familiar with the checklist, staff can monitor him but allow him
to do the checklist himself. As Arnold becomes reliable about completing
the checklist, staff can make covert spot checks, but Arnold should be
essentially independent in cooking and using the checklist.
4. Data should be kept on whether Arnold completes each item correctly on
his checklist. Arnold's self-rating can be used for this data along with a
note by the counselor verifying that it was done correctly.

Results   Figure 7.2 shows the percentage of safety steps successfully
followed during intervention and reveals a steady increase in kitchen safety
following implementation of the training plan. After three trials, Arnold reliably received 100% with only one exception.

Case 7

Harold was a 24-year-old man with autism who had a low-average intelligence level and was fully verbal. He lived in a group home under the
supervision of trained counselors. He was allowed to have short periods of
unsupervised time including riding public transportation.

Harold had been noted to have peculiar behavior while out on his own. For example, he had been observed at a bus stop rocking, pacing rapidly, swinging his arms, and talking to himself. In order to teach Harold to behave in a more acceptable manner in public, a checklist was developed and reviewed with him before each outing.

Procedures Harold was instructed to rate himself on each item on the checklist at the end of an outing. The instructions for this procedure are as follows:

1. Harold should be given a written checklist with the following items: arms at side, silent unless spoken to or in need of assistance, and good posture.
2. The checklist should be reviewed with Harold at the following times: before leaving home in the morning, before leaving work, and before each independent outing.
3. When reviewing the checklist with Harold, the counselor should explain to him what each item means and demonstrate for him. For example, Harold should be told that "good posture" means standing upright without rocking.
4. Harold should be reminded that he needs to follow these rules on the checklist while out in the community.
5. Harold should be told to evaluate himself at the end of each outing.

Results Covert observations of Harold on outings revealed 100% compliance with his checklist items after the checklist evaluation system was put into effect.

Case 8

Max was a 19-year-old male with autism. He lived in a group home in the community and attended a school for adolescents with severe autism. His IQ was 82 as measured by the WAIS—R. Max's symptoms of autism included abnormal speech melody, perseverative language, difficulty establishing and maintaining relationships with others, and ritualistic behaviors. He established minimal eye contact; spoke in a monotone; engaged in finger flicking, head shaking, and chin banging; compulsively ordered his belongings; and demonstrated repetitive, stereotyped use of leisure time.

Max displayed a number of behaviors in the classroom that interfered with his ability to complete tasks and relate to others. These behaviors were noted in Max's record for 14 years prior to intervention. The behaviors of concern included perseverative questions on bizarre topics, such as restraint, socks, and washing machines; jumping out of his seat; running out of the classroom; staring at female feet; writing answers to written questions without reading them; refusing to begin tasks; and stopping mid-task to self-stimulate or to pursue perseverative activities such as note writing.

At the beginning of the intervention, Max was a full-time student in the classroom and had been for 8 months. Initially, Max worked 2 hours per day at the public library under the supervision of an assistant instructor from his school program. After about 1 year, when Max turned 21, he began work full time at the library under the supervision of a job coach. A plan was developed that allowed for systematic control over Max's behavior by his teacher, with a gradual shift in control away from the teacher to Max.

Procedures   Instructions for implementing Max's plan are as follows:

Baseline   A list of six target behaviors was developed that was considered to be incompatible with Max's problem behaviors. These behaviors were as follows: begins work, works steadily, works accurately, remains in assigned location, has interesting conversation (defined as absence of perseverative questioning), and visually attends to task. During baseline, Max was covertly rated on each behavior at the end of each hour. He was given two points for items that he initiated and performed independently, one point for those items requiring one prompt, and zero points if two or more prompts were necessary. This baseline was taken for 5 days.

Checklist: Teacher Ratings   A checklist was designed for Max that consisted of hourly ratings on the six behaviors. At the end of each hour, the teacher would provide Max with verbal feedback on his performance on each item.

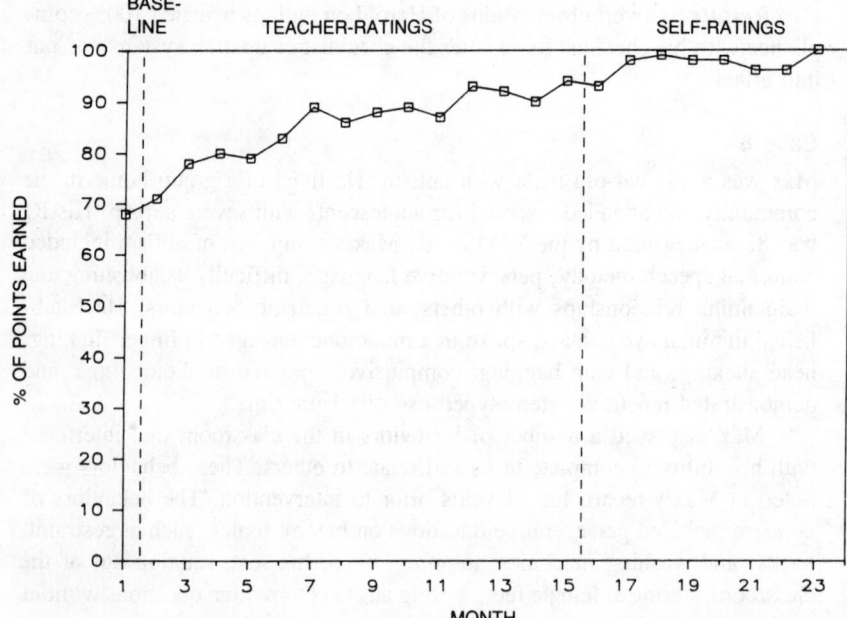

Figure 7.3. Percent of report card points that Max earned during baseline, teacher ratings, and self-rating.

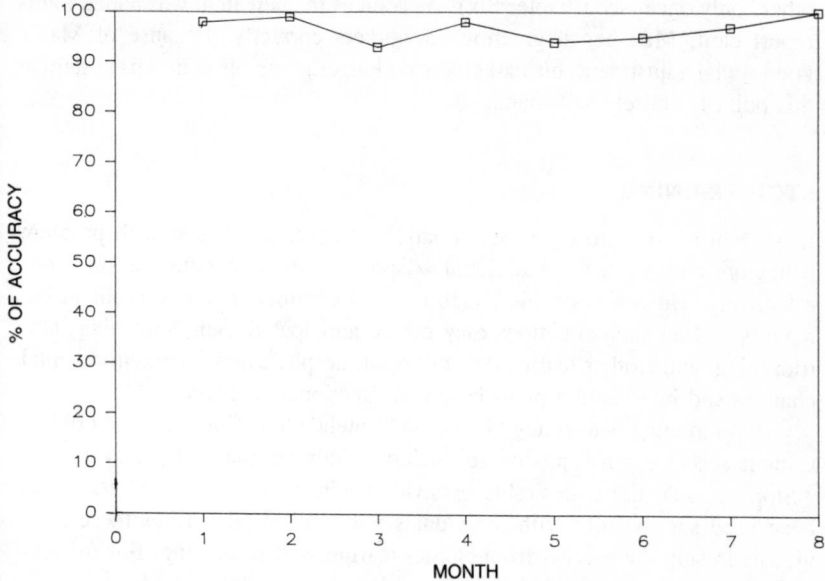

Figure 7.4. Percent of agreement between Max's ratings and staff ratings.

Report Card: Self-Ratings Following 12 months of teacher ratings, a fading procedure was begun whereby Max began to rate himself. Initially, the teacher would stand with Max, ask him to rate himself, and praise him for accuracy. After 2 months of rating himself with the teacher standing nearby, Max was told that he was responsible for rating himself each hour.

Results The percent of points Max earned is shown by month in Figure 7.3, with the exception of the baseline period which was a 4-day period. During the baseline period, Max earned 68% of the total possible number of points. By month 13, Max earned over 93% of the total possible number of points. Max continued to earn over 90% of the points following the shift from teacher-rating to self-rating in month 18.

Max's level of accuracy is shown in Figure 7.4. The percent of agreement between Max's rating and his teacher's rating was computed by dividing the number of agreements by the total number of agreements plus disagreements and multiplying the quotient by 100. Max's level of accuracy has been consistently above 95%.

Two Years Later After approximately 2 years of full-time work at the library, Max changed jobs. He took a job in the stockroom of a clothing store under the supervision of a job coach. Max had one new problem at his new job—a tendency to greet co-workers repeatedly at they walked by. This behavior was addressed by adding a new item to his report card entitled, "works quietly." Additionally, he was given social skills training on greeting others only once (see Chapter Six). As soon as the new item was added to his report card, Max began greeting co-workers correctly. Because of Max's good social adjustment, his caregivers no longer graph his data. His system at this point is entirely self-managed.

STOP TRAINING

It is often possible to eliminate situations that are associated with problem behaviors and teach the individual adaptive skills to handle the situations effectively. However, certain situations may continue to evoke problem behaviors and all such situations may not be anticipated. Self-scratching, tantrumming, and clothes tearing can still occur despite extensive environmental changes and intervention plans based on functional analyses.

Stop training is a strategy based on Cautela's Self-Control Triad (1983). Cautela's self-control procedure includes training the individual to say "Stop" should the undesirable behavior begin to occur. This strategy has been used successfully with individuals with autism. It teaches these individuals to stop themselves from clothes tearing, self-scratching, finger flicking, tantrumming, accosting women, and staring at feet.

The strategy, as used with adults with autism, consists of telling the individual to begin to do the behavior (e.g., scratch), then firmly saying "Stop! Hands down." As the individual complies, he or she is enthusiastically praised. For example, the individual is told, "Good, you put your hands down. You stopped yourself from scratching." This practice is conducted three times in a row, twice per day.

In addition to the regular, daily practices, the individual might also be rewarded for behaviors or conditions that are incompatible with the misbehavior. For example, in the case of self-scratching, the skin can be checked daily. If there are no new marks, the individual is given a small reward, such as a favorite snack or an opportunity to engage in a favorite activity. Throughout the day, the individual is praised for attractive, clear skin (if it is clear).

Case 9

Margo was a 31-year-old woman with autism who had an IQ of 54 as measured by the WAIS—R. She had been living in a group home for adults with autism for approximately 1 year under the supervision of a residential counselor. Margo's symptoms of autism included self-injury, aggression, ritualistic behavior, impaired language and communication abilities, difficulty establishing and maintaining relationships with others, and difficulty adjusting to change.

The target behavior of stop training was skin picking. Margo would scratch her arms and legs, a behavior that had been evident throughout her stay in the group home. At the time the study was begun, her arms and legs were covered with self-inflicted scratches. Previous unsuccessful attempts to decrease the self-scratching included rewards for clear skin and prompts to stop scratching.

Procedures   Regular daily practice was used to teach Margo to refrain from self-scratching. Two sessions daily, one in the morning and one in the evening, were conducted by the residential counselor. The counselor instructed Margo to begin to pick at her arm. As she was about to pick, the counselor said, "Stop!" If Margo stopped herself, the counselor said, "Good, you stopped picking."

This same procedure was conducted with the legs as well as with the arms for a total of three practices per session. After the first session, Margo was encouraged to say "Stop" herself. A role reversal was also done in which the counselor would begin to pick her own arm, then stop herself. Margo was encouraged to say "Stop" when the counselor began to self-scratch. If no new marks were apparent at morning skin checks, then Margo was allowed to listen to music while preparing for work. If no new marks were apparent at evening skin checks, she was given a favorite food as a snack and could choose from a special snack menu. Additionally, praise was given for clear skin. The instructions to staff are as follows:

1. Check Margo's skin (hands, arms, and legs) twice per day, once in the morning and once in the evening.
2. If her skin has no fresh marks at the morning check, praise her and allow her to listen to music until leaving for work. If her skin has no new marks at the evening check, praise her and allow her to select a snack from a special menu. Snacks listed on the treat menu, in picture form, should include: canned fruit, coffee, tea, and cheese. Other favorite snacks should also be included.
3. When presenting the morning music and evening special snack, Margo should be told that these treats are rewards for clear skin.
4. Stop training is to be done once in the morning and once in the evening. The counselor is to say, "Margo, start to pick your arm." As she is about to pick her arm, the counselor says, "Stop!" If Margo complies, the counselor should say, "Good, you stopped picking!" Repeat three times. Practice with legs as well as arms.
5. In subsequent practice sessions, have Margo say "Stop" as she stops herself.
6. The counselor can reverse roles. That is, the counselor says, "I'm going to start to pick my arm." The counselor then starts to pick, then says, "Stop!" and stops herself. This can be repeated and Margo can be encouraged to tell the counselor to stop.
7. For each skin check, record whether there are any new marks.

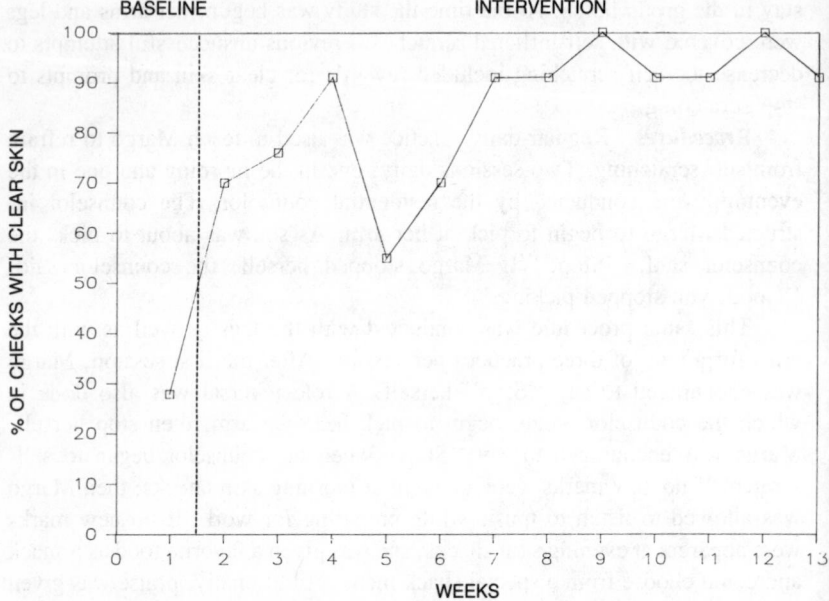

Figure 7.5. Percent of checks with clear skin during baseline and intervention for Margo.

Results Figure 7.5 shows the percentage of rating periods in which there were no new scratch marks. The percentage was computed by dividing the number of rating periods where there were no new marks by the total number of rating periods and multiplying the quotient by 100. An immediate increase in observations of clear skin over baseline occurred during the first week of intervention. The data indicate a steady increase with the exception of week 4 where there was a recurrence of self-scratching, although not to the baseline level. It should be noted that Margo's father died that week. Following week 8, a steady increase is again noted with a leveling off above 90%. A 5-month follow up indicates that her skin remained clear during all checks in the 2-week follow-up probe.

Case 10

Adam, a 25-year-old man with autism, had an IQ of 69 as measured by the WAIS—R. He exhibited a behavior that jeopardized his employment at a print shop. Although he could learn and perform job tasks, he was at risk for losing his job. Adam would leave his work area to rush over to visiting female customers and grab them by the arm. When asked to return to his work area, he would grab his counselor, shake him or her, yell, and jump up and down. Previous attempts at modifying the behavior included verbal instruction, removal from the work area following an incident, praise for acceptable behavior, and threats of being fired.

Stop training was used with Adam. Two sessions of stop training were held daily. During these sessions, Adam was told to pretend a female visitor was passing by and to begin to go toward her. As he began to leave the table, he was told, "Stay!" in a firm voice. After the first practice, he was told to say "Stay!" himself. Three practices were held per session.

During the baseline period there were two female visitors to the work-site, and Adam accosted both of them. During the first month of intervention, he remained at his work table during three of four visits by female customers. During the subsequent 10 months, out of 14 visits, he left his workstation a total of three times to accost visitors. Prior to intervention when told to return to his work area, Adam would flap his arms, scream, and grab at his job coach. Following stop training when he did accost visitors, he immediately responded to verbal instruction to return to his work area. A 30-month follow up revealed that Adam was staying at his work station for all visits by female customers.

Case 11

Carl was a 30-year-old man with severe autism and low-average intelligence. He had a long history of tantrums that composed of arm flapping, rapid, loud shouting, and occasional self-abuse or aggression. Carl's tantrums were often instigated by certain news events, certain words that he associated with certain news events, or certain topics such as death. Carl's tantrums occurred at work, at home, and in public.

Stop training was used with Carl. In his training he was told to pretend he was about to become very upset and flap his arms, and he was then told "Stop!" Practice sessions were held once per day where he would role play the beginning of a tantrum and then terminate it by saying "Stop!"

Figure 7.6 shows the total number of tantrums Carl had each month in the group home during 10 months of baseline and the total number once stop training was instituted. Following 5 months of stop training, tantrums were eliminated in the group home. Occasionally, minor hand flapping and rapid verbalizations occurred at his job, however, he has held the same job for several years and is considered a valued employee. A covert observation of Carl on the subway revealed that he began to get upset and raise his arms, then he quietly said, "Stop," put his arms down, and sat quietly for the remainder of the trip.

Some Considerations

The use of stop training has several advantages for changing problem behaviors in community settings. One advantage is that it seems to teach individuals to control their own behavior (i.e., to stop themselves from performing the behavior). Reports from caregivers suggest that at least in some cases participants did in fact learn to interrupt the behavior. This feature is particularly

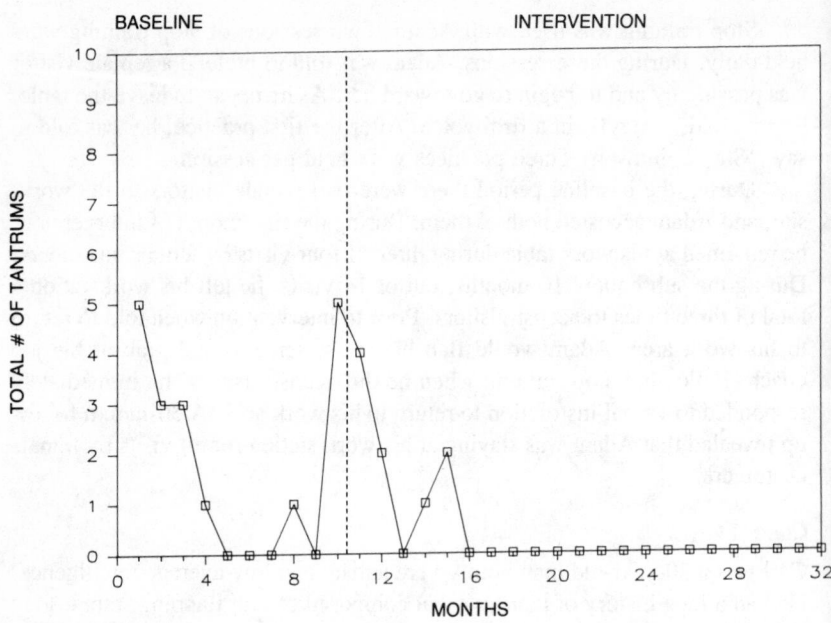

Figure 7.6. Total number of tantrums that Carl had per month during baseline and intervention.

important in cases such as self-scratching or clothes tearing in which the individual performs the behavior in private. Teaching individuals to begin the behavior chain, then to interrupt it by stopping themselves, may be a valuable approach to modifying behavior problems in community settings.

As a rule, this strategy should be used in conjunction with a strategy that teaches the individual a more effective way of interacting with the environment. The strategy described here teaches the individual what not to do (e.g., not to self-scratch), as well as what to do. An individual may tear his or her clothes or scratch him- or herself when having difficulty with a task. If this is the case, the person might need to be taught to stop self-scratching, but might also need to be taught to ask for assistance. When using the strategy of teaching an individual to stop a problem behavior, it is also generally necessary to teach a new, more constructive behavior in its place.

The use of routine practices to teach self-control should also be accompanied by positive feedback for participating in the practice, as well as for showing improvement throughout the day. So, for example, an individual who is learning to refrain from self-scratching should be complemented on having clear skin; a person who is learning to refrain from clothes tearing should be complemented for wearing attractive, intact clothing.

A final point is that the practices are held as a daily part of the individual's routine and are conducted in a friendly and pleasant manner. These practices are not implemented immediately after the behavior problem is observed. These practices are preventative and are not used as a consequence for the misbehavior.

THAT'S TOO BAD

Most people, when confronted with a minor setback or disappointment, continue with their life. A person may find the bank unexpectedly closed but that does not prevent him or her from going to work. A person might even have a fender bender, then proceed with the day.

People with autism occasionally have a hard time carrying on after minor disappointments or unexpected changes. A person with autism may go to the bank, find it closed, then head bang. Another might wait for a parent who does not come then rip his or her shirt. Sometimes these individuals need to learn that even though some minor setback has occurred, life must go on. They must learn to take disappointments with a, "That's too bad attitude," then continue with their day. The that's too bad strategy is illustrated below.

Step 1: Recognize Signs of Discontent

First, the caregiver must recognize that the individual is upset by noticing signs such as agitated talking, complaining, increased pacing, or refusal to do a task.

Step 2: Recognize Antecedent or Setting Events

Second, the caregiver must be alert to the antecedent or setting event that caused the individual to become upset. It could be an unexpected change, a disappointment, or some minor catastrophe (e.g., the dryer breaks at laundry time).

Step 3: State the Problem

Third, the caregiver asks the individual if he is upset. In some cases, it might be better to simply state the problem to the individual. For example, the caregiver might say, "Stan, are you upset because the dryer is broken?" Stan is given a chance to respond.

Step 4: That's Too Bad

Finally, the caregiver says, "That's too bad. It's just too bad that the dryer is broken." Although this sounds heartless, this is said in a sympathetic tone. This statement is said instead of what many caregivers attempt to do, and that is talk the person out of his or her feelings. If an individual is upset because a dryer is broken, or his or her parents did not come, it is difficult to explain that it is not a reason to get upset. "That's too bad" acknowledges the individual's feelings, but communicates that nothing can be done to change the situation.

Step 5: Direct Ongoing Activity

The individual is then directed to the ongoing activity. In other words, life must go on. The caregiver actually says, "Stan, that's too bad that the dryer is broken. But the next task on the schedule is to set the table. So now it's time to set the table."

Step 6: Follow-Up Supervision

Initially, it may be necessary to follow up the "that's too bad" with additional supervision. Once the signs of agitation are gone, the supervision can revert to what it is normally.

The that's too bad program is illustrated in Case 3 in Chapter Twelve on modifying self-injurious behavior. In that case the individual rapidly learned to say, "That's too bad," for himself. The caregiver's role was quickly reduced.

That's too bad has been used successfully to teach people to manage themselves in a crisis. Adults with autism have learned to say "That's too bad" and then carry on with the day, despite the minor upsets and circumstances that had previously resulted in behavior problems.

Some Considerations

Typically, this procedure has been used successfully with individuals with autism who can express themselves verbally. Although its usefulness is limited to those with a certain level of verbal and cognitive skills, it does have several advantages with that group. This approach helps verbal adults with autism learn how to self-manage in difficult situations. It provides them with a response (that's too bad) and a course of action (carry on).

Initially, the caregiver must be closely involved. The caregiver in effect carries out the management by identifying the problem and giving the individual specific instructions on what to say and how to act. Over time, the individual may learn how to handle the situations independently.

Care must be taken to use the that's too bad approach in circumstances that really are beyond anyone's control to change. The purpose of this program is not to discourage people from making changes where changes can be made nor is it to discourage individuals from asking for assistance or trying to better their circumstances. The purpose is to teach individuals that in some situations there is no choice. Life must go on.

SUMMARY

Self-management training has been done extensively with people without autism and people with mild handicaps. Work with individuals with autism during the 1980s has indicated that they can also benefit from training in self-management. Browder and Shapiro (1985) suggested that self-management training be provided to people with severe handicaps as a component of all instruction for community independence.

A variety of procedures have been presented that have been useful when teaching self-management to individuals with autism. Training in asking for assistance, self-disclosure, decision making, self-recording, self-evaluating, and self-stopping have all been effective. Self-management strategies might be effective alone, or they might serve as only one component of an intervention plan. Self-management strategies, like all other strategies covered, should derive from a functional analysis. In some cases, although the strategy cannot stand alone, it might be critical for the effectiveness of the intervention plan.

REFERENCES

Ackerman, A., & Shapiro, E. (1984). Self-monitoring and work productivity with mentally retarded adults. *Journal of Applied Behavior Analysis, 17*, 403–407.

Agran, M., Salzberg, C.L., & Stowitschek, J.J. (1987). An analysis of the effects of a social skills training program using self-instructions on the acquisition and generalization of two social behaviors in a work setting. *Journal of The Association for Persons with Severe Handicaps, 12* (2), 131–139.

Browder, D., & Shapiro, E. (1985). Applications of self-management to individuals with severe handicaps: A review. *Journal of The Association for Persons with Severe Handicaps, 10* (4), 200–208.

Cautela, J. (1983). The self-control triad: Description and clinical applications. *Behavior Modification, 7*, 299–316.

Connis, R. (1979). The effects of sequential pictorial cues, self-recording and praise on the job task sequences of retarded adults. *Journal of Applied Behavior Analysis, 12*, 355–361.

Gardner, W.I., Clees, T.J., & Cole, C.L. (1983). Self-management of disruptive verbal ruminations by a mentally retarded adult. *Applied Research in Mental Retardation, 4*, 41–58.

Gardner, W., Cole, C., Berry, D., & Nowinski, J. (1983). Reduction of disruptive behaviors in mentally retarded adults: A self-management approach. *Behavior Modification, 7*, 76–96.

Harvey, J.R., Karan, O.C., Bhargava, D., & Morehouse, N. (1978). Relaxation training and cognitive behavioral procedures to reduce violent temper outbursts in a moderately mentally retarded woman. *Journal of Behavior Therapy and Experimental Psychiatry, 9*, 347–351.

Sowers, J., Verdi, M., Bourbeau, P., & Sheehan, M. (1985). Teaching job independence and flexibility to mentally retarded students through the use of a self-control package. *Journal of Applied Behavior Analysis, 18*, 81–85.

Wehman, P., Schutz, R., Bates, P., Renzalia, A., & Karan, O. (1978). Self-management programmes with mentally retarded workers: Implications for developing independent vocational behavior. *British Journal of Social Clinical Psychology, 17*, 57–64.

Chapter Eight

SELF-STIMULATION

Some people with autism occasionally engage in unusual behaviors that seem to serve no other purpose than to provide stimulation to the individual. Such behaviors are called self-stimulatory behaviors and/or stereotypic behaviors. Rocking, pacing, jumping, hand flapping, and finger flicking are all examples. Other behaviors that also appear to be self-stimulatory include rectal digging, shredding fabric, smearing saliva, and staring at spinning objects.

Self-stimulatory behaviors present several practical problems in community settings. Although self-stimulation does not necessarily jeopardize community placement, it can jeopardize job placements, and it can interfere with the acquisition of functional living skills. First, self-stimulation can interfere with other tasks that the individual should be doing. If an adult with autism is hired to work at a printing company, he is expected to bind books, not rock and pace. Second, self-stimulation looks abnormal. A person walking down the street rocking and finger flicking is apt to arouse the interest of others. Finally, self-stimulation occasionally involves destruction of property or materials. People with autism might shred clothing or blankets in order to produce strings to look at.

Although there are behavior problems that are more serious than self-stimulation, this problem is still worthy of attention, and in some cases its control is mandatory for optimum success at school, work, and in the home. The purpose of this chapter is to examine strategies for reducing self-stimulation that are based on functional analysis.

RESEARCH ON SELF-STIMULATION

It has been reported that up to two-thirds of persons with developmental disabilities who live in institutions self-stimulate (Berkson & Davenport, 1962). This widespread behavior has been widely studied and reported. Punishment procedures have been used extensively to reduce the frequency of self-stimulation. Baumeister and Forehand (1972) reported on the use of

129

electric shock to eliminate body rocking in a mentally retarded boy. Several researchers, including Koegel, Firestone, Kramme, & Dunlap (1974) and Romanczyk (1977) used slaps to control such behavior. Other punishment procedures have included the use of water mist, lemon juice, and vinegar (Friman, Cook, & Finney, 1984), and a forced oral hygiene procedure with an oral antiseptic (Singh, Manning, & Angell, 1982).

Modification of self-stimulation with punishment has no basis in the functions or purposes of the behavior. Fortunately, a number of researchers have reported on successful management of self-stimulation based on purposes of the behavior. When intervention is based on function, then there is no need for punishment.

A number of researchers have been able to reduce self-stimulation by using environmental enrichment or positive reinforcement of other behavior. Singh, Dawson, and Manning (1981) reduced self-stimulation (rocking, mouthing, and complex motor movements) by providing reinforcers for set intervals without self-stimulation. Foxx, McMorrow, Fenlon, and Bittle (1986) reported on the elimination of public masturbation by reinforcing other behaviors. Horner (1980) demonstrated that maladaptive behavior, including self-stimulation, could be significantly reduced by enriching the environment with toys and objects and by reinforcing use of those objects.

FUNCTIONS OF SELF-STIMULATION

Repp, Felce, and Barton (1988) suggested that people engage in self-stimulation for a variety of reasons. Durand and Carr (1987) pointed out that the reasons can in fact change over time. Self-stimulation can serve more than one purpose for one individual. It is useful to examine some of the purposes that self-stimulation can serve; then intervention plans can be based on the functions identified for each individual.

Escape

Self-stimulatory behavior can serve the function of allowing the individual to escape from a task. Durand and Carr (1987) demonstrated that by allowing the individual to escape from the task as a result of hand flapping and body rocking, the behaviors increased. In other words, the individuals learned to use these behaviors to escape from a task. Repp et al. (1988) found that for children whose purpose was escape from a task, reduction was achieved when rewards were provided for cooperation.

Social Attention

Self-stimulation can in some cases serve a social function. Durand and Carr in their 1987 study of self-stimulation found that by teaching the individuals to ask for assistance with difficult tasks, self-stimulatory behaviors during those tasks decreased. Repp et al. (1988) found that for children whose self-stimulation served the purpose of gaining adult attention, the successful intervention consisted of extinction by giving no attention to self-stimulation.

Sensory Stimulation

Research has suggested that for some individuals the behavior serves the purpose of providing sensory stimulation. A number of researchers have reported that self-stimulation itself is reinforcing, thereby serving its own function. Rincover (1978) noted that self-stimulation could be reduced by eliminating the sensory consequences of the behavior. Hung (1978) demonstrated that self-stimulation could serve as a reinforcer for another behavior, namely appropriate speaking.

Several researchers have found that providing other forms of sensory stimulation can reduce self-stimulatory behaviors. Barmann (1980) found that providing a 6-year-old boy with vibration resulted in decreased hand mouthing and rumination. Favell, McGimsey, and Schell (1982) reduced self-stimulation by providing similar but more acceptable sensory experiences. Smith (1986) reported decreases in rectal digging followed by finger sniffing when a woman with autism was provided with other items to smell, such as perfumes.

STRATEGIES FOR REDUCING SELF-STIMULATION

Strategies for reducing self-stimulation need to be based on the information obtained from a functional analysis. Different strategies can be used depending on the function of the behavior. For cases where the behavior serves more than one function, it might be necessary to use more than one strategy. The final intervention plan may be a combination of several strategies woven together as a workable plan for use at home, work, or school.

Scheduling

Self-stimulatory behavior can be closely tied to scheduling issues. These scheduling issues have to be examined individually, as each has different implications for intervention.

Too Little to Do   Too much free time and too few structured activities can result in too much self-stimulation. The individual may be using the self-stimulation to fill a void left by an austere environment. If this is the case, then an intervention plan must address scheduling issues. A busy, constructive schedule becomes an important part of the plan. Providing a variety of home-care and self-care activities, as well as a school or work day filled with activities, can crowd the self-stimulation right out of the individual's day.

It may also be necessary to include additional recreational and leisure activities to provide the stimulation that the individual is currently getting from the self-stimulation. Nonverbal individuals with relatively low cognitive skills might enjoy puzzles, crafts, painting, and simple games, as well as shopping, bowling, swimming, movies, and other recreational activities. Persons who are verbal, with good cognitive skills, might enjoy more complex games, cards, taking classes in the community, and painting, as well as activities such as swimming, bowling, and skating. The intervention plan might need to specify exactly what types of activities should be available, the types of materials available, the amount of assistance needed to carry out activities, and the timing of the activities.

Too Much to Do   Likewise, too many activities, or activities that are too difficult, can also result in self-stimulation. Self-stimulation could be serving the function of providing a way out, a means of escape. If too much activity is the problem, then the intervention plan might need to include breaks at designated times. Some individuals can work all morning without needing a break, while others may begin to finger flick after 20 minutes, and so may need to have short breaks scheduled every 15 minutes. If short breaks are needed, they should be scheduled to occur before the individual begins to try to escape. In other words, if a person can work 15 minutes with no problem, but begins to self-stimulate after 20, then breaks should be scheduled every 15 minutes. The length of work time can be gradually increased.

Rewarding Better Behavior

Sometimes making other activities available is all it takes to reduce self-stimulation. However, sometimes it is necessary to provide the individual with a reason for participating in these other activities. Rewards for participating in more acceptable behavior might be necessary, and might be particularly critical in cases where the self-stimulation served the purpose of escape. If the individual was self-stimulating in order to escape from a task, it might mean he or she had no useful purpose for doing the task. By providing a reward, the individual is provided with a reason. He or she has a reason for staying on task, and the self-stimulation is no longer necessary as a way to escape. Even in cases in which self-stimulation did not serve the function of escape, it still might be necessary to reward other behavior. While a job coach in a supported work program might understand why the individual should bind books rather than rock, the reason might not be clear to the worker with autism. For whatever reason, the individual might prefer to rock. Providing reinforcers for binding books provides the individual with a reason for working, rather than rocking.

Although in many cases tangible rewards are necessary, some individuals will respond well to praise alone. Providing specific praise for engaging in the correct behavior can often be sufficient to eliminate self-stimulatory behavior.

If reinforcement schedules are necessary, a number of issues must be addressed. The timing of the reinforcer, the types, and the behavior to be reinforced all need to be specified in the intervention plan. Chapter Four discusses these issues in some detail.

Alternate Sensory Stimuli

Types Self-stimulation might serve the simple purpose of providing a sensory pleasure to the individual. At times, the stimulation provided by the behavior is not otherwise or easily available in the environment. Even though the individual has a full schedule of constructive activities, with rewards for participating in those activities, the self-stimulatory behavior might still serve a sensory purpose that is not provided elsewhere.

If the sensory component seems to be a function in maintaining the behavior, then a valuable intervention strategy might be to provide similar, but more acceptable stimulation. Alternate sensory stimuli can be easy to find and practical to use with individuals with autism.

A number of self-stimulatory behaviors involve tactile stimulation, like self-scratching and self-picking. Similar sensory stimuli can be easily found that provide tactile stimulation. Some examples are: hand lotion; aftershave; massage oil; back scratches; hand shakes; vibrators; briskly rubbing the skin with a feather, brush, terry cloth, sponge, or silk fabric; powder to rub into the skin; or a warm damp cloth for skin massages. Providing interesting textured items to hold or feel can also provide alternate stimulation, such as cotton balls, dried leaves, shaving cream, and clay. Some individuals enjoy cold sensations, and a cold water bottle or cold cloth is considered enjoyable stimulation.

Self-stimulation occasionally occurs around water. Water related self-stimulation in the toilet is particularly unacceptable, such as splashing in the toilet or watching the toilet flush. Alternate water activities can provide good substitutes. Allowing water play or activity in the sink, or even extra baths can be useful.

Some forms of self-stimulatory behavior provide olfactory stimulation (i.e., the opportunity to smell). Rectal digging followed by finger sniffing is an example. Another example is the drooling or spitting of saliva in order to smell it. Alternate, more acceptable scents are readily available. Scented lotion, perfume, scented aftershave, and cologne can all be rubbed into the skin and provide pleasant scents. Other scented items, such as spices, extracts (vanilla extract and orange extract), and sachets can also be used.

Self-stimulatory behaviors such as rocking and pacing often do not need alternate forms of stimulation. These behaviors typically reduce sufficiently with full schedules and rewards for other behaviors. However, it is often not practical to schedule every minute of the day and evening, and people with rocking, jumping, and pacing behaviors will often resort to these behaviors during unscheduled leisure time. Alternate forms of gross motor activity can then be helpful, such as the opportunity to take walks, jog, swim, and ride a bicycle or an exercise bike. Rocking chairs are a good source of alternate stimulation for some people and rocking in a rocking chair looks more acceptable than rocking on a stationary sofa. One young man who jumped wildly and continuously throughout his house was provided with a mini trampoline. Although he still jumped, at least the jumping was confined to the mini trampoline in the rec room.

Scheduling   Alternate sensory stimuli can be provided as a reward on a reinforcement schedule, or freely throughout the individual's day. In addition, the stimuli should be present at all times. For example, lotions or scents can be kept on a shelf in the home or at the worksite, and the stimuli can be provided at certain time intervals, such as once per hour or once per day.

Timing considerations are similar to those involved in choosing reinforcement schedules. The caregiver should note approximately how often the individual engages in the behavior, then alternate stimuli can be provided on roughly the same schedule.

Teaching Time and Place

It's difficult to provide substitutes for some forms of self-stimulation. Certain ritualistic self-stimulatory behaviors such as calculating fall into this category. An adult with autism who has calculating skills might spend hours per day calculating to the exclusion of other activities. Masturbation and compulsive note writing are two other examples. Self-stimulatory behaviors such as these can often be managed by providing designated times and places during which these behaviors can occur. The individual can be taught when and where these behaviors are acceptable by verbal instructions, written schedules, or both. For example, a man with autism who preferred calculating over any other activity was provided with a daily written schedule that included allowed time for calculating.

Individuals who cannot speak or read can sometimes learn to limit self-stimulatory behaviors by the use of picture schedules. For example, nonverbal adults with autism can be allowed private time in their rooms at certain times during the day or evening. This private time can be designated, in order of occurrence, on a picture schedule that includes photographs of the individual engaged in the chores and recreational activities.

Simply providing individuals with allowed time and space to engage in ritualistic self-stimulatory behaviors such as calculating or note writing might be sufficient to reduce it. At other times, however, it might be necessary to provide additional incentives in the form of rewards for participating in required tasks and activities, or for restricting the self-stimulation to the times designated on the schedule. In other words, following the schedule may need to be specifically reinforced.

Verbal Instructions

Occasionally, giving the individual specific instructions prior to an activity, and praise during the activity, can prevent the self-stimulatory behavior. These instructions should state exactly what the individual should do, not what he should not do. For example, Alex often rocked vigorously when walking. This behavior was conspicuous on walks through the community. Before each walk, he was instructed to walk with good posture and to keep his back straight; throughout the walk he was praised for having good posture. This intervention was sufficient to teach Alex to walk without rocking.

Extinction

Self-stimulatory behavior may serve many functions. Depending on the function, it might not be feasible or practical to actually put the behavior on extinction. This is the case when the behavior is maintained by its sensory consequences. In those cases, other strategies should be used to effect change. At times, however, self-stimulatory behavior does serve purposes that can be controlled. For example, when it serves as a means of escape then it is possible to put the behavior on extinction.

Placing self-stimulatory behavior on extinction simply involves the caregiver proceeding with the ongoing schedule or activity as if the behavior were not occurring. No social consequences or changes in schedule would be provided as a result of the behavior. This means that nothing should be said to the individual about the self-stimulatory behavior. If the behavior does serve the purpose of obtaining attention, then even telling the individual to stop can actually be rewarding. If the caregiver is speaking to the individual, the conversation can continue, however, the self-stimulatory behavior should not be mentioned.

If the individual is given a task, or is in the middle of a task and begins to self-stimulate, the caregiver should simply redirect the individual back to the ongoing activity. Again, nothing should be said about the self-stimulation. The only words spoken should involve redirection to the task. In some situations, it might be sufficient to simply point to the task, without having to give verbal instructions. Some individuals, however, might need more structured prompting.

The prompt hierarchy, a system of least prompts, can be useful for directing the individual back to task without addressing the self-stimulation. Some individuals might need a variation of the prompt hierarchy. For example, the prompt hierarchy as described in Chapter Five contains physical guidance as the last step. (Physical guidance might need to be omitted with individuals who would respond aggressively to such prompts.) This series of prompts can begin once the individual stops working and becomes involved with self-stimulation. It is as follows:

1. No help: Wait about 5–10 seconds for the individual to return to task independently. For some individuals a longer wait time might be appropriate. If no correct response, then go to Step 2.
2. Nonspecific verbal cue: Say, "What's next?" and wait about 5–10 seconds. If no correct response, then go to Step 3.
3. Specific verbal instruction: Give specific verbal instruction, breaking down the task into steps. Wait 5–10 seconds. If still no correct response, then go to Step 4.
4. Gestural cue: Use a gesture and specific verbal instruction. Wait about 5–10 seconds. If no correct response, then go to Step 5.
5. Physical guidance: Gently provide physical guidance to assist the individual in doing the activity or the task. Do not use physical guidance in a forceful way or in a manner that will create a power struggle or aggression.

Caregivers occasionally see self-stimulatory behavior, and in order to stop it, they provide the individual with something acceptable to do. Providing new tasks or changing the tasks as an immediate result of self-stimulation could actually reward the behavior. The individual would then learn to self-stimulate as a way of getting new or different activities. If the individual self-stimulates during a nonstructured time, then the behavior should not be addressed and the individual should not immediately be presented with something new to do, unless the schedule called for a new activity at that time.

Too much unstructured time leading to self-stimulation should be treated with a busier schedule, but new activities should not be instantly initiated just because self-stimulation has begun. It is best to have an adequately structured schedule, rather than to provide activities as an immediate response to self-stimulation. Providing alternate activities immediately after the self-stimulation could be reinforcing and so would not be consistent with putting the self-stimulation on extinction.

Extinction can be an important part of an intervention plan for self-stimulation; however, it should not be used alone. Self-stimulatory behaviors, as all behaviors, should be seen as serving a purpose. The plan must include other ways for the individual to serve that purpose. Extinction, combined with other procedures can be essential. Extinction used alone can be dangerous and counterproductive, particularly in integrated community settings.

Self-Management Procedures

Several of the self-management procedures described in Chapter Seven can be considered for use with self-stimulation. Stop training, self-monitoring, and self-evaluation might all prove useful in the management of self-stimulatory behavior.

CASE 1

Max was a 20-year-old male with autism. His symptoms of autism included abnormal speech melody, perseverative language, difficulty establishing and maintaining relationships with others, ritualistic behaviors, and self-stimulatory behavior.

A high frequency behavior that interfered with his work and with his social relationships was his finger flicking. He would bring his fingers up to his face and rapidly flip them for periods up to 1 minute. Previous attempts at reducing the finger flicking included prompts to keep his hands down, praise for incompatible behavior, and reminders. Since it was noted that the behavior often occurred after Max made a mistake or when he had difficulty with a task, he was taught to ask for assistance and correct mistakes. Although he improved in these skills, the finger flicking behavior remained a problem.

Procedures

Stop training was instituted to teach Max to keep from flicking his fingers in his face. Sessions were held twice daily, once in the morning and once in the afternoon. Max was told to put his hands to his face, then told, "Stop! Hands down." Max was praised for putting his hands down, and for keeping them away from his face. This exercise was repeated, and Max was encouraged to say "Stop" himself. Each session contained three practices.

Results

Figure 8.1 shows the percent of 15-minute time blocks where Max flicked his fingers in his face. The percentage was computed by dividing the number of time blocks during which finger flicking occurred by the total number of time blocks in the day and then multiplying the quotient by 100. Data are presented for each day of data collection, daily during baseline and twice per week during intervention.

During the baseline period, the percentage of time blocks during which flicking occurred ranged from 58 to 100. After stop training was instituted, the percentage never exceeded 42% and went as low as 10%. Intervention percentages were consistently below the baseline range.

CASE 2

Paula, a 25-year-old woman with autism, had no verbal language and was considered to be profoundly mentally retarded. She exhibited rectal digging, followed by finger sniffing, at a baseline rate measured as high as seven times

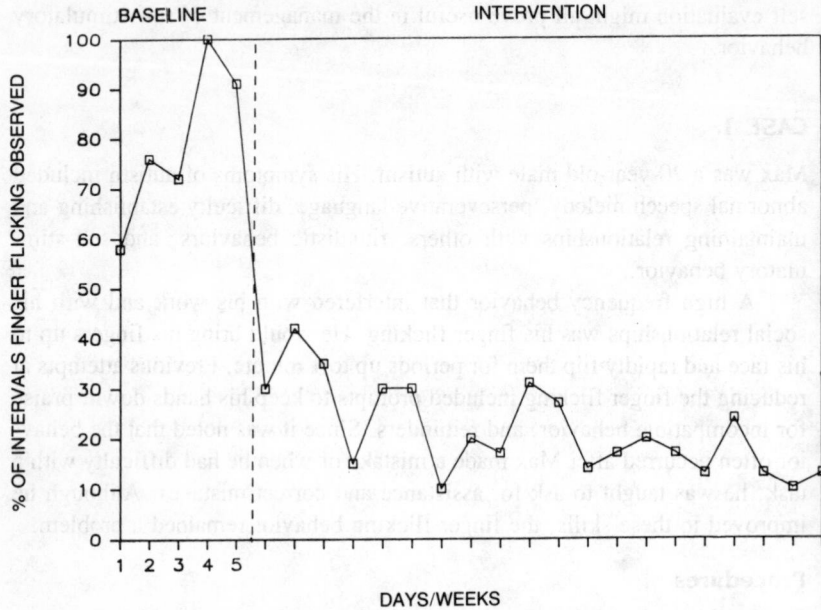

Figure 8.1. Percent of 15-minute intervals per day in which Max finger flicked during baseline and intervention.

per hour. According to her records, this behavior had been present for most of her adult life.

Data Collection

Staff recorded the times that rectal digging occurred each day. The purpose of this was to determine approximately how often Paula seemed to want something to smell.

Functional Analysis

Paula was on an intervention plan for aggression that provided her with frequent edibles, attention, and favorite activities approximately every 15 minutes. Since her needs for food, attention, and activity were being met, it seemed that the purpose of the rectal digging must have been the smell that was produced. The fact that Paula would sniff her fingers afterwards suggested that this was the function.

Procedures

The most humane and effective approach seemed to be to provide Paula with alternate, more acceptable items to smell. Paula's intervention plan involved providing her with scented hand lotion, perfume, sachets, and scented lipstick. Self-stimulation occurred at a high rate, so these appropriate, alternate scents were provided fairly frequently on a scheduled basis with the only requirement being that Paula not be engaged in rectal digging during or for a short time prior to delivery of the scent. If Paula asked (by gesturing) for the scent, then the scent was provided. This strategy is based on the premise that if the desired stimulation is freely available, then the individual will no longer have to engage in the self-stimulatory behavior to obtain the stimulation.

Prior to intervention, Paula engaged in rectal digging about every 15 minutes. The intervention plan in this case consisted of presenting her with acceptable scents approximately every 10–15 minutes. The instructions given to the counselors who implemented Paula's intervention program are as follows:

1. Paula will be given a number and a variety of scented items that are appropriate to smell, for example, perfume, scented lotions, sachets.
2. The only criterion for delivery of scented items is that it not be during a hands-to-pants-to-nose sequence and that it follow such a sequence by no less than 2 minutes. That is, if Paula sniffs her hands after putting them in her pants, she should not be given a scented item for at least 2 minutes. Otherwise, scented items will be delivered according to the intervention schedule.
3. This program should be in effect, if possible, throughout Paula's waking hours.

Results

The results are shown in Figure 8.2. The mean number of incidents per day are graphed for each month beginning with the baseline month and continuing

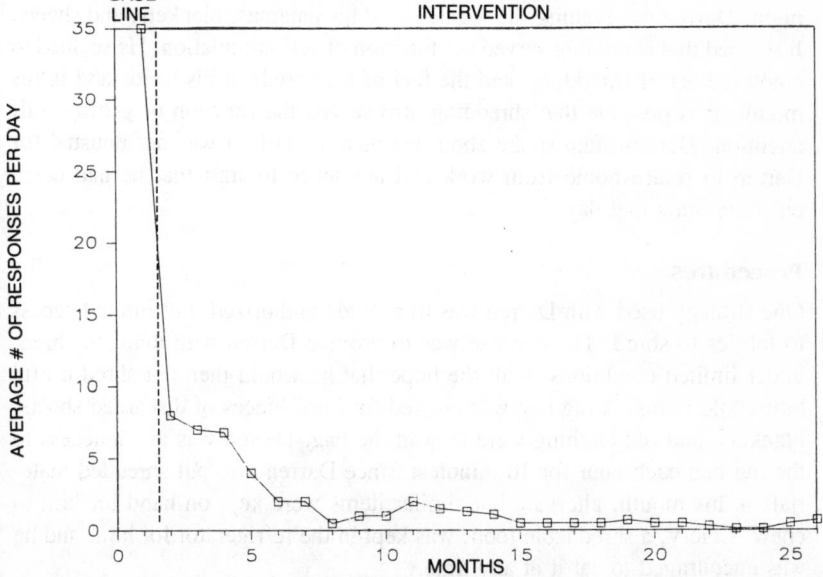

Figure 8.2. Average number of incidents of rectal digging during baseline and intervention. (Adapted from Smith [1986].)

through month 26. Inspection of the graph reveals a decrease, to levels below baseline, following intervention. The daily total decreased from a mean of 35 (month 1) to a mean of less than 1 incident per day. A follow-up probe 3 years later revealed no incidents of rectal digging in the month probed. Paula's intervention plan has remained in effect.

CASE 3

Darren was a 25-year-old man with severe autism and moderate mental retardation. Darren lived in a group home with three other men with autism under the supervision of a residential counselor. He could read and speak, although his words were often unintelligible. Darren's self-stimulatory behavior consisted of shredding fabric, then examining and chewing on the shred. Darren shredded clothing, blankets, and sheets.

Data Collection

A 30-minute time block procedure was used to determine the frequency of the shredding. For each 30-minute period of the day, staff recorded whether or not Darren shredded fabric.

Functional Analysis

Darren had a structured, busy schedule. Shredding mainly occurred during periods without structured activity, and at every possible opportunity, Darren would go to his bedroom and shred. It also occurred when he was in his bed at night. During the evening, he would shred his pajamas, blankets, and sheets. It seemed that shredding served the function of self-stimulation. He seemed to enjoy the act of shredding, and the feel of the shreds in his hands and in his mouth. It is possible that shredding also served the function of getting staff attention. Darren often spoke about his pica to staff. It was not unusual for Darren to return home from work and announce to staff that he had eaten cigarette butts that day.

Procedures

One strategy used with Darren was to provide authorized, but limited access to fabrics to shred. The purpose was to provide Darren with items to shred, under limited conditions, with the hope that he would then not shred useful household items. A rag bag was created for him. Pieces of discarded sheets, blankets, and old clothing were kept in the bag. Darren was given access to the rag bag each hour for 10 minutes. Since Darren also put shredded materials in his mouth, alternate but similar items were kept on hand for him to chew. Celery, a shreddable food, was kept in the refrigerator for him, and he was encouraged to eat it at any time.

Darren's schedule was also targeted for change. The intervention plan recommended a busy schedule, since the busier he was the less likely he was to shred. Since shredding typically occurred in his bedroom, staff were instructed to encourage Darren to remain in the living room during leisure time.

Staff attention also seemed to play a role and so staff were instructed to chat with Darren regularly, as well as praise him often. Finally, a reinforcement schedule was included to provide incentive for Darren to behave cooperatively and to engage in activities other than shredding and pica. The only shredding that was rewarded was his use of the rag bag. The instructions for Darren's intervention plan are as follows:

1. A variable interval schedule of reinforcement will be used for any of the following non-pica behaviors: having a clean, empty mouth (i.e., no inedibles in mouth), working on a task with the maximum amount of independence of which he is capable, staying in assigned location and/or living room, maintaining acceptable distance from television, wearing clothes in an attractive manner (i.e., shirt tucked in, belt buckled), reading, keeping hands on objects other than household shreddables (i.e., blankets), working with rag bag.

2. Every 30 minutes (plus or minus 10 minutes) Darren will receive a reinforcer when he is exhibiting any cooperative, social, non-pica behavior. Specific verbal praise will accompany the delivery of the reinforcer. Reinforcers to be used should include: food or drink (any nutritional foods or drinks that Darren enjoys, e.g., apples and celery) and favorite activities (special time with the counselor or the opportunity to engage in favorite activities compiled by the staff and attached to this program). Reinforcers should be alternated to ensure variety and to keep Darren interested, and should be delivered while Darren is displaying a target behavior, or in the case of a task, immediately after the task is finished. In the case of leisure time, Darren should be provided with a reinforcer only if he is not shredding or eating a nonedible. If possible, most of the rewards should be delivered while Darren is in the public areas of the house. No rewards should be given during pica or shredding behavior, or within 5 minutes of such behavior.

3. Darren should be told why he is getting the reinforcer. Specific behavioral praise should accompany delivery of the reinforcer. Darren should be praised about every 15 minutes for cooperative or social behavior, or any behavior that is not pica behavior or shredding behavior as long as he is in compliance with the house routine. He can also be praised for good grooming, such as shirt tucked in, belt buckled, and so forth. He should be specifically told how nice he looks with a clear mouth.

4. Darren enjoys positive attention from staff, and this attention should be provided in the form of praise and reinforcement as described above.

Social interactions between Darren and staff should occur at least twice per hour. Staff can chat with Darren, provide him with information, ask him about what he's doing, and so on. Staff should talk with Darren when he arrives home from work, telling him what they did that day and asking Darren what he did.

5. Every effort should be made to keep Darren in the main areas of the house as he is more likely to shred and eat nonedibles when alone in his room. Staff should provide activities and events for him in the living areas. If necessary, his schedule should be revised in accordance with this suggestion.

6. If Darren attempts to talk with a counselor about eating nonedibles, this conversation should be ignored.

7. A rag bag should be assembled for Darren that contains rags and pieces of fabric he can shred. He should be given access to this rag bag during any leisure periods and told that he can shred the fabric, but that he needs to keep it out of his mouth. He needs to be supervised to ensure that he does not put the threads in his mouth, and he can be praised for shredding and for keeping the fabric out of his mouth. If he puts the threads in his mouth, the bag should be removed.

8. Darren should be given unlimited or at least frequent access to celery, since he seems to enjoy shredding and chewing celery.

Results

Prior to intervention, Darren shredded during 60%–80% of the 30-minute time blocks throughout the afternoon and evening. Following intervention, Darren shreds in only 2%–3% of the half-hour time blocks each month. Darren now gets his rag bag independently on an hourly schedule.

CASE 4

Clark was a 20-year-old man with severe autism and profound mental retardation. He was nonverbal. Clark lived in a group home with two other young men with autism under the supervision of a residential counselor. When the intervention plan was developed, Clark was a student in a school for adolescents with autism. When he reached 21 years of age, he entered a supported work program and began a job in an organization that rented party supplies.

Clark had several problem behaviors, including aggression, grabbing at others, and self-stimulation. His self-stimulatory behavior occurred in two forms. He was fascinated with water and often splashed in the toilet. A more serious behavior was his skin picking. He would pick at his skin until he bled, then smear the blood on his desk.

A number of unsuccessful attempts had been made over a 2-year period to decrease the skin picking. These attempts included frequent treats for incompatible behavior and ignoring the skin picking. A mild punishment procedure had been tried unsuccessfully (i.e., wiping his face with a cold cloth). Posey mitts had also been tried. Contingent use of the mitts did not discourage the behavior; noncontingent use made the behavior impossible, but was discontinued because their bulkiness prevented him from engaging in useful work. Because of the frequent bleeding, rubber gloves were used; however, even the rubber gloves did not prevent him from drawing blood and smearing.

Data Collection

Aggression and skin picking were recorded on a 15-minute time block format. For each 15-minute period of the day staff would record whether or not aggression or skin picking occurred. Observations were also made to determine antecedents and consequences of the behaviors.

Functional Analysis

Clark's self-stimulatory behavior seemed to serve several functions. It was possible that it was maintained for social attention. Each time he picked, since he drew blood, staff felt obligated to tell him to stop. However, since skin picking did not result in a termination of tasks, the behavior did not seem to be for the purpose of escaping tasks. The behavior did appear to be more frequent during unstructured times, so it is possible that free time was a setting event for the behavior. The behavior also seemed to fill a sensory function as he would often engage in picking and smearing to the exclusion of assigned activities.

Procedures

Structured Schedule A highly structured schedule was created for Clark. He was provided with a minimum of at least two activities every half hour in the group home. At school, tasks and leisure activities were presented at least twice every half hour. Once he began his supported job, he was provided with work continuously throughout the day, except for short snack and lunch breaks.

Rewards for Cooperative Behavior Clark was rewarded about every 15 minutes for cooperating with scheduled activities and keeping his hands on his assigned activities. Since he enjoyed water activities, water-related activities were used as reinforcers, as were favorite foods and drinks. All rewards were given with praise, so that attention was also provided frequently.

Alternate Sensory Stimulus Lotion was provided as an alternate sensory stimulus to skin picking and blood smearing. Clark was provided with a small container of lotion every 15 minutes and was taught to take the lotion and rub it into his skin.

Extinction Face picking was ignored. The behavior was not discussed with him in any way. If the behavior persisted during tasks for more than 2 minutes, Clark was redirected to task using the prompt hierarchy. The procedures for the intervention plan are as follows:

1. A variable interval schedule of reinforcement will be used. Target behaviors include any on task behavior, cooperative behavior, or any acceptable behavior that is incompatible with aggression or self-injury, such as: working on task with the maximum amount of independence he is capable of, staying in assigned location, keeping hands on his work or to himself when being instructed, keeping hands off his face during leisure or work activities.

2. Every 15 minutes (plus or minus 10 minutes) Clark will receive a reinforcer contingent on a cooperative behavior. Specific verbal praise will accompany the delivery of the reinforcer. Reinforcers to be used include: food or drink (small amounts of nutritious, low calorie food that Clark enjoys) and activities (water play in the sink, water-related activities, blowing bubbles, and other activities that Clark enjoys). These reinforcers should be alternated to ensure variety and to keep him interested, and should be delivered while Clark is engaging in the cooperative behavior. If Clark grabs at others or picks his face, there should be no reinforcer for at least 10 minutes.

3. Specific praise should accompany the delivery of the reinforcers. Clark should be told exactly what he did to earn the reinforcer, such as engaging in assigned or appropriate activities approximately every 10 minutes. Clark should especially be praised for any independence on tasks or activities, such as any work that he does for which he did not wait to be prompted, but he should not be praised while agitated (hand flapping, rapid noise making, head shaking).

4. Clark should be given lotion to rub on his face every 15 minutes. Lotion should not be given within 5 minutes of face picking.

5. Any self-stimulatory behavior such as hand flapping and face picking should be ignored. These behaviors should not be discussed with him. If behaviors persist during tasks for more than 2 minutes, he can be redirected to task using the prompt hierarchy.

6. If Clark grabs at staff, staff should attempt to block the grab in a low-key, nonaggressive manner.

7. When a task is first presented to Clark, if he does not immediately begin the task, the counselor should begin to do the task. When Clark joins in he can be given positive feedback, such as, ''That's right, you're folding laundry.''

8. Clark should engage in a minimum of one supervised and one leisure time activity every half hour throughout the day. Supervised activities are

to be listed on his schedule and include such items as dressing, making breakfast, grocery shopping, and cleaning the refrigerator. After completing the supervised task for 10–25 minutes, the remaining time in the half hour should be used for leisure activities that require the use of his hands. Examples of leisure time activities include paints of all kinds, puzzles, weaving, water play, collage making, and projects using a variety of materials. It is important to vary the leisure activities and try new things from hobby shops and art stores.

Results

Prior to intervention, Clark picked his face then smeared the blood almost continuously. Following intervention, face picking decreased to only several times per day. His sores healed and blood smearing ceased to be a problem. Clark remains free of skin picking as long as his intervention plan is in place. During periods of unstable staffing in his group home and unreliable implementation of the plan, face picking returns.

SUMMARY

Self-stimulatory behaviors can serve many purposes, only one of which is actually self-stimulation. Intervention plans for self-stimulation should be based on identified functions. A variety of procedures can be used once functions are identified. These strategies include enriched environment, scheduling of tasks, picture schedules, written schedules, rewards for more acceptable behavior, stop training, and alternate sensory stimuli.

In all cases of self-stimulation presented in this chapter, the individuals were provided with a structured environment that included training in work tasks, home chores, and frequent outings. Positive reinforcers, including praise, and in some cases food and drink, were provided for participation in training, work, home, and leisure activities.

The management of self-stimulation might require several strategies in combination. The successful use of strategies such as alternate sensory stimuli or stop training might depend on the use of positive reinforcement to strengthen more acceptable behaviors. In many cases, individuals with autism can learn to self-manage their self-stimulatory behavior. For example, Paula, in Case 2, had no verbal language, but she learned to acquire more acceptable scented materials. Similarly, Darren, in Case 3, learned to obtain his own rag bag and celery when desired. Although self-stimulation might not be totally eliminated, it can be significantly reduced in adults with autism. Even individuals with severe autism can sometimes learn self-management of self-stimulation.

REFERENCES

Barmann, B. (1980). Use of contingent vibration in the treatment of self-stimulatory hand-mouthing and ruminative vomiting behavior. *Journal of Behavior Therapy and Experimental Psychiatry, 11,* 307–311.

Baumeister, A.A., & Forehand, R. (1972). Effects of contingent shock and verbal command on body rocking of retardates. *Journal of Clinical Psychology, 28,* 586–590.

Berkson, G., & Davenport, R.K. (1962). Stereotyped movements in mental defectives: I. Initial survey. *American Journal of Mental Deficiency, 66,* 849–852.

Durand, V.M., & Carr, E.G. (1987). Social influences on "self-stimulatory" behavior: Analysis and treatment application. *Journal of Applied Behavior Analysis, 20,* 118–132.

Favell, J., McGimsey, J., & Schell, R. (1982). Treatment of self-injury by providing alternative sensory activities. *Analysis and Intervention in Developmental Disabilities, 2,* 83–104.

Foxx, R.M., McMorrow, M.J., Fenlon, S., & Bittle, R.G. (1986). The reductive effects of reinforcement procedures on the genital stimulation and stereotypy of a mentally retarded adolescent male. *Analysis and Intervention in Developmental Disabilities, 6,* 239–248.

Friman, P., Cook, J.W., & Finney, J. (1984). Effects of punishment procedures on the self-stimulatory behavior of an autistic child. *Analysis and Intervention in Developmental Disability, 4,* 39–46.

Horner, R.D. (1980). The effects of an environmental "enrichment" program on the behavior of institutionalized profoundly retarded children. *Journal of Applied Behavior Analysis, 13,* 473–491.

Hung, D.W. (1978). Using self-stimulation as reinforcement for autistic children. *Journal of Autism and Developmental Disabilities, 8,* 355–366.

Koegel, R., Firestone, P., Kramme, K., & Dunlap, G. (1974). Increasing spontaneous play by suppressing self-stimulation in autistic children. *Journal of Applied Behavior Analysis, 5,* 381–387.

Repp, A., Felce, D., & Barton, L. (1988). Basing the treatment of stereotypic and self-injurious behaviors on hypotheses of their causes. *Journal of Applied Behavior Analysis, 21,* 281–289.

Rincover, A. (1978). Sensory extinction: A procedure for eliminating self-stimulatory behavior in developmentally disabled children. *Journal of Abnormal Child Psychology, 6,* 299–310.

Romanczyk, R. (1977). Intermittent punishment of self-stimulation effectiveness during application and extinction. *Journal of Consulting and Clinical Psychology, 43,* 730–739.

Singh, N., Dawson, M.J., & Manning, P. (1981). Effects of spaced responding DRL on the stereotyped behavior of profoundly retarded persons. *Journal of Applied Behavior Analysis, 14,* 521–526.

Singh, N.S., Manning, P.J., & Angell, M.J. (1982). Effects of an oral hygiene punishment procedure on chronic rumination and collateral behaviors in monozygous twins. *Journal of Applied Behavior Analysis, 15,* 309–314.

Smith, M. (1986). Use of similar sensory stimuli in the community-based treatment of self-stimulatory behavior in an adult disabled by autism. *Journal of Behavior Therapy and Experimental Psychiatry, 17,* 121–125.

_____ *Chapter Nine* _____

MODIFYING INAPPROPRIATE VERBALIZATIONS

A person with autism does not look much different from anyone else. Many adults with autism are average or even good looking people. Their autism is not obvious in the way they look, dress, or walk. However, as soon as they open their mouths to verbalize, the autism is obvious.

Autism is a disorder of communication, and it affects communication in a number of ways. Some people with autism might not have any verbal language at all, while others might speak in short phrases, have echolalia, abnormal speech melody, or poor grammatical structure. Some individuals with autism can have fluent speech, but difficulty with abstract terms. Autism, then, can involve an absence of normal communication, or it can be associated with the presence of abnormal verbalizations. Individuals with severe autism might scream, hoot, shriek, yell, or hum. Individuals with some language might have incessant talk, incessant questioning, and perseverative speech that might be directed at others or at no one. Individuals with autism might also provide lengthy replays of past conversations (their own or others').

Presence of certain types of verbalizations can create serious adjustment problems for persons with autism. Some types of verbalizations are merely annoying, such as humming. Others can be frightening, such as loud hooting or screaming, or highly disruptive, such as shrieking. The problem is not how to decrease or eliminate verbalizations, but how to teach and encourage acceptable verbalizations. Teaching and encouraging verbalizations and other forms of communication comprises an entire field in the education of persons with autism. Detailed instructional programs for language are beyond the scope of this book. For information on interventions for language development, the reader is referred to the many texts and research articles on language development of persons with developmental disabilities. The purpose of this chapter is to present strategies for managing unacceptable verbalizations that might be associated with autism. This chapter examines the measurement, functional analysis, and management of unacceptable verbal behavior.

PINPOINT THE BEHAVIOR

Verbal behavior does not have to be seen, it only needs to be heard, because it is audible, it is measurable. As with all behaviors, the first step in intervention is to pinpoint the behavior. Verbal behavior has several dimensions. Pinpointing verbal behaviors involves making decisions about these several dimensions.

Volume

One dimension that must be considered is volume. At times, the critical aspect of the behavior is the volume. In some cases, it is the only important consideration. For example, an individual might have some speech skills, however, he or she might yell at times. A fluent individual might raise his or her voice at certain times, or an individual who speaks in short phrases might shout words. The problem is not what is said, but the volume at which it is said. Similarly, nonverbal individuals might make sounds such as humming or hooting. Only when these sounds reach a certain volume do they cause problems.

In community settings it is typically not possible to measure volume in any scientific manner. Some subjectivity is unavoidable. However, it is important that staff be consistent in their definition of the target behavior. All caregivers involved should come to an agreement on the target volume. This can be done by a joint observation of the individual, or staff can meet and a demonstration of desired volumes can be provided.

Nature of the Sound

Some people with autism make unconventional sounds, such as humming, hooting, and shrieking. These sounds are most common in individuals who have no speech. The target behavior and the goal will depend on the setting. In certain situations, it might be desirable to eliminate the sound. Hooting is an example. Jim hoots, and hooting in the group home is not a problem so no goal is needed for that setting. However, Jim has a job in a supported employment program working in a factory. Co-workers find the sounds disturbing, and in fact, Jim has previously lost several jobs because of his loud hooting. An intervention plan might need to target hooting at work. A desirable goal might be either low hooting or no hooting.

Content

The content of the verbal behavior may be the target for change. Some adults with autism speak on topics that are upsetting to themselves or others, and often such topics signal that more serious behaviors such as aggression might follow. Examples of such content include talk about harming others, talk about destroying property, talk about past institutional placements, and talk about past incidents of aggression. Content might be embarrassing rather than upsetting. For example, an individual might ask a stranger personal questions, such as how old one is, or is one married, if not, why not, and so forth. If content of this type is creating problems in the home or work setting, it would be legitimate to target this type of behavior for change.

When pinpointing content, the content and the setting must be clearly defined. It is not sufficient simply to target "inappropriate conversation." Rather, the plan must target specifics, such as "personal questions defined as questions about marriage, money, and sex." The target might also include the audience, for example, "personal questions defined as questions about marriage, money, and sex, directed to strangers or new acquaintances."

Frequency

The issue in many cases is not the nature of the sound or the content since the sound might be plain English and the content a simple request, question, or statement. The problem is that the frequency is annoying or disruptive to all concerned. Martin's case provides a good example of this problem. Martin asked his group home counselor when his team meeting was scheduled, and the counselor told him. However, over the next several weeks, Martin asked this same question hundreds of time. The frequency was the issue that needed to be addressed.

Repeated demands is another example of a behavior that might need change. People with autism certainly have the right to make requests. However, when these requests are made hundreds of times per day, an intervention plan might be needed.

DATA COLLECTION

Verbalizations can be measured in the same way that other behaviors are measured. Measurement must achieve the purposes of providing some indication of the frequency of the behavior and some information on the circumstances. Some frequently used measures of verbalizations are briefly described.

Tally

Tallies can be used when the frequency is less than 5–10 times per day, and staff have time to record the occurrence of each verbalization. Occasional shrieking might be suitable for tally. For example, Eleanor shrieks about five times per day and staff record each instance of shrieking.

Time Block

When the behavior occurs many times per day, it might be inconvenient to record each instance. For example, some individuals might shriek or hoot up to 100 times per day. Since staff probably do not have the time to record each incident, a time block can be a reliable and sufficient alternative.

Behaviors that stretch out over time with little clear beginning and end are also suitable for time block, rather than tally. Screaming is a good example. An individual might scream for an hour. He or she might take a breath or two, then continue. It would be difficult for staff to determine how to break the incident up into separate behaviors and count them. Time block of course does not require the counting of separate incidents. The caregiver simply marks in each block whether or not the behavior occurred and does not need to make decisions about how many separate incidents were involved.

Percent of Opportunities

Certain verbal behaviors only occur given certain opportunities. For example, an individual might only ask personal questions when new visitors come to the worksite. If no visitors come, there are no opportunities to ask personal questions. The relevant type of data may be to count the total number of visits by new visitors and compute the percentage of those visits in which the individual asked personal questions.

Structured Diary

A structured diary or a regular diary will be necessary in order to obtain information on antecedents and consequences of the targeted verbal behavior. If the behavior occurs more than about five times per day, a structured diary might need to be done on a time sample basis.

FUNCTIONS OF VERBALIZATIONS

Many verbalizations are appropriate to the setting and situation, and their functions are clearly stated. People with autism can be skillful in asking questions or making statements or requests that clearly communicate their purposes. These purposes are often acceptable in the setting and respectful of others. Appropriate, clear communications are not the target of this chapter, and the many acceptable functions that such communications serve are not discussed here. Verbalizations that are considered unacceptable in content, frequency, or nature must be analyzed in regard to their function. As with other behaviors, their functions or purposes must be determined.

The function of bizarre verbalizations might be no different than the functions of other problem behaviors. The individual might not have acceptable behaviors to achieve his or her purposes, so somehow, he or she has learned to use bizarre verbalizations instead. This chapter provides a description of some functions of bizarre verbalizations. This list is not meant to be inclusive, but simply suggestive of some possibilities.

Attention

Adults with autism who have no speech might use unconventional verbalizations to gain or maintain attention of others. Several researchers have suggested that bizarre verbalizations serve the purpose of gaining social attention. Ullmann et al. (1965) reported that social attention in the form of nods, smiles, and signs of interest increased the frequency of psychotic speech. A study by Hunt, Alwell, and Goetz (1988) suggested that talking to and about people who were not present may have served social functions.

Shrieking, hooting, screaming, or crying can all serve the purpose of obtaining attention. Often such noises result in caregivers meeting needs, giving reprimands, making comments, or giving instructions. Any response from the caregiver is a form of attention. In settings where there is little other social interaction between caregivers and the individual, attention becomes a strong suspect as the function. Also, if the individual has no speech skills, such noises might be the only possible means of obtaining attention. Verbal individuals might use repeated questioning, repeated demands, and repetitive verbal rambling as a way of gaining and maintaining attention. Such verbal behaviors might be the most effective means that they have to obtain attention.

Escape

Verbal behavior, either coherent or incoherent, can serve the purpose of escape. The individual has learned that hooting, screaming, shrieking, crying, or yelling is an effective way to end a task or be permitted to leave an area. Similarly, a verbal individual might find that by shouting, threatening, or speaking about past aggressive incidents or frightening topics, an unpleasant task can be ended, or staff may leave the area or send the individual to his or her room. In all cases, the individual might have learned that certain types of conversations can effectively end unpleasant situations, or the behavior has allowed him or her to leave the setting.

Durand and Crimmins (1987) published evidence that the psychotic speech of a 9-year-old boy with autism served the purpose of escape for him. They found that when task demands increased, so did the frequency of bizarre talk. The child had quickly learned to use the bizarre talk to end certain tasks.

Assistance

Many people with autism have difficulty using language well. If an individual is having difficulty with a task or situation, then using language, which is normally difficult, becomes even more so. He or she might have learned that shrieking, crying, or yelling is a fast, easy way to get help. Such noises might be the only means that he or she has to obtain assistance.

An individual with verbal skills might use bizarre or repetitive verbalizations to gain assistance. Asking for assistance, a fairly easy skill for most people, might be unknown or difficult for an individual with autism. When having difficulty with a task, the individual might begin to talk repetitively about certain topics, make threats, or make other unpleasant statements in order to get assistance.

Smith and Coleman (1986) worked with a young man with autism who was employed at a printing company. Despite the fact that this man had fluent speech, he occasionally screamed at work. A functional analysis revealed that screaming occurred when he was having difficulty with a task. One function of the screaming appeared to be to obtain assistance. If the target verbalizations occur during tasks, especially new tasks or difficult tasks, and if such verbalizations are sometimes followed by assistance from others, then it is possible that the purpose of the verbalizations is to obtain assistance.

Desired Items or Activities

The purpose of the verbalizations might be to obtain a certain item or activity. Perseverative demands such as "soda please, soda please, soda please," might be taken at face value—the individual wants a soda. Others might not be able to say "soda please"; instead, they hoot, scream, shriek, or cry. Verbalizations might also serve the purpose of requesting a certain activity. "Swim please, swim please, swim please," is clear. The individual wants to go swimming. If the individual does not have the verbal skills to ask, other noises might be used instead.

Schedule changes or changes in routine can often be the setting events or antecedents for increased verbalizations. In such cases, the verbalizations might serve the function of attempting to return to the original schedule or routine.

Self-Stimulation

The function of verbalizations might be self-stimulation. Certain odd vocalizations, humming or talking to oneself, might possibly serve the function of self-stimulation. It is difficult to verify this function; however, if the possibility exists that self-stimulation is the function, then certain implications are implied for intervention. Wong et al. (1987) published a study that supported the environmental influences on stereotypic verbalizations. However, these authors also presented evidence that certain types of verbalizations are self-maintaining.

Unconventional or unpleasant verbalizations can serve a variety of functions. These functions can vary across individuals and also within individuals. An individual might use hooting or shrieking in a variety of situations to serve several purposes. Likewise, a verbal individual might use repetitive questioning to serve different functions in different circumstances. As with all behaviors that are targeted for change, the functions must be determined before proceeding with an intervention plan.

CAUTION: CONSIDER GOALS CAREFULLY

Care must be taken when designing plans that involve verbal behaviors. In many cases, the verbal behavior, whether it is screaming, hooting, or shrieking, is the only way in which the individual communicates needs, discomfort, or even joy. Goals must be carefully selected. It serves no humane purpose to attempt to eliminate an individual's only means of verbal expression.

A careful analysis must be made of the purpose of the behavior, and the individual's abilities to learn more conventional verbal behavior. An adult with autism with no speech might shriek for joy when pleased. Such shrieking might not be a legitimate target for behavior change unless a specialist is quite certain that a more acceptable response can be taught. Similarly, a nonverbal adult who occasionally cries might have no other way to express sadness or discomfort. Again, unless a specialist is quite certain that a more acceptable response can be taught, the behavior should not be tampered with.

Similar considerations must be given to individuals who have verbal problems. People with autism often use perseverative questioning or rambling as their only known means of carrying on conversations with others. Simply targeting reduction of rambling or questioning would deprive these individuals of their only learned means of social conversation. It is critical that more acceptable conversational skills be taught.

STRATEGIES FOR REDUCING DISRUPTIVE VERBALIZATIONS

Intervention plans that involve verbalizations must thoroughly address functions. Failure to adequately address the functions can actually result in escalation of the behavior or a change in the form. Instead of simply screaming or crying, the individual might begin to self-injure or strike out. Caregivers, then, must proceed with caution in goal setting, design, and implementation of plans involving verbalizations.

Descriptions of a variety of strategies are presented. Although the strategies are presented individually, as with all intervention plans, a combination of strategies might be necessary. The cases provided at the end of the chapter present examples of combining strategies to deal with verbalization problems.

Teach Acceptable Alternatives to Nonverbal Individuals

Unconventional verbalizations such as hooting, squealing, and shrieking often serve the functions of obtaining food, attention, assistance, escape, activities, or objects. Teaching acceptable alternatives can be a critical part of an intervention plan. Adults with autism who have no speech might be limited in the amount of conventional speech that they can acquire. However, they may be able to learn a combination of signs, words, or sounds that approximate words in order to communicate. Communicating with picture boards or similar arrangements might also be possible.

A variety of strategies have been used with some success with persons with autism to teach communication skills. Strategies for actually teaching language are beyond the scope of this book. However, in any plan that involves verbalizations of people with autism with either limited or no speech, language specialists should be consulted to develop strategies for language development.

Several factors should be considered when teaching language to persons with autism. First, efforts to build language should be ongoing throughout the day. Removing an individual from his or her setting to devote a short period of time to a "language lesson" will most likely not be as effective as ongoing efforts. Language training, particularly with adults, must be functional. Bizarre verbalizations serve specific functions for these people. Communication training must serve obvious functional purposes if these adults are to give up their odd verbalizations and adopt new methods. The connections between the new forms of communication and the functions the individual has been trying to achieve must be close and obvious.

Carlton provides a good example. When Carlton needed to go to the bathroom, he grabbed his crotch, pounded his chest, and squealed. Teaching him to say or sign "bathroom" in segregated language lessons by showing him pictures of a bathroom was too abstract and theoretical for him. However, teaching him the correct signs when taking him to the actual bathroom was practical and functional.

Ellis provides another example. Ellis hooted when he wanted food. A language instructor attempted to teach Ellis to sign for food by showing him pictures of food. The instructor even tried showing him food items during their language session. However, when in the kitchen of his group home, Ellis would still hoot and grab for food. Ellis needed to be taught more conventional ways of asking for food while actually in the kitchen throughout the day and evening.

Teach Acceptable Alternatives to Verbal Individuals

Persons with autism who have verbal skills can usually use conventional language to make requests for objects and activities. Their verbal problems typically become evident in two types of situations: 1) social situations or situations in which they are seeking attention, and 2) situations in which they are experiencing problems such as difficulty with a task, denial of a request, and change in routine. Any of a variety of setting events and antecedents that can set the stage for problem behaviors can also be associated with inappropriate verbalizations.

Individuals with autism who have bizarre verbal behaviors can learn better ways of using language to replace their more bizarre methods. The strategies depend on the individual, the behaviors, and the setting. Some useful and practical strategies are described below. This list is not inclusive, and a language specialist might have more ideas for individual cases.

Social Skills Training   Social skills training can be useful to teach individuals with autism how to initiate conversations with others, ask for assistance, reveal problems, and defend their rights. Social skills training is described in detail in Chapter Six. Whenever bizarre, repetitive, threatening, or otherwise unacceptable verbalizations can be replaced by more acceptable language, and if the individual is capable of learning and using improved language, social skills training should be considered.

Self-Disclosure Training   Unacceptable verbalizations such as screaming, crying, threatening, and perseverative talking might occur when an individual with autism has a problem. The individual might have difficulty expressing the problem to others because of either lack of skill or fear. Routine training in self-disclosure can teach the individual acceptable alternatives to unacceptable verbalizations in target situations. Self-disclosure training is covered in detail in Chapter Seven.

Discrimination Training   In some cases the individual with autism does not realize that the verbalizations are unacceptable. In these cases, discrimination training can be useful. At regular times each day, the individual is provided with a list of acceptable verbalizations and unacceptable verbalizations for specific situations.

Discrimination training might be useful for cases like that of Mona. Mona often had awkward and embarrassing conversations with co-workers. She would talk about her past experiences in an institution, her parents who abandoned her at age three, and her problem behaviors. Mona's job coach compiled a list of acceptable and unacceptable topics for conversations with co-workers. Acceptable topics included work, the weather, the weekend, dinner, the news, and other topics that would be of interest to co-workers. Unacceptable topics included the institution, her parents, and her problem behaviors. After several months of discrimination training, Mona's conversations with co-workers became consistently acceptable.

Training in Conversation Skills   Individuals with autism sometimes use repetitive questioning, personal questioning, or irrelevant questioning in order to initiate and maintain conversations with others. Training in initiating conversations might be useful as a means of teaching more acceptable conversations. A sample strategy for training in conversational skills is provided in Chapter Six.

Modeling   Individuals with autism are not adept at learning social behaviors from watching others. If they were, they would most likely not have such severe social deficits. However, just because they learn slowly or incompletely does not mean that they do not learn at all from watching others.

Modeling can be particularly useful to teach individuals to speak in lower voice volumes. Some individuals with autism speak in loud tones, shrill tones, or even shriek their words. Caregivers can model soft tones by standing near the individual when speaking and speaking in very soft tones. Similarly, caregivers of such individuals must be conscientious to avoid shouting themselves to avoid modeling the behavior that they want to eliminate. Caregivers of individuals with autism can teach acceptable alternatives by the way in which they use language. Whatever skills are targeted, whether they are skills in asking for assistance, skills in starting conversations, or skills in greeting others, caregivers should serve as models for acceptable handling of such situations. The modeling referred to here is not the contrived modeling in social skills training, but modeling by doing throughout the day.

Remove or Reduce Setting Events

Certain setting events might be associated with intense outbursts of bizarre verbalizations. For example, a nonverbal individual with autism might need to wait for his laundry to finish drying. After several minutes of waiting, hooting, shrieking, or wailing might occur. Another individual might see a Soda and start shrieking in a high pitched tone, "Soda, Soda, Soda." Removing or reducing setting events might be a practical way to prevent unacceptable verbalizations. However, not all setting events can be eliminated, but for those that can, removal or reduction should be considered as a strategy.

Provide Picture and Written Schedules

Verbal outbursts might occur when the individual is unclear about what is expected. Such outbursts might occur when the individual wants to do an unscheduled activity or does not want to do a scheduled activity. Providing picture or written schedules of the individual's day and evening can be helpful in communicating what is expected. Also, such schedules provide clear cues on when desired activities will be available.

Repetitive questions and demands related to activities can also be helped by picture or written schedules. Mitchell is a young man with autism who asked group home staff multiple times per day when upcoming activities would occur. For days he would ask the date of his team meeting. Once the team meeting passed, he began to repeatedly ask the date of an upcoming ice skating trip. Since Mitchell has some reading skills, he was given a calendar. Important events were recorded on his calendar. When Mitchell asked about an event, he was referred to his calendar. After several days, he learned to check his calendar rather than ask staff.

Provide Active Schedules

An active schedule with constructive activities can be an important component in an intervention plan for bizarre verbalizations. Individuals with autism who are left alone or who lack constructive, meaningful activities for long periods of time are likely to engage in a variety of unacceptable behaviors, including bizarre verbal behaviors.

Provide Choices

Verbal outbursts may serve the function of allowing the individual to escape from an activity. Providing individuals with autism with choices throughout the day can help eliminate verbal outbursts. Providing choices in leisure activities, chores, special events, and timing of such activities can help reduce the need for outbursts. Teaching individuals to say no, to ask to stop an activity, or to ask for a break can also help reduce verbal outbursts.

Provide What the Individual Wants

Verbal outbursts can often be avoided in individuals with autism by simply providing frequent access to those items, activities, or events that the individual is attempting to acquire by the outbursts.

Motivate for More Acceptable Verbalizations

It might be necessary to provide motivation for more acceptable verbalizations. Nonverbal individuals who hoot, shriek, or make other loud verbalizations may need to be motivated to have softer verbalizations. Verbal individuals with autism who scream, yell, or shriek their words may need to be motivated to speak in quieter tones. A variety of reinforcement schedules can be used to encourage quieter verbalizations. Quieter verbalizations can often be achieved with individuals who have no speech by using variable interval schedules of reinforcement as described in Chapter Four.

Verbal individuals who can read can often be motivated to speak lower or to have more acceptable conversations using a checklist. The individual can be rated at set intervals on relevant criteria. Checklist items to encourage lower volume might include "working quietly" or "low voice volume." Checklists or report cards are described in Chapter Four, and self-evaluations are described in Chapter Seven. Verbal individuals whose conversations include unacceptable content can also sometimes benefit from checklist rating systems. Checklist items might include "interesting conversation" or "polite language." The caregiver will define interesting conversation and polite language.

Extinction

Certain types of verbalizations might be targeted for decrease. Although speech or acceptable communication should not be discouraged, in many cases it might be necessary to discourage screaming, loud hooting, shrieking, and other disruptive communications. Extinction might be needed in order to discourage unacceptable verbalizations. If the individual uses hooting or shrieking to obtain certain items or outcomes, then the connection must be broken between the verbalization and those outcomes.

Targeted verbalizations are put on extinction as any other behavior. Caregivers should ignore the behavior. For example, if the individual hoots, shrieks, or yells during a task, the caregiver should continue to present the task. If the behavior occurs during leisure, the caregiver proceeds with the ongoing activity or schedule without mentioning the verbalizations or changing the activity.

Extinction Plus Structured Conversation

A person with autism might have a conversation and in the midst of the conversation begin the targeted unacceptable verbalizations. For example, while speaking with a visitor, the individual with autism might begin to ramble about past placements or other perseverative topics. Caregivers can discourage such topics by being very structured in the conversation. If the individual with autism begins to speak about the undesirable topic, the caregiver simply continues to speak about some acceptable topic. Nothing is said about the undesirable topic. The topic is, in effect, put on extinction. However, the person with autism is not ignored. Rather, the caregiver carries on the conversation by continuing with an approved topic.

An example of this type of structured conversation follows. Earl, a young man with autism, is holding a conversation with his nonhandicapped friend, Raymond. Earl is perseverating on a person from his past. Raymond continues to speak with Earl, but does not directly address the unacceptable topic. Instead, Raymond keeps the conversation focused on the here and now.

> **Raymond:** "Hi Earl, it's good to see you."
> **Earl:** "Raymond, do you know Ray Sands from Oakview? Do you Raymond? Do you know Ray Sands?"
> **Raymond:** Earl, I can't believe how cold it is outside. I was freezing out there. Were you cold out there?"
> **Earl:** "Yes, its cold out there. Do you know Ray Sands from Oakview?"
> **Raymond:** "Earl, I had such a busy day today. And guess who I saw at the office? I saw your friend Pete."
> **Earl:** "You saw Pete? Did you see Pete, Earl?"

After many conversations held in this manner, Earl can gradually learn to talk about current topics, rather than perseverate on people or places from his distant past.

Respond to Verbalizations as a Sign of Aggression

Caregivers should be aware of certain verbalizations that tend to signal that a more serious outburst is likely. Some individuals with autism might talk about past placements; threats; past aggressive incidents; or violent, destructive, or aggressive behavior. Such topics might signal a more serious outburst. Caregivers should become aware of verbal signs that can be clues to possible escalation. The intervention plan would then need to include instructions on how to respond to these signs of aggression.

CASE 1

Danielle was a 38-year-old female with autism who was untestable by the traditional standards of intellectual ability. Her symptoms of autism included severe language deficits, her speech was limited to one-word phrases, and shrieking, squealing, and hand flapping occurred frequently. Danielle was employed as a stock clerk at a department store under the supervision of a job coach. Her job was to remove the plastic covering from clothes to prepare them for display. She maintained this job for over 4 years.

Procedures

Data Collection Danielle's vocational counselor kept a tally of incidents of shrieking and squealing. A total number of incidents per day was calculated from this tally.

Functional Analysis A functional analysis was done, using information provided by the job coach. Presentation of tasks frequently preceded shrieking, and attempts to quiet Danielle usually followed. Shrieking was primarily a task avoidance behavior. A second function may also have been to obtain attention.

Intervention Plan An intervention plan was developed that provided positive reinforcement, including attention, for soft verbalizations and quiet working. The plan also called for continued presentation of task despite shrieking. The intervention strategy had several components.

Variable Interval Schedule A variable interval 15-minute schedule of positive reinforcement was implemented. The job coach gave Danielle a positive reinforcer about every 15 minutes when she exhibited any of the target behaviors. Reinforcers included favorite foods or drinks, favorite activities, favorite objects, and short breaks. If Danielle shrieked, paused in her work, or left location during a task, there was at least a 5-minute period during which no reinforcers were delivered. No reinforcers were given during off-task or shrieking behavior.

Praise Danielle was told why she was given the reinforcer. Specific behavioral praise accompanied delivery of the reinforcer. Also, within each hour period Danielle was praised several times for working quickly and working quietly.

Staff Response to Shrieking Staff ignored shrieking. If a task was presented and Danielle shrieked, staff continued to present the task. The instructions for staff are as follows:

1. Danielle should be rewarded for on-task, quiet work behavior. Sample target behaviors include: working on task with the maximum amount of independence that she is capable of; staying in assigned location; working on task for as long as possible; moving quickly from one task to the next; taking the initiative on any work-related behavior; working quietly; working quickly; responding to greetings with a wave, a smile, or friendly "hello."
2. Danielle will earn a reinforcer on a variable interval 15-minute schedule contingent on quiet, productive work behavior. Approximately every 15 minutes (plus or minus 10 minutes) she will receive a reinforcer when working well. Specific praise will accompany delivery of the reinforcer.
3. Reinforcers to be used are: food or drinks that Danielle enjoys, using nutritious foods if possible; activity reinforcers such as going for walks or short breaks (the job coach should compile a list of possible reinforcing activities); and object reinforcers that Danielle likes, such as pennies. Reinforcers should be alternated to ensure variety and to keep her interested, and should be delivered while Danielle is engaging in the target behavior, or in the case of a task, as soon as she is finished. If Danielle shrieks, pauses, or leaves location, or is noncooperative in any way, there should be at least a 5-minute period during which no reinforcers are delivered.
4. Danielle should be told why she is getting the reinforcer. Specific behavioral praise should accompany delivery of the reinforcer. It is important that within each hour period Danielle be praised several times for working quickly and working quietly.
5. A sign can be paired with the praise, such as thumbs up and a smile, and eventually, the verbal praise can be faded out and Danielle can be rewarded with thumbs up and a smile.

Results

The average number of incidents of shrieking per day are shown in Figure 9.1 for the week of baseline (preintervention period during which there was no systematic response to either shrieking or cooperative behavior) and for 12 weeks of intervention. During the baseline week, Danielle averaged 60 incidents of shrieking per day. By week 7 of intervention, she averaged less than 10 incidents per day with a decreasing trend noted as the plan continued. A follow-up probe done 3 years later revealed an average of 1.5 incidents of squealing per day for the month probed.

CASE 2

Elaine was a 39-year-old female with autism who had an IQ of 17 as measured by the Stanford-Binet Intelligence Scale, Form L-M. Her symptoms of autism

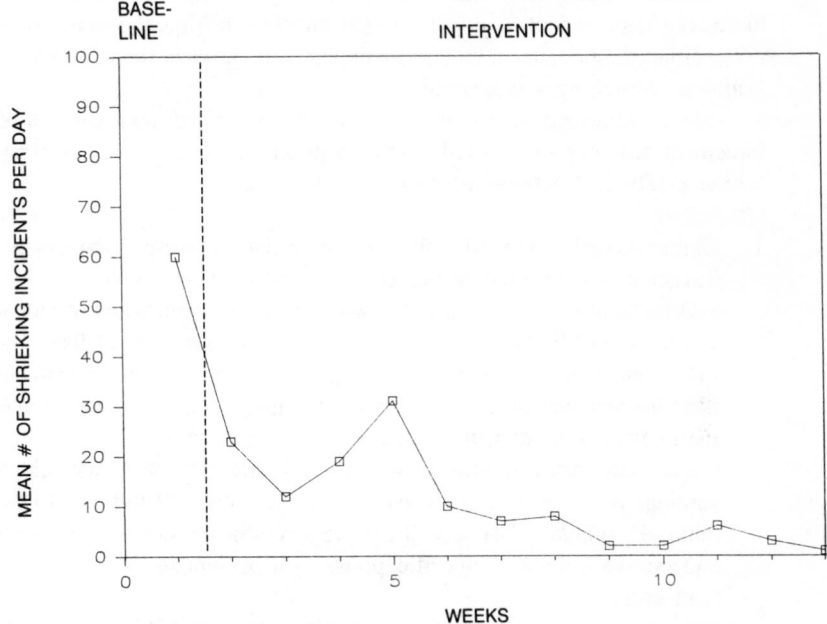

Figure 9.1. Mean number of shrieking incidents by Danielle per day during baseline and intervention.

included difficulty in establishing relationships with other people, severe language deficits (i.e., verbal expression limited to two- and three-word phrases), ritualistic behaviors, aggression, and self-injury. Elaine would also frequently shriek loudly when requesting something, usually food or drink.

Procedures

Data Collection   The number of incidents of shrieking per day was recorded and tallied.

Functional Analysis   It was noted that Elaine usually shrieked for food or drink. At times Elaine was given what she wanted, or she was prompted to ask for the item nicely, then was given what she wanted. It appeared, then, that the function of Elaine's shrieking was to obtain food, drink, or any other object or event that she desired.

Intervention Plan   Since Elaine frequently shrieked to obtain food and drink, the intervention plan consisted of offering her such items when she was quiet. As the item was offered, she was asked quietly if she would like it. If she replied quietly that she did want the item, it was given to her. The objective of this plan was to eliminate the need to shriek by frequently providing Elaine with desired items. She could then learn a more acceptable response (quietly asking).

Desired items were offered approximately every 30 minutes. Furthermore, if Elaine independently requested an item in a quiet voice, she was given either the item or an immediate explanation of when the item would be available. Shrieking was ignored.

Since Elaine also had problems with self-injury and aggression, a reinforcement schedule was included to provide incentive for more cooperative behavior. The instructions for staff are as follows:

1. Elaine should be rewarded for any appropriate, nonaggressive behavior. Target behaviors include but are not limited to any of the following: involvement in any task or chore with the maximum amount of independence of which she is capable; sitting quietly, dancing, or listening to music during leisure time; staying in assigned location; sitting or working near housemates in a nonaggressive manner; clear skin (i.e., no new marks from self-scratching); speaking softly.

2. Elaine will earn a reinforcer on a variable interval 30-minute schedule contingent on cooperative behavior. About every 30 minutes (plus or minus 10 minutes) Elaine will receive a reinforcer when exhibiting any cooperative behavior. Specific praise will accompany delivery of the reinforcer.

3. Reinforcers to be used are: food or drink reinforcers that include iced tea, small amounts of nutritional foods that she enjoys, juices, and soda; activity reinforcers that include rest, quiet time, or other favorite activities (staff should compile a list of other possible activity reinforcers); and sensory reinforcers such as lotion and scents should be tried to determine whether they might serve as reinforcers. It is recommended that staff use these listed reinforcers as a starting point, and attempt to expand the lists. Food reinforcers should be used in small quantities. All reinforcers should be alternated to ensure variety and to keep Elaine interested, and should be delivered while Elaine is engaging in the behavior, or in the case of a task, as soon as she finishes. If Elaine is aggressive, or destructive, or shrieks, there should be at least a 10-minute period during which no reinforcement is delivered. No reinforcement is to be given during aggressive or noncooperative behavior.

4. Elaine should be told why she is getting the reinforcer. Specific praise should accompany delivery of the reinforcer. Elaine should be praised approximately every 15 minutes for cooperative behavior. The counselor should be at eye level with Elaine when praising her. For example, if Elaine is sitting, the counselor should sit next to her while praising her; if Elaine is standing, then the counselor should stand next to her. Praise can be either brief or involve a long conversation. Staff need to gauge whether Elaine would be more appreciative of short or long interactions. This may vary from day to day.

5. If Elaine begins to go off task or display preaggressive behaviors, she should be directed back to task. No reinforcers should be delivered during these behaviors.

6. If Elaine has been aggressive or has displayed preaggressive behavior, and then she returns to task, she should not be praised. However, she can be given feedback, such as, "That's right, you're washing the dish." There should be at least a 10-minute delay between aggressive behavior and praise, and at least a 3-minute delay between self-picking and praise.

7. If Elaine becomes aggressive or destructive, she should be given verbal instruction to return to task. If she does not respond to verbal instruction, and is about to injure someone else or destroy property, then she should be physically redirected back to task with verbal instruction on what she should do with her hands to return to task.

8. Elaine's shrieking should be completely ignored. Counselors should not attend to her in any way if she shrieks. Eye contact should not be made with her, and if possible, the counselor should turn away from her. Talking quietly should be responded to by addressing the issue she brings up. If she asks softly for food, drink, or something else, she should be answered and told whether she can have it. If she cannot have it, she can be told, "Now it's time for (task or activity)."

9. When Elaine is presented with something she likes, she should be prompted to ask softly for it (e.g., if she is given a glass of juice, the counselor should first prompt Elaine to ask for it, and as soon as she asks for it quietly, the counselor should enthusiastically say, "Here's juice," then give it to her). Elaine should be offered drinks or snacks about every half hour, with the prompts as described.

Results

The average number of screaming incidents per day are reported for the baseline month (month 1) and for the following 13 months in Figure 9.2. The average number of incidents per day was nine during the month preceding intervention, and a steady decline was noted in the following months. An increase was noted in month 4. Elaine broke her arm that month, and it appears that the discomfort associated with a broken arm and the necessity of wearing a cast accounted for the increase in screaming during that month. By month 6, her first month without the cast, shrieking had declined to approximately one incident per day. In a follow-up probe done 2 years later, Elaine averaged three incidents per day.

CASE 3

Linda was a 25-year-old woman with autism. She had lived in a state institution for the mentally ill from ages 3 to 23, when she entered a community-

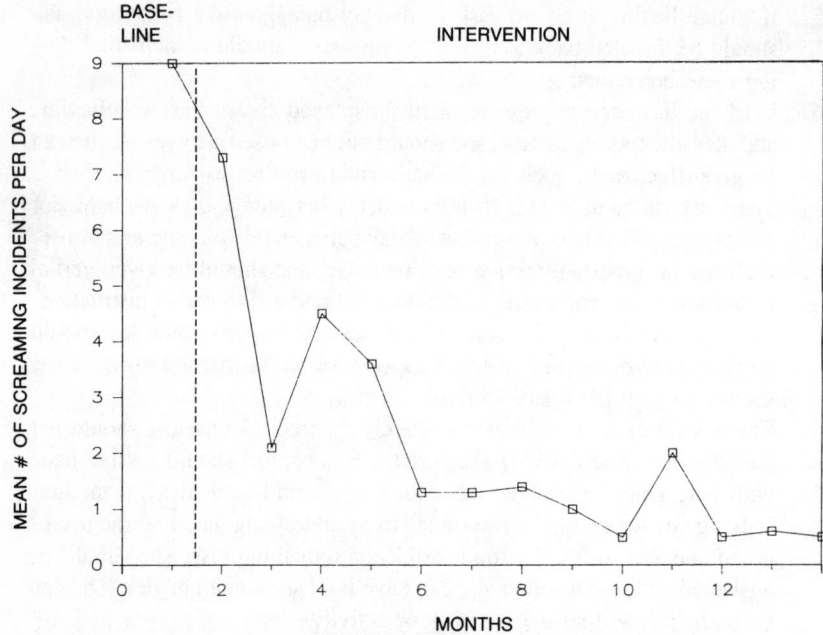

Figure 9.2. Mean number of screaming incidents by Elaine per day during baseline and intervention.

integrated group home and supported employment program. She was fully verbal with a low-average IQ. Linda's symptoms of autism included difficulty establishing relationships with others, communication problems including unusual rhythm and inflection, and difficulty adjusting to change with dramatic responses to even small changes in the environment.

Linda had numerous incidents at work involving bizarre conversations with co-workers. She would talk about being reunited with her parents, who had abandoned her at age three, about her institutional placement, and about sex in a socially unacceptable manner. Occasionally she would yell and cry at work.

Procedures

Data Collection Antecedent and consequence data were collected on incidents of bizarre conversation.

Functional Analysis At work, the conversations resulted in expressions of interest and sympathy from well-meaning co-workers. Therefore, it appeared that the unacceptable conversations served the function of gaining attention, sympathy, and contact with others.

Intervention Plan An intervention plan was developed that sought to teach Linda to discriminate acceptable from unacceptable topics. She was provided with frequent attention from her job coach since attention seemed to be a motivating factor. Finally, a reward system was put into place to motivate her to initiate more acceptable conversations.

Discrimination Training A list of interesting topics and uninteresting topics was compiled by the job coach for Linda. These topics were for use with co-workers on the job. Interesting topics included leisure activities, work, meals, vacation plans, weekend plans, the news, and the weather. Uninteresting topics included the institution, her parents, sex, and violence. Each morning and several times each day, the job coach reviewed the list with Linda. Linda was encouraged to talk with co-workers about topics from the list.

Report Card A rating system, called a report card, was developed. Linda was rated several times per day on the following behaviors: respects others, respects self, normal voice volume, interesting conversation, follows directions, and works steadily. Linda received one point for each item if she met the criteria for success, and a zero if she did not.

Self-Disclosure Training Linda was given self-disclosure training, as described in Chapter Seven, three nights per week. The purpose of this training was to teach her to discuss her problems with her job coach or group home counselor.

Extinction Any bizarre talk was absolutely ignored. Linda's job coach and residential counselors simply helped her continue with the scheduled activity, but did not directly respond to her bizarre talk.

Linda had serious problems with aggression. Her plan including instructions to staff on implementation is presented in detail in Chapter 10.

Results

Linda's bizarre conversations with co-workers virtually disappeared after several months of plan implementation. During major changes or disappointments, she might speak in a threatening manner. However, these conversations are directed at her caregivers and not at co-workers. After several months, Linda was able to participate in rating herself, and discrimination training was dropped. Self-disclosure training continues indefinitely.

SUMMARY

Shrieking, squealing, and screaming might be present in persons with severe autism. These behaviors are aversive to others but may be indispensable to the individuals in order to achieve their goals or to meet their needs. Frequently, the aversive nature of the behavior prompts caregivers to find some way to quiet the individual, and once the caregiver finds a way to quiet the individual, he or she is likely to use that method the next time the individual shrieks.

Unfortunately, many attempts to quiet the individual with autism teach him or her that screaming is a useful behavior. For example, in the case of an individual screaming for desired food items, caregivers will often ask the individual to request the item nicely. When the individual asks nicely, the item is given. The following chain of behavior is established: 1) individual screams for cookie, 2) individual is prompted to ask nicely, 3) individual asks nicely for cookie, 4) individual is given cookie. The individual learns that screaming eventually pays off in cookies with an intervening behavior of asking nicely.

When this type of situation has been established, it is important that intervention efforts have two components. First, the individual must be taught that screaming will not result in rewards. Usually this can be achieved by not giving the requested item following screaming and not prompting the individual at that time to ask nicely. Second, the individual needs to be taught an alternate way of requesting desired items. If caregivers simply refuse to respond to screaming and do not teach an alternate behavior, then the individual will most likely find an equally unpleasant way of requesting what is wanted.

Individuals can be taught alternate ways of requesting items by a variety of methods. The method presented in Case 2 was to provide desired items to Elaine frequently, always with an instruction on how to ask nicely. The goal was to teach Elaine that: 1) screaming does not pay off, 2) it is not necessary to scream for what you want—desired items are plentifully available, and 3) an effective way to obtain a desired item is to ask quietly.

The case of Danielle illustrates the use of screaming to end tasks. Often, instructors will end the task in order to end the screaming. The individual then learns that screaming is indeed an effective way to end tasks. Intervention efforts again must be twofold. First, the individuals need to learn that screaming is not an effective way to end tasks. This might be taught by continuing to present the task despite screaming. Second, the individual's refusal to engage in the task must be examined. The plan may call for modifying the task in some way, providing more frequent breaks, or as in the case of Danielle, providing motivation to do the task.

In Case 3, although Linda is considered to have low-average intelligence and good verbal skills, she frequently screamed and shouted at work, and her conversations were often considered bizarre by co-workers. Linda benefited from systematic training in conversation skills and self-disclosure skills. Her plan also included a motivational component for working quietly and having interesting conversations.

Strategies for modifying disruptive verbalizations will need to be individualized to account for the individual's purposes in screaming and the demands of the situation. A variety of strategies are identified to deal with disruptive verbalizations in individuals without spoken language. Additionally, suggestions are provided for individuals with spoken language. This chapter tackles the problem of disruptive verbalizations from a behavior management perspective. An active, functional language acquisition plan might also be necessary to augment gains that can be realized from a behavioral management approach.

REFERENCES

Durand, V., & Crimmins, D. (1987). Assessment and treatment of psychotic speech in an autistic child. *Journal of Autism and Developmental Disorders, 17,* 17–27.

Hunt, P., Alwell, M., & Goetz, L. (1988). Acquisition of conversation skills and the reduction of inappropriate social interaction behaviors. *Journal of The Association for Persons with Severe Handicaps, 13* (1), 20–27.

Smith, M., & Coleman, D. (1986). Managing the behavior of adults with autism in the job setting. *Journal of Autism and Developmental Disorders, 16,* 145–153.

Ullmann, L.P., Forsman, R.G., Kenny, J.W., McInnis, T.L., Unikel, I.P., & Zeisset, R.M. (1965). Selective reinforcement of schizophrenic interview responses. *Behavior Research and Therapy, 2,* 205–212.

Wong, S.E., Terranova, L.B., Bowen, L., Zarate, R., Massel, H.K., & Liberman, R. (1987). Providing independent recreational activities to reduce stereotypic vocalizations in chronic schizophrenics. *Journal of Applied Behavior Analysis, 20,* 77–81.

Chapter Ten

MODIFYING AGGRESSION

Most people will not disagree with the idea that all people are entitled to life, liberty, and the pursuit of happiness. Many, however, will argue that if a person hits, kicks, bites, pulls hair, and pinches another individual then maybe liberty is not such a good idea. It follows, then, that people with these behaviors are not at liberty to enjoy integrated community life. Individuals with autism have been profoundly affected by this segregation and thus, they are at risk for institutionalization. A major reason may be that some people with autism tend to hit, kick, pinch, and commit other unpleasant acts against those who love and care for them.

Aggression is one of the most challenging problems facing those who serve persons with autism. Aggression can take any form, including hitting, kicking, biting, pinching, pulling hair, or scratching. Head banging, tearing of clothes, throwing objects, and shoving are also common behaviors. Aggression occurs at varying rates. Many people with autism are not aggressive, some are very infrequently aggressive (perhaps having one incident every year), some are aggressive every few months, some every few weeks, some every couple of days; and some are aggressive on a daily or hourly basis.

Aggression is a challenge to all concerned. Often it is not clear why the aggression has occurred. Even when it is clear, it does not make the behavior any more tolerable. Parents of aggressive children, particularly adult children, often live in fear and depend on neighbors, relatives, and friends to help out in crisis situations. When children become full-grown, aggression can often become unmanageable in the home, resulting in the need for outside placements. Direct care staff and instructors who live and work with aggressive individuals often must take pain and discomfort in stride. Caregivers of people with autism might see more aggression in a month than the average person sees in his or her entire adult life. The ideals and values of staff are often sorely stretched as a result of physical assaults.

Aggression is also a challenge to the person with autism. When the individuals can talk, they usually express sorrow and regret at their own behavior, and when the individuals cannot talk, they express regret in other ways. These individuals often cannot say why they behave the way they do, but they clearly say that they do not like it.

On the surface, the situation looks bad. How can a person who hits, kicks, pinches, scratches, and head bangs live in an apartment, ride the bus, eat at a restaurant, shop at a mall, and work at a department store, print shop, or library? Although it seems unlikely, it is not impossible. In fact, people with autism and high rates of aggression can make good neighbors, good workers, and good friends.

The purpose of this chapter is to demonstrate that: 1) aggression can serve a purpose for the individual, 2) it is best modified in the real environment, and 3) people with autism can live and work successfully in the community. All of this can be accomplished despite problems with aggression.

INTERVENTION IN THE COMMUNITY

Aggression has traditionally been considered incompatible with community integration. If a person hits or kicks, how can he or she work? If a person scratches or pinches, how can he or she live with others? From this philosophy comes the idea to wait until the person no longer has aggression before moving him or her into the community to live and work. There are a number of problems with this approach.

The Waiting Game

It might seem to make sense to wait for Johnny to stop kicking before getting him a job, or to wait for Maura to stop scratching and pinching before moving her into a group home. But there is one major problem. While waiting, Johnny might always kick, Maura might continue to scratch, and no one will ever get anywhere. Waiting becomes the name of the game.

Getting from Here to There

People with autism have a hard time generalizing. They can learn how to behave in one setting, but they need to learn all over again for the next setting. For example, they can learn to count change at their dining room table, but once at McDonald's, they might need to learn all over again. Similarly, they can learn to follow instructions from Mr. Smith, but when Mr. Jones takes over, they must learn all over again.

The most efficient approach to this problem is to teach these individuals in the setting where they will need the skills. If Mary needs to learn to order dinner, she can be taught in a restaurant. If Phil needs to learn to ride the bus, he can be taught at the bus stop and on the bus. The same goes for behavior. If Jim needs to learn to control hitting at a job, he can learn on the job. If Ava needs to learn to control scratching in a home setting, she can learn in her group home.

If acceptable behavior is taught directly in the situation in which it is desired, then there is no need to worry about problems with generalization. If a person needs to learn to keep hands to him- or herself, and if he or she needs a job, the most efficient approach is to get him or her a job, and teach the skills needed on the job.

Functional Analysis

A critical part of an intervention plan is the functional analysis. It is important to learn the purpose that the behavior serves for the person. To find out the real purpose, it is necessary to look at the setting. The reason a person hits others in a day activity center might be different from why he or she would hit them at a job, or at home. To adequately manage the behavior, then, it is necessary to know the purpose that the behavior serves in that setting. Finding the purpose that the behavior serves in a training setting might allow management of the behavior in that setting. When the person goes to work, there might be a new purpose for the behavior in the work setting. The functional analysis needs to be done in that setting, so it makes sense to place the person where he or she will ultimately be. The intervention plan can then be carried out where it is needed.

Imitation

A compelling reason for getting people with aggression out into integrated community settings is that the community is filled with people who are not aggressive (or so it is hoped). In segregated settings, aggression can be the norm. In restaurants, shopping malls, and integrated jobs, aggression is rare or nonexistent. The adult with autism will look around and will not see hitting, pinching, scratching, or biting. Although these people do not learn solely by imitation, to the extent that they do, the teachers are there: the grocer, the banker, the waitress, the nonhandicapped co-worker, the employer, and the bus driver to name a few. These are people from whom people with autism can learn by watching. It is hoped that they will learn that people get through the day without hitting, scratching, and kicking.

Natural Curriculum

One strategy for modifying aggression is a busy schedule, especially one rich with preferred activities. People who have a lot of what they want have little need to hit or kick. The community is filled with reinforcers—reinforcers for people without autism, and reinforcers for people with autism. Ice cream shops, bakeries, restaurants, swimming pools, parks, movies, and bowling alleys are all activities enjoyed by people with and without autism. When people are doing things they enjoy, they are less likely to strike out. Printing companies, manufacturing firms, libraries, and stores are all places where people with autism can work and can even like their work. When people like their work, they are less likely to hit, kick, or pinch and are less likely to want to escape.

The community is a natural curriculum. It is filled with cues for acceptable behavior. It is packed with work and leisure activities and is replete with reinforcers. People with autism, given the same opportunities as others to work in busy and diverse communities and with the aid of caregivers, can find attention, preferred activities, and reinforcers they might otherwise seek through aggression. The community can provide a rich environment and a natural curriculum in which aggression becomes an obsolete activity.

It Has Been Done

The idea of getting a job for a person with aggression might seem unrealistic. However, it has been done. In fact, over 70% of adults with autism and aggression served in a supported employment program have been employed over half of the time that they have been in the program (Juhrs & Smith, 1989). People have had problems with hitting, kicking, scratching, pinching, and biting, but these problems have not stopped them from working in printing plants, warehouses, restaurants, manufacturing firms, retail stores, and a variety of other places.

MANAGEMENT OF AGGRESSION

Aggression has been widely treated with the use of punishment. A variety of punishers have been used, including water mist (Gross, Berler, & Drabman, 1982), electric shock (Birnbrauer, 1968), shaving cream in the mouth (Conway & Bucher, 1974), tickling (Greene & Hoats, 1971), Tabasco sauce in the mouth (Altmeyer, Williams, & Sams, 1985), loud noise (Charlop, Burgio, Iwata, & Ivancic, 1988), and loud reprimands (Van Houten & Rolider, 1988). However, during the past several years, studies have demonstrated the effectiveness of nonaversive management plans based on a functional analysis. Smith (1986) achieved significant reductions in aggression in two adults with autism with a multi-part intervention plan based on a functional analysis.

Several studies have achieved success by either manipulating antecedent events or providing rewards for cooperative behavior. Gardner, Cole, Berry, and Nowinski (1983) and Cole, Gardner, and Karan (1985) reported on reductions in aggression by teaching coping and self-management skills. Slifer, Ivancic, Parrish, Page, and Burgio (1986) presented a case in which aggression was reduced by rewarding cooperative behaviors.

Aggression can be managed in individuals with autism without the use of aversive procedures. However, the management of aggression, like all behaviors, is based on the functional analysis. Once the purpose of the behavior is known, then an intervention plan can be developed. Neither the type of aggression nor the severity of the aggression change the process of behavior management. Whether an individual spits, hits, or kicks, the procedures for changing the behavior are the same.

DEFINE THE BEHAVIOR

The behavior must be defined in ways that are observable and measurable. A bad temper, hostility, depression, or lack of self-control cannot be targeted. Behaviors must be seen and measured. Goals should seek to increase keeping hands and feet to self, keeping hands on tasks, keeping 1-foot distance from others, and should seek to decrease hitting, kicking, pinching, pulling hair, biting, or similar behaviors that can be seen and measured.

DATA COLLECTION

Once the behavior is defined, then data can be collected. In cases of aggression, it is important to get information on the antecedents and consequences of the behavior. Antecedents include when and where the behavior occurred and the events that preceded the behavior. As discussed, certain antecedents have been shown to precede aggression, such as making demands, difficult tasks, absence of attention, and difficult social situations. The presence of another person who is aggressive or screaming can also be the antecedent for aggression. Data must give information on exactly what situations preceded aggression and should also describe what happened after the behavior occurred. Exactly what staff and others did as a result of the behavior must be examined. What was said? How was it said? Who said it? What exactly was done? Who did it? Data collection might also examine setting events that were ongoing or that preceded the behavior. Certain setting events might typically set off aggression; therefore, it is helpful to quickly take an inventory of setting conditions.

Physiological Events

In nonverbal clients, physiological conditions such as hunger, thirst, being ill, feeling hot, or feeling tired may make the individual more likely to be aggressive. Physiological states involving overmedication, undermedication, or missed medication might also result in aggression. The role of psychotropic medication in the presence or absence of aggression must be carefully explored.

Environmental Events

Other setting events that can lead to aggression in adults with autism involve scheduling of activities and lack of activities. For some people, too many activities and demands can result in aggression, and for others, too few activities and demands can result in aggression. Interactions with others in the environment must also be examined. For some people, too few interactions will result in aggression, and for others, too many can cause problems. The type of interactions are also important. Making demands, speaking critically, and speaking in a harsh tone can all lead to aggression.

The weather can also be a setting event that plays a role in aggression. Change of weather or change of seasons can lead to aggression, and certain types of weather, like rain or thunder, can also be associated with aggression. For example, some adults with autism become very upset during thunderstorms and aggression may then be likely.

Changes in routine, disappointments, and waiting situations can lead to aggression in both verbal and nonverbal adults with autism. Unexpected changes or changes for which the person has not been prepared, disappointments, like expecting a parent or a friend who does not come, or delays in expected appointments can all result in aggression. Nonverbal clients in particular might become aggressive in waiting situations, such as waiting for laundry to be done, waiting in traffic jams, or even waiting at traffic lights.

FUNCTIONAL ANALYSIS

Researchers have studied purposes, or functions, that aggression serves. Carr, Newsom, and Binkoff (1980) identified purposes of aggression for two children with retardation and autism. They found that when demands were made on the children, aggression was likely to occur, however, when demands were not made, aggression rarely occurred. When the children were allowed to leave the demand situation following aggression, rates of aggression increased, but if the children were not allowed to leave the situation, even if they were aggressive, then aggression decreased. Carr and his associates concluded that aggression could serve the purpose of escape.

Carr and Durand (1985) demonstrated that aggression was most likely to occur when there was a low level of adult attention as well as when tasks were difficult. A second purpose that aggression might serve is to acquire adult attention, particularly in situations where attention is low. Aggression can also serve the purpose of obtaining food or other items. Smith (1986) reported on two adults with autism who used aggression to obtain food and attention, as well as to escape from demands.

Researchers have identified a number of purposes of aggression. Clinical experience has provided examples of many of these purposes, including: escape from a noisy setting, removal of a noisy peer, change of routine, change of activity, change of staff, and addition of staff.

Nonverbal Individuals

Clinical experience has suggested that nonverbal individuals tend to use aggression in a variety of situations for the purposes of obtaining food or drink, gaining attention, escaping from a task, or escaping from a setting. Because of the lack of language skills, it is possible that aggression becomes an all-purpose way of achieving results.

Verbal Individuals

Although a person with autism can have good language skills, he or she might still find aggression useful. Usually, the purposes are somewhat less concrete and less obvious than with nonverbal clients. For example, it is rare for a verbal adult with autism to hit in order to obtain food or drink. Instead, aggression seems to occur in more complex social situations.

Margaret, a 31-year-old woman who is verbal with low-average intelligence, occasionally becomes aggressive toward staff and roommates. Her aggression often occurs around holiday times. She is without parents, and her aggression seems to occur when her roommates spend holiday time with families. Aggression serves the purpose of communicating jealousy and dislike for the situation. It has resulted in staff going to great lengths to work out pleasing holiday arrangements for her.

John is a 51-year-old man who becomes aggressive when he does not receive expected letters from his parents when they are out of town. Aggression then results in reassurances from staff, additional supervision, and extra attention. John's loneliness or disappointment might spark the aggression, and well-meaning staff reward it with attention and comfort.

Smith and Coleman (1986) reported on a 27-year-old man with autism whose aggression at work occurred during difficult tasks. Often, the aggression resulted in his getting extra help or being sent home. Aggression, then, served the purpose of getting assistance or escape from what had become an unpleasant situation.

Analyzing the Behavior

Once the data are collected, a functional analysis can be done as for any other behavior. Using the information on setting events, antecedents, and consequences, it is possible to generate ideas about when the behavior occurs and the purpose it serves for the individual. Aggressive behaviors that are very severe or dangerous might look like they serve no useful purpose, but it is important to view them as if they do. The data should be analyzed to determine the purpose the behavior might serve.

MANAGEMENT STRATEGIES

Once data are collected and a functional analysis is done, then strategies can be selected. As with all behaviors, a comprehensive plan must be designed to address all identified functions and to motivate the individual to behave more acceptably. When the target behavior is serious, as aggression always is, it is wise to select as many strategies as possible and integrate them into a feasible plan. Depending on outcome of the functional analysis, any of the strategies described in Chapter Four can be useful for the management of aggression. Obviously, any given plan will not use every possible strategy. However, aggression plans will probably need certain strategies in order to ensure safety, so the plan might include all of the following strategies.

Sufficient Supervision

The amount and nature of supervision necessary must be specified in order to prevent injury. For example, if the individual is dangerous and could harm others, then continual close supervision is needed. Some individuals are likely to be aggressive only in the presence of certain antecedents or certain setting events. These events and conditions should be identified and the plan should call for increased supervision under these conditions. Other individuals display certain behaviors prior to aggression that can help predict the onset of the aggression. Mabel's signs of aggression provide an example. First, she cries and threatens to urinate on the floor, then she does urinate on the floor and verbally threatens others. Most likely to follow is an attempt to hurt someone else. When those "pre-" behaviors are present, then supervision is increased.

Another example is George's case. George, who is nonverbal, often lies on the floor, or sits with his head down, and refuses to follow instructions. When he behaves this way he is likely to hurt anyone who comes near him. When such behaviors are present, staff increase his supervision, but are careful not to get too close. If signals of aggression are known, then they should be listed.

Teach Alternatives

Verbal individuals can often be taught more acceptable ways to handle situations in which they would normally be aggressive. For example, a person who hits others when his or her work is too hard can be taught to ask for assistance; or a person who grabs at female visitors to the worksite can be taught to stay in the designated work area and simply greet the visitors with a wave. These skills can usually be taught by social skills training, as described in Chapter Six. The individual might also benefit from self-management training, as described in Chapter Seven.

Nonverbal individuals may have to be taught alternative behavior through contingencies. Cooperative behavior may need to be specifically rewarded. Through such a system, the individual can be indirectly taught that cooperative behavior pays off. Such reward systems must be carefully considered and worked out for maximum benefit.

Reward Cooperative Behavior

It is possible that behavior can be changed without a reinforcement component. Social skills training or even self-management training might be sufficient. Addressing scheduling issues or rearranging setting events might also be sufficient. Despite the potential effectiveness of these other strategies, most aggression plans will include some reward system for cooperative behavior. The rationale is simple: Positive reinforcement strengthens behavior. In people who act aggressively, the goal is to strengthen acceptable behavior as quickly as possible. Positive reinforcement can provide added incentive for the individual to cooperate with any other strategies that might also be used, and since rapid change is necessary, it often seems prudent to include strong positive reinforcers as part of an intervention plan.

The rewards must be delivered fairly frequently in the cases of high-frequency aggression. Rewards chosen must be valuable to the individual and can include favorite food, drinks, special activities with staff, access to favorite objects, access to favorite sensory activities, attention, and physical affection. Reinforcement systems that have been useful for individuals with autism are described in more detail in Chapter Four. To summarize here, variable interval schedules have worked well with many individuals with autism without verbal language. Individuals with autism with verbal language often do well on report card systems.

Provide What Is Wanted

Providing the individual with an ample supply of what he or she wants might be a critical part of an aggression plan. If an individual is aggressive for food or attention, then by freely providing these, the aggression becomes obsolete. Snacking programs can be useful for a person with autism who is aggressive in order to obtain food. Providing frequent snacks, or a snack bowl, gives the individual ample access to food. Aggression, then, is no longer necessary in order to get food.

If the plan includes a component for providing what is wanted, it is important that these items or events not be provided as a direct result of aggression. Rather, they should be available routinely or on a schedule. They should, of course, not be provided directly during or after an aggressive episode.

Avoid Criticism

In many cases, taking a critical approach with an individual with autism can be an antecedent to aggressive behavior. Using a harsh tone or using criticism can often lead directly to aggression. Telling the individual with autism that he or she has done something wrong, or that he or she must redo something, or telling him or her not to do something can lead to aggression. The following recommendations are crucial in avoiding aggression.

Avoid a Harsh Tone Some individuals with autism react aggressively when caregivers use harsh tones with them. Firm tones can be tolerated; however, yelling at the individual or using an unduly harsh tone can lead to aggression. Therefore, caregivers should speak in firm, but gentle tones.

Avoid a Negative Approach   As a rule, it is better to tell an individual with autism what to do, rather than what not to do. This principle is essential if the individual is already upset. For example, if an individual is about to spill milk, rather than shout, "Don't spill that milk!" the caregiver should say, "Pour carefully. Keep the milk in the glass." Similarly, if an individual with autism is about to hit someone, it is better to say, "Put your hands down," rather than, "Don't hit." One individual with autism when told not to hit, kicked instead.

Avoid a Critical Approach   When speaking to some individuals with autism, it is important to avoid a critical approach. Some people who have problems with aggression also have problems with criticism. For those individuals, criticism can be an antecedent to aggression. Criticizing or having the individual redo the task or undo what was done wrong can be an antecedent to aggression. If such an individual is having difficulty with a task or process, it is better to provide additional gentle assistance without being critical.

Saul's case provides an example. Saul is a young man with mental retardation and autism. Taking a critical or negative approach with Saul, or using harsh tones, often leads directly to property destruction or aggression. A group home counselor learned this lesson the hard way. One night Saul was eating dinner with his fingers, and the counselor said, "Saul, eat with your fork." Saul complied. The counselor should have stopped then; however, the counselor then went on to say in a critical tone, "You know you're not supposed to eat with your fingers." The critical tone and negative approach was an antecedent to aggression. Saul jumped up and smashed the counselor's head into a wall. The interesting thing about Saul is that when he is supervised by counselors who tell him in gentle tones what to do, without mentioning what not to do, and when his report card program is reliably run, he can go years without aggression.

Extinction

As with any undesirable behavior, it is important that aggression be put on extinction, that is, the behavior must not pay off. This is achieved by not directly addressing the aggressive behavior. There are no promises, threats, or other discussions of the behavior; likewise, the individual is not asked to apologize or make up in any way since any of these responses might provide some pay off for the behavior.

Some behavior plans fail because rewards are scheduled too close to the aggressive behavior. For example, the schedule might call for a reward after 2 minutes of calm behavior. This type of schedule does not really put the aggression on extinction. In fact, the reward that occurs 2 minutes after aggression might actually reward aggression. Therefore, the plan must specify a reasonable waiting period between aggression and the delivery of the next reward. If aggression is often, the wait might only be 10 minutes. For verbal clients with infrequent aggression, the delay might be several hours.

One consideration when dealing with aggression is that the individual and others must be kept safe from harm. The following guidelines, considered emergency procedures, are recommended in order to prevent injury from aggression. Although there is some possibility that preventing injury might somehow be rewarding to the individual, safety must come first in all situations.

Emergency Procedures

If an individual is about to injure self, others, or cause significant damage to property, the following guidelines should be followed:

1. If time permits, use verbal instruction. Tell the individual exactly what to do with arms, legs, and so forth. For example, if an individual is about to hit, say, "Put your arms down." If an individual is about to throw a chair, say, "Put the chair down." If an individual is about to kick, say, "Keep your feet on the floor."
2. Avoid telling the individual what not to do. For example, do not say, "Don't hit." Instead, tell the individual what to do.
3. Avoid vague phrases such as "calm down" or "relax." Instead, use specific phrases, such as, "Keep your arms still."
4. If verbal instructions are ignored and the individual continues with the behavior, attempts to harm others, or damages property, then the individual should be physically prevented from causing damage or injury. It might be necessary to go directly to physical management if there is not time to give verbal instructions.
5. If possible, use techniques such as positioning or blocking to prevent the individual from harming others or injuring self.
6. Keep the individual's arms or legs still if necessary in order to prevent injury. Procedures demonstrated by a specialist in physical management of aggressive behavior should be followed in these situations. While following these procedures, give one verbal instruction, such as, "Keep your arms still. When your arms are still I will let you go." Say no more until the individual's limbs have relaxed, then physical assistance can be gradually withdrawn.
7. Gradually withdraw physical assistance as the individual begins to comply with verbal instructions. If the individual becomes violent again, physical prevention should be reinstituted.
8. Physical management should be used only to prevent imminent injury or damage and should be withdrawn as soon as the situation is deemed safe.
9. If necessary, call for help. Try to do so in a low-key manner. Ask for assistance in a quiet and matter of fact manner, and do not sound agitated or upset.
10. If more than one staff person is involved, staff should work together

quietly and should not discuss the individual in the third person. Only very necessary coordinating instructions should be spoken.

11. Physical assistance should not be used as a punishment and should not be used to force individuals to do something that they do not want to do, unless there is immediate danger of injury or damage.
12. Physical management should not be used for nondangerous, nondestructive behaviors such as arm flailing or jumping up and down.
13. Caregivers who may need to prevent injury from aggression or self-abuse must be trained and competent in the physical management of aggression by a specialist in the field.
14. If caregivers cannot manage the individual in order to prevent injury, then additional emergency steps should be taken, such as calling additional staff or the police. Each agency should have its own procedures for whom to call in such emergencies.

CONSIDERATIONS AT WORK AND IN PUBLIC

Adults with autism who have aggressive behavior can live and work in the community. However, staff must ensure the safety of all concerned. It is absolutely essential that the following criteria are met:

Supervision: Adequate supervision must be in place to prevent injury.

Planning: A comprehensive intervention plan based on functional analysis must be in place.

Training: All staff involved must be trained and competent to implement the intervention plan. Additionally, all staff involved must be trained by an expert in physical prevention of injury, and they must be competent in physical management of aggression.

Back-up System: The agency must have a back-up system in the event that should staff need help to prevent injury, such assistance can be easily called and quickly available. It may be necessary for back-up assistance or supervisors to wear beepers in order to be reached in emergencies.

Outings to Work and to Play: Persons with aggression might become upset at work, at a mall, in a restaurant, or wherever they may be. If there is a risk of aggression, these people must be accompanied by staff who are qualified to prevent injury and who are competent to run the intervention plan under all conditions. Employers of persons with aggression have stated that they do not worry about the aggression when they can trust job coaches to handle the situations.

Following are three cases studies of individuals with aggression.

CASE 1

Jim was a 22-year-old man with severe autism and profound mental retardation. His symptoms of autism included difficulty in establishing relationships with other people, severe language deficits (i.e., verbal expression limited to two-word phrases, mostly echolalia), ritualistic motor behavior, and aggression. The targeted aggressive behaviors included hitting and kicking others. Aggression could be serious, and on one occasion Jim broke a staff member's cheekbone. Prior to intervention, there were about 10 incidents of aggression each hour.

Procedures

Data Collection Data were kept on the antecedents and consequences of each incident of aggression.

Functional Analysis A functional analysis was done to determine the purpose of Jim's aggression. The data suggested that the aggression served several purposes for Jim: 1) when presented with a task, Jim would become aggressive in an attempt to avoid the demands and to escape from the task; 2) when around food that he could not have, Jim was often aggressive in order to obtain food; 3) when Jim wanted attention, he became aggressive, as he often smiled at staff when they became involved with him during aggressive episodes; and 4) when unfamiliar staff on duty, noise, chaos, or disturbances in routine were present, Jim became aggressive, possibly to be removed from the situation.

Intervention Plan An intervention plan was developed that sought to teach Jim more acceptable ways of obtaining favorite foods, drinks, and attention. Expectations were made clear and a routine was established through the use of a picture schedule. A reward system was also instituted for following the picture schedule. The prompt hierarchy was used to redirect Jim to task during periods of stalling. Staff were trained to respond to aggression in a low-key manner with as little disruption to the ongoing schedule as possible. Setting events such as unfamiliar staff, noise, chaos, or disturbances in routine were avoided as much as possible. The intervention plan is as follows:

1. Cooperative behavior is to be rewarded on a variable interval schedule of positive reinforcement. Target behaviors are any appropriate, cooperative, nonaggressive behavior that includes: involvement in tasks with the maximum amount of independence that he is capable of; sitting on the sofa during leisure time; staying in assigned location; having good table manners; waiting while others are served; correctly using property; coming to task; communicating with signs, pictures or verbal language; sitting near others in a nonaggressive manner; being near others' food or drink without taking it.

2. Every 15 minutes (plus or minus 10 minutes) Jim will receive a reinforcer contingent on a cooperative behavior. He will receive the reinforcer while displaying one of the target behaviors. Specific verbal praise will accompany the delivery of the reinforcer. Vary the target behaviors that are being reinforced. For example, if on one occasion he

is rewarded for keeping his feet on the floor, next time he might be rewarded for working well on a task.

3. Reinforcers to be used include: food or drink reinforcers such as small amounts of nutritious food, and favorite foods or drink that Jim enjoys; and activity reinforcers such as being sung to, listening to music, and special attention from staff. Reinforcers should be alternated to ensure variety. Specific praise should accompany the delivery of the reinforcers. Jim should be told exactly what he did to earn the reinforcer. Use his name to get his attention and be enthusiastic when praising him.

4. Reinforcers should be delivered while Jim is displaying a target behavior, or in the case of a task, immediately after the task is finished. For example, Jim is washing dishes. After he has washed three dishes with only verbal prompting, he is given a pretzel and told, "Good washing, Jim." Do not give Jim a reinforcer within 5 minutes of aggression, task refusal, screaming, or any other dangerous or noncooperative behavior. No reinforcer should be given during aggressive or noncooperative behavior.

5. Reinforcers should not be promised in advance. They should be delivered spontaneously during periods of good behavior. Do not mention reinforcers when Jim is misbehaving, and do not discuss Jim's misbehavior with him.

6. Praise cooperative behavior about every 1–10 minutes. All praise should be specific, making exact reference to what Jim did to earn the praise. It is correct to say, "Good washing," but incorrect to say, "Good job." Similarly, it is better to say, "Nice sitting, Jim," rather than saying, "Nice, Jim." Praise should be given during the task, at the time of good behavior. Jim should not be praised while refusing to cooperate or while aggressive.

7. Jim's daily activities are to be posted in order of occurrence on a picture schedule in the group home. Each activity, meal, task, leisure period, or event should have its own picture. Prior to each event or activity, Jim should be taken to the picture schedule and shown the next activity and told "Look, it's time for (task or activity)."

8. After completing each task or activity, Jim should be told, "Since you're done with . . . it's time to check the schedule to see what's next." Jim should then be taken to the schedule. A velcro tab should be placed over the picture of the completed activity and Jim should be rewarded with a ring on a ring pole. He should then be shown the next picture to determine his next task or activity. At the end of the evening, if Jim has followed his picture schedule, his ring pole should be complete. He should then be given a special snack treat for earning all of his rings. He should be told that it is for following his picture schedule all day.

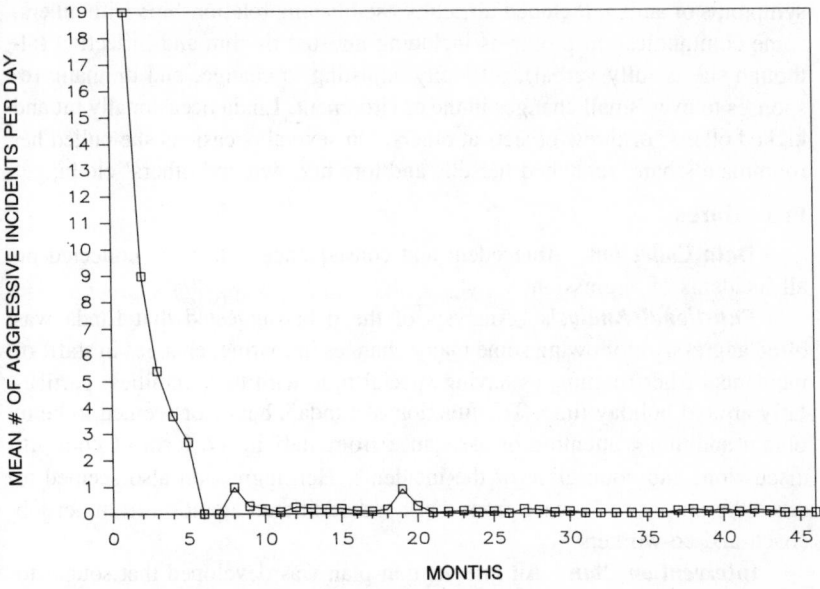

Figure 10.1. Mean number of incidents of aggression per day for Jim.

9. The prompt hierarchy should be followed for all activities that Jim knows how to perform. In cases of new activities, he should be given a demonstration or graduated guidance as necessary until he learns the task. The prompt hierarchy is discussed in Chapter Five.
10. Keep a record of the date, time, reinforcer, and behavior that was reinforced. Keep a daily frequency count of each instance of aggression and self-injury. Describe each incident of aggression on an ABC sheet.

Results

The mean number of aggressive incidents per day is shown for each month of this intervention plan in Figure 10.1. Reliable collection of frequency data was not begun until the first day of implementation of the plan so all data presented should be considered data during intervention.

As shown in Figure 10.1, the mean number of aggressive incidents per day was 19 the first month, and diminished to a mean of less than 1 per day by month 6. A follow-up probe done at month 63 revealed no incidents during the month.

CASE 2

Linda was a 25-year-old woman with autism with a low-average IQ. She had lived in a state mental institution for 20 years. At 23, she entered a community-integrated group home and supported employment program. Her symptoms of autism included difficulty establishing relationships with others, some communication problems including unusual rhythm and inflection (although she is fully verbal), difficulty adjusting to change, and dramatic responses to even small changes in the environment. Linda occasionally hit and kicked others, or threw objects at others. On several occasions she pulled her roommate's hair, scratched herself, and tore her own and others' clothing.

Procedures

Data Collection Antecedent and consequence data were collected on all incidents of aggression.

Functional Analysis Analysis of the data suggested that Linda was often aggressive following some major changes in routine, changes in staff, or incidents of her roommates having special time with their families, particularly around holiday time. The function of Linda's behavior seemed to be to obtain additional attention or assistance from staff in the form of comfort, discussion, and counseling of the incidents. Her aggression also seemed to serve the purpose of escape from work and additional attention from her job coach and co-workers.

Intervention Plan An intervention plan was developed that sought to teach Linda more acceptable behaviors for gaining attention and assistance in difficult situations. A reward system was put into place that quickly changed to a self-management plan. It should also be noted that Linda attended weekly therapy sessions. Her therapist was a social worker who had expertise in providing counseling to individuals with autism as described in Chapter Thirteen. Linda's intervention plan is as follows:

1. Linda's behavior will be rated on a report card. The purpose of this report card is to provide a gentle reminder on a consistent basis of the rules of behavior, to provide consistent feedback on compliance with those rules, and to provide motivation for following the rules. Linda should be rated three times per day, in the morning before leaving for work, at the end of the work day, and at the end of the evening on each of the following items: respects others by keeping hands and feet to herself; respects self by not injuring hands and face, and not tearing clothing; maintains normal voice by keeping her volume to a normal speaking level; holds interesting conversation by speaking only on interesting and acceptable subjects; follows directions by listening attentively to directions relating to work and household tasks; works steadily by not stopping except for breaks and to ask for assistance.

2. At each report card time, staff should review with Linda her rating on each item. If Linda complied with the item, she should be given a "1" and specific praise. It is very important that she be told why she earned each point. For example: "Linda, you respected others. You got along

with everyone you worked with this morning. That's great. You earn '1' for respecting others.'' Linda should not be threatened with loss of points, rather, if she loses a point, she should just be given a zero at rating time. If she earns a zero she should just be told why, very briefly, with no further discussion.

3. At all times, Linda will carry with her a data sheet that will be used to summarize her behavior throughout the day.

4. Linda will be praised for receiving a successful rating. Whenever she arrives at home, the group home counselor will praise her for points she earned at work and her therapist will praise her for accomplishments on her report card.

5. The job coach will develop with Linda a list of interesting and uninteresting topics of conversation. Each morning the job coach will review the list with her and remind her to choose topics from the "interesting" list when she speaks to co-workers.

6. Linda will have daily self-disclosure training as described in Chapter Seven. If Linda brings up a problem, and a staff member can assist with a solution, he or she should do so.

7. If Linda's behavior becomes uncooperative, such as refusal to follow directions, cursing, verbal threats, or other disturbing but not dangerous behaviors, then the behavior should be ignored. Linda can be gently redirected to the activity at hand. If she refuses or persists in other nondangerous, uncooperative behaviors, staff should not respond to those behaviors, but keep her under close watch. In several minutes they should again gently redirect her to the ongoing activity. There should be no discussion of her uncooperative behavior, no threats, no arguing, and no power struggles.

8. If Linda becomes aggressive or is about to cause significant damage to property, if possible, give specific verbal instructions telling her exactly what to do (e.g., "Linda, put your hands down."). If she is in danger of injuring herself or others and she does not respond to verbal instructions, then staff should physically prevent injury.

9. While Linda is being physically prevented from causing injury, she should be told exactly what to do (e.g., "Keep your arms down. Keep your arms still."). This instruction should only be given once if she continues to struggle. As she complies, she can be gradually let go. Any staff who may need to provide physical intervention in order to prevent injury must be trained in nonaversive physical management of aggression by a specialist in that field.

10. Once Linda is again willing to respond to verbal instructions, she should be redirected to the ongoing activity. There should be no discussion with her about the incident.

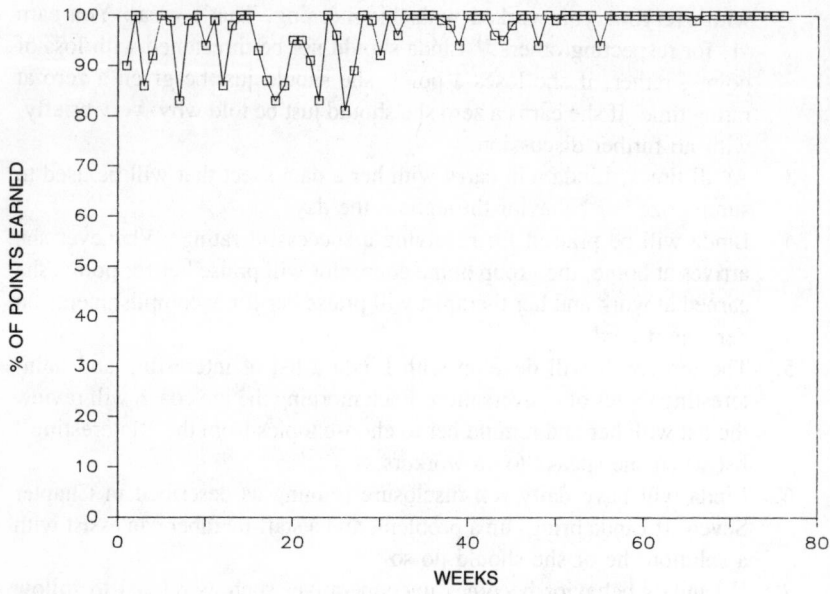

Figure 10.2. Percent of points earned by Linda per week during baseline and intervention.

Results

Prior to intervention Linda had at least weekly incidents of self-injury (scratching face and hands), aggression (hitting and kicking others), yelling, and bizarre conversation. After intervention, Linda's incidents decreased to one every several months. The percentage of points Linda earned each month from baseline (week 1) through week 76 are shown in Figure 10.2. After several months, Linda was taught to self-rate. Under self-rating, Linda rates her own behavior with praise and feedback from staff. Linda has maintained a job in competitive employment, under the supervision of a job coach, for the past 7 years. A follow-up probe done 3 years later revealed that Linda earned 99% of her points in the month probed.

CASE 3

Ernest was a 16-year-old student with autism who was severely disabled. He was nonverbal and occasionally had tantrums that consisted of head banging, hitting, kicking, and spitting. Ernest attended a community-based school for adolescents with autism. He lived in a group home in the community where he was supervised by trained residential counselors.

Procedures

Data Collection Data were collected on structured diary forms on which the antecedents of each tantrum, a description of the tantrum, and consequences of the tantrum were recorded.

Functional Analysis A functional analysis of the behavior indicated that aggression and self-injury typically occurred when Ernest was presented with a task. The data also indicated that the tantrums might be maintained by staff attention for the simple fact that the tantrums were invariably followed by an increase in attention from staff.

Intervention Plan The intervention plan was essentially a reinforcement schedule in which Ernest was presented with special staff attention, such as singing with him for a minimum of 5 minutes contingent on cooperative behavior. The reinforcing events were to be delivered approximately every 2 hours.

In addition to the reinforcement schedule, a list of signs of aggression was compiled along with staff instructions should these signs occur. In case of signs of aggression, such as hanging his head down or lying on the floor, staff were advised to avoid physical contact with Ernest, since touching him at such times was likely to result in aggression. Actual instances of aggression were handled as described in Case 1.

Results

The results are shown in Figure 10.3. During the baseline period, Ernest had between 10 and 16 tantrums per month. Following implementation of the intervention plan, tantrums occurred between 1 and 5 times per month. Additionally, prior to intervention, several staff had been injured by Ernest. Following intervention, there were no episodes involving injury to staff. A 2 year follow-up indicated that Ernest had three tantrums in the month probed.

SUMMARY

This chapter presents three cases of adults with autism. Their aggressive behaviors were reduced through multi-part intervention plans that emphasized nonaversive programming designed to meet their specific needs. Progress was made by using paraprofessionals in the direct implementation of the intervention strategies. The results suggest that paraprofessionals can be taught to implement intervention plans for aggression. Furthermore, intervention plans can be devised that are practical and safe for use in community settings.

Although it appears that the multi-part nature of the plans contributed to the successful outcomes, the relative contribution of each separate part cannot be assessed. Since the aggressive behaviors were of high frequency and long duration, and put the individuals and staff at risk of injury, the conservative

BASELINE   INTERVENTION

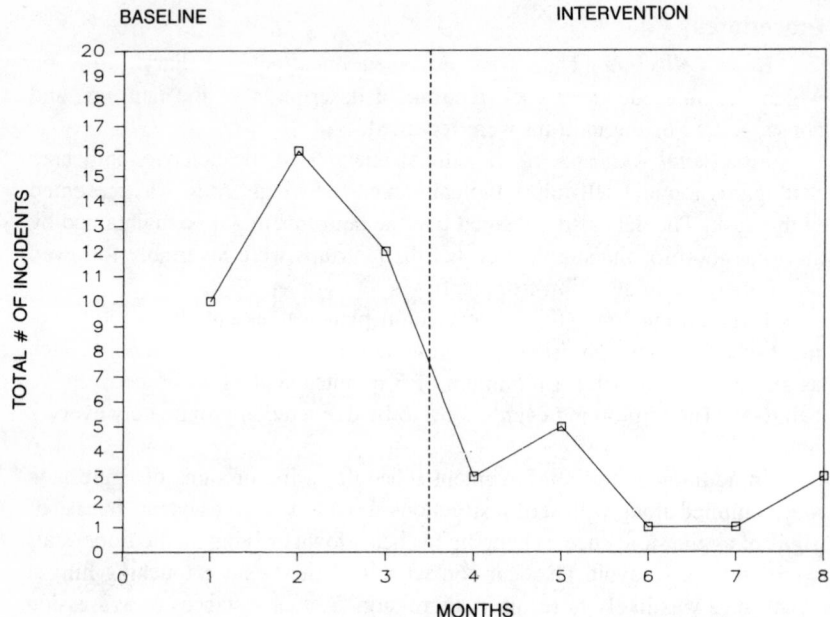

Figure 10.3. Total number of incidents of aggression by Ernest per month during baseline and intervention.

approach appeared to be to cover as many of the functions and apparent needs as possible when developing the plan. Any intervention plan for aggressive behavior needs to be individualized for each person. The guidelines and the sample intervention plans discussed were appropriate for the cases presented, but may not be appropriate for other cases.

Staff must be trained in all aspects of a behavior management plan. Caregivers who train and work with people who exhibit aggressive behavior must also be trained to prevent injury should aggression occur. At times, caregivers may find it necessary to physically prevent individuals from injuring themselves or others, and it is important that the staff be trained to follow established procedures in a safe, efficient, and nonaversive manner. Furthermore, it is imperative that enough staff be assigned to persons who have a history of aggression to ensure safety.

When working with aggression, it is important to collect continuous data so that progress can be reliably assessed. Failure of an individual to progress should result in a review of all aspects of the intervention plan, and modifications should be made if necessary. Failure to progress should be considered suggestive of an inadequate intervention plan, as this viewpoint incorporates the impetus to try a new way. When working with people with autism and high rates of aggression, it might be necessary to keep a successful plan in place indefinitely. Since the risks of fading too soon are high (i.e., the return of aggressive behavior), it is suggested that caregivers be overly conservative in fading out intervention.

A final consideration when working with individuals who exhibit aggressive behavior is that it might be unreasonable to expect to eliminate aggression totally and permanently. Although reduction in rate can reasonably be expected in most cases, if not all, outcomes may vary. Some individuals can be taught alternative behaviors and aggression can be permanently eliminated. Some people might be expected to exhibit some level of aggression despite well designed and faithfully implemented plans. However, if caregivers are trained to handle the aggression in a safe, nonaggressive manner, if the individual is directed back to the business at hand as soon as possible, and if adequate support is available to prevent injury, then such an individual might achieve a successful and permanent adjustment to life in the community despite the fact that aggression is not permanently suppressed.

REFERENCES

Altmeyer, B.K., Williams, D.E., & Sams, V. (1985). Treatment of severe self-injurious and aggressive biting. *Journal of Behavior Therapy and Experimental Psychiatry, 2,* 159–167.

Birnbrauer, J. (1968). Generalization of punishment effects: A case study. *Journal of Applied Behavior Analysis, 1,* 201–211.

Carr, E., & Durand, V. (1985). Reducing behavior problems through functional communication training. *Journal of Applied Behavior Analysis, 18,* 111–126.

Carr, E., Newsom, C., & Binkoff, J. (1980). Escape as a factor in the aggressive behavior of two retarded children. *Journal of Applied Behavior Analysis, 13* (1), 101–118.

Charlop, M.H., Burgio, L.D., Iwata, B.A., & Ivancic, M.T. (1988). Stimulus variation as a means of enhancing punishment effects. *Journal of Applied Behavior Analysis, 21,* 89–96.

Cole, C., Gardner, W., & Karan, O. (1985). Self-management training of mentally retarded adults presenting severe conduct difficulties. *Applied Research in Mental Retardation, 6,* 337–347.

Conway, J., & Bucher, B. (1974). "Soap in the mouth" as an aversive consequence. *Behavior Therapy, 5,* 154–156.

Gardner, W., Cole, C., Berry, D., & Nowinski, J. (1983). Reduction of disruptive behaviors in mentally retarded adults: A self-management approach. *Behavior Modification, 7,* 76–96.

Greene, R., & Hoats, D. (1971). Aversive tickling: A simple conditioning technique. *Behavior Therapy, 2,* 389–393.

Gross, A.M., Berler, E.S., & Drabman, R.S. (1982). Reduction of aggressive behavior in a retarded boy using a water squirt. *Journal of Behavior Therapy and Experimental Psychiatry, 13,* 95–98.

Juhrs, R., & Smith, M. (1989). Community-based employment for persons with autism. In P. Wehman, & J. Kregel (Eds.), *Supported employment for persons with disabilities* (pp. 163–175). New York: Human Sciences Press.

Slifer, K.J., Ivancic, M.T., Parrish, J.M., Page, T.J., & Burgio, L.D. (1986). Assessment and treatment of multiple behavior problems exhibited by a profoundly retarded adolescent. *Journal of Behavior Therapy and Experimental Psychiatry, 17* (3), 203–213.

Smith, M. (1986). Managing the aggressive and self-injurious behavior of adults disabled by autism in the community. *Journal of The Association for Persons with Severe Handicaps, 10,* 228–232.

Smith, M., & Coleman, D. (1986). Managing the behavior of adults with autism in the job setting. *Journal of Autism and Developmental Disorders, 16,* 145–153.

Van Houten, R., & Rolider, A. (1988). Recreating the scene: An effective way to provide delayed punishment for inappropriate motor behavior. *Journal of Applied Behavior Analysis, 21,* 187–192.

Chapter Eleven

MODIFYING SELF-INJURY

Some people with autism have problems getting along with others. At times, these problems escalate into aggression. Individuals with autism may also have difficulty getting along with themselves. At the extreme, these problems escalate into self-injury. Self-injury is a thoroughly studied but poorly understood behavior. It can take many forms, including self-hitting, self-scratching, self-pinching, self-kicking, self-biting and head banging. Self-injury can also be less direct, but as dangerous, in the form of pica (i.e., eating nonedibles).

Self-injury, along with aggression, is one of the most challenging problems facing persons with autism and those who serve them. Self-injury occurs at varying rates. Some people with autism have no self-injury, others have very infrequent self-injury with maybe one incident every few months, and still others, as with aggression, are self-injurious on a daily or hourly basis. In severe cases, self-injury can appear to be almost constant.

It is possible that the most bizarre behavior associated with autism is self-injury, and it is certainly one of the most frightening. Self-injury appears to preclude successful integration into the community. It is hard to imagine a person with high rates of head banging working at a department store, or a person who eats metal objects working in a stock room. The purpose of this chapter is to demonstrate that self-injury can serve a purpose for the individual and although this individual inflicts self-injury, he or she can be managed in integrated community settings with the help of intervention plans. This chapter shows how.

MANAGEMENT IN THE COMMUNITY

Self-injury is not incompatible with community integration. Persons with problems with self-injury can go to work and live in the community just like anyone else. They can work even though they head bang, self-scratch, self-pinch. The goal is to help these people to achieve adjustment and to reduce the severity of the problem.

191

The reasons provided in Chapter Ten for managing aggression in the community are valid for self-injury as well. In fact, they may be even more valid. Individuals must learn to control their self-injury directly in the situations in which they work and live. Functions must be identified and intervention procedures must be implemented directly in target situations.

Persons with self-injury can learn by watching those without self-injury. There are very few people out and about who self-injure. Chances are, a person with self-injury who visits a shopping mall or a grocery store will not see other people self-injuring. As with aggression, the adult with autism will look around, will not see self-hitting, head banging, or self-pinching, and by seeing multitudes of others who respect their own bodies, he or she can be helped to learn to do so too.

Self-injury often occurs in the absence of competing activities. The community is filled with activities that can be incompatible with self-injury since it offers limitless opportunities to learn more acceptable behaviors, as well as a variety of reinforcers for those behaviors. As with aggression, self-injury has not precluded employment. Over 70% of adults with autism and self-injury have been employed over half the time that they have been in a supported work program (Juhrs & Smith, 1989). People have had problems with head banging, self-hitting, self-scratching, self-kicking, self-biting, and pica, but these problems have not stopped them from working in such places as recycling plants, manufacturing firms, libraries, restaurants, and department stores.

MANAGEMENT OF SELF-INJURY: BRIEF RESEARCH REVIEW

Self-injury has been treated extensively with punishment procedures. Punishment procedures have included the use of electric shock (Romanczyk & Goren, 1975; Yeakel, Salisbury, Greer, & Marcus, 1970), aromatic ammonia (Baumeister & Baumeister, 1978; Tanner & Zeiler, 1975), lemon juice (Favell, McGimsey, & Jones, 1978), contingently applied protective equipment (Luiselli, 1986), and water mist (Dorsey, Iwata, Ong, & McSween, 1980). Pica has been treated with visual screening (Singh & Winton, 1984) and brief physical restraint (Singh & Bakker, 1984).

Despite the extensive use of punishment procedures, studies have also documented the successful intervention of self-injury without the use of punishment. Intervention plans based on a functional analyses are receiving more attention. Carr and Durand (1985) reported the reduction of behavior problems, including self-injury, by teaching children other ways to communicate their needs. Mace and Knight (1986) successfully treated pica in an adolescent with mental retardation by performing a functional analysis of the behavior and then basing intervention recommendations on the results of that analysis.

Berkman and Meyer (1988) reduced self-injury in a 45-year-old man who had been institutionalized for the majority of his life. Community-based intervention strategies included a structured schedule of functional work and leisure activities, instruction, and communication training. This man became a successful employee in a supported employment program. Willis and La-Vigna (1988) successfully reduced self-injury in a 17-year-old boy. The boy had both autism and a profound hearing impairment. He had been removed from an unsuccessful program that used extreme punishments. Willis and LaVigna created a multi-part intervention plan based on a complete environmental assessment and functional analysis. Intervention involved changes in the boy's living situation, instructional programming, and reinforcement contingencies. Self-injury dropped from 50 incidents an hour to 0 an hour.

Smith (1987) successfully treated a young man with autism who had life-threatening pica. This young man ate metal objects and had been hospitalized for internal damage from the metal. The pica was treated by rewarding behaviors incompatible with eating metal and providing alternate sensory stimulation in the form of access to crunchy snacks.

PINPOINT THE BEHAVIOR

Self-injury, because it is such a dramatic behavior, is fairly easy to target. In most cases, the behavior is readily observable and measurable as in self-hitting, self-kicking, self-pinching, and head banging. If an individual has several self-injurious behaviors, it might be best to lump them into one behavioral class referred to as self-injury. Taking separate data on each of the forms of self-injury in one individual can be difficult to interpret. Self-scratching might go down, but if self-hitting goes up, then interpretation can be confusing. It is often simplest to take data on the class of behaviors and look for decreases in totals.

In some cases, the behavior itself is not observable because the individual does the behavior in private. Some individuals, particularly verbal individuals, engage in self-injury when their caregivers are not in sight. Behaviors such as self-scratching, self-hitting, or head banging might be done in the privacy of the bedroom or bathroom, and when self-injury is done in private, it might be necessary to target marks on the body, rather than the behavior itself.

DATA COLLECTION

Self-injury is assessed by any combination of relevant methods described in Chapter Three. For only occasional incidents, a tally might be possible; for high-frequency self-injury, a time block would be more feasible; for self-injury that occurs in private, checking for marks on the body would be the most reliable method. Checks can be made at regular intervals, such as each morning and each evening.

Antecedent, behavior, and consequence data can be collected for each incident of self-injury. If the frequency is high, ABC data might need to be collected on a sample basis. Analysis of setting events, antecedents, and consequences often follows the same course as the analysis for aggression. The same setting events and antecedents that are associated with aggression are also associated with self-injury, and in fact, many individuals will engage in self-injury and aggression almost simultaneously.

FUNCTIONAL ANALYSIS

Recent years have seen a number of studies on the functions of self-injury. Although self-injury may serve different purposes for different individuals, it is helpful to be aware of typical purposes. Carr (1977) suggested that self-injury can be a function of different sources of reinforcement. In other words, self-injury is a behavior that is maintained by reinforcement. Since then, a number of researchers have provided evidence for different specific functions of self-injury.

Self-Stimulation

Iwata, Dorsey, Slifer, Bauman, and Richman (1982) found that self-injury did appear to be functional, and these functions were varied across individuals. They reported that self-injury was highest when children were left alone, leading them to speculate that self-injury may be a form of self-stimulation. Iwata and his colleagues found that the lowest rates of self-injury occurred when toys were available, when there were relatively few demands, and when other behaviors were reinforced.

Burke, Burke, and Forehand (1985) reported that self-injury was less likely to occur following positive interpersonal interactions, and more likely to occur following the absence of interpersonal interactions. The authors concluded that programs to reduce self-injury should maximize interpersonal interactions and minimize time in which no interpersonal interactions occurred.

Favell, McGimsey, and Schell (1982) found that self-injury was most likely to occur when the individuals had nothing to do. Favell and her colleagues concluded that self-injury was maintained by its sensory consequences. By providing alternate sensory activities, the researchers were able to greatly reduce self-injury. Taylor and Chamove (1986) reported on the successful reduction of self-injury through the use of alternate stimulation. They used vibration and visual stimulation (a flashing red light) to achieve decreases in self-injury.

Attention

Lovaas, Freitag, Gold, and Kassorla (1965) demonstrated that self-injury could serve the function of obtaining social attention. Carr and Durand (1985) provided additional evidence of social attention serving as a purpose for self-injury.

Escape

Self-injury can also serve the purpose of providing the individual with a way to escape from an unpleasant situation. Carr and Durand (1985) demonstrated that self-injury is more likely to occur when difficult tasks are presented. Self-injury often provides the individual with a way out of an unpleasant situation.

Favorite Events or Activities

Observations and informal discussions with caregivers provide many examples of misguided but well-intentioned staff who inadvertently rewarded self-injury. Staff and family members have reported using favorite drinks and foods, back rubs, soothing music, and favorite activities to terminate episodes of self-injury. Increases in self-injury following such intervention suggest that it can serve the purpose of getting the individual certain desirable items or events.

INTERVENTION PLAN

All of the considerations discussed in Chapter Ten for aggression can be valid in a discussion of self-injury. The critical elements of an intervention plan are also the same. A plan for management of self-injury will most likely need to address these topics: supervision, teaching alternative acceptable behaviors, rewarding cooperative behavior, and providing a way for the individual to achieve his or her functions without self-injury. Critical considerations in the management of self-injury include scheduling issues, motivation, sensory consequences, interventions with verbal individuals, extinction, prevention of injury, and pica.

Scheduling Issues

Plans for high-frequency self-injury will need to emphasize scheduling issues. As many researchers have reported, absence of activity can be a setting event for self-injury. Management plans will often need to specify active, functional schedules.

Motivation

If self-injury serves the purpose of escape, the behavior plan might need to include motivation for cooperating with the schedule of tasks and activities and engaging in behaviors that are incompatible with self-injury. The plan might also include motivation for keeping the skin or body parts in healthy condition. Motivation can be provided through schedules of positive reinforcement. These schedules were presented in Chapter Four.

Sensory Consequences

Management of self-injury may also need to address the sensory aspects of the problem. As discussed, several researchers have demonstrated that self-injury can be reduced by providing alternate sensory stimuli. Although not all self-injury is maintained by its sensory consequences, this possibility is difficult to rule out; therefore, for nonverbal individuals with frequent self-injury, it seems prudent to include alternate sensory experience in the environment and on the schedule.

Considerations for Verbal Individuals

Plans for individuals with autism with verbal skills and moderate mental retardation may need to emphasize the teaching of alternate responses to setting events and high risk antecedent conditions. Plans might need to include training on how to ask for assistance, how to disclose problems, how to respond to others' teasing, how to accept criticism, and how to respond to disappointments or changes. Examples of these strategies are covered in Chapter Seven on self-management.

Extinction

As with aggression, a method for putting the self-injury on extinction must be included. The plan should call for no direct verbal response; that is, no comment should be made about the actual self-injury except for possible redirection to task. If the individual has marks from the self-injury, no comment should be made about the marks. If necessary, medical attention can be given, but no verbal attention. The limits to extinction are in cases where the individual might cause harm to him- or herself. Light tapping on the face or head might not be of concern but violent head banging on a table is a problem.

Prevention of Injury

Prevention of injury can sometimes be accomplished by blocking. The caregiver can be alert to the onset of self-injury, then physically block the blow. For example, if an individual is about to hit him- or herself in the ear, the counselor can block the blow to the ear. Positioning can also help. If an individual is known to bang his arm on a table, the caregiver can walk between the individual and the table.

Sometimes the self-injury can be prevented by providing verbal instructions and feedback during risky situations. For example, Milton had a habit of getting into the car, then slamming his head into his knees. This behavior was prevented by instructing him, as he entered the car, to sit upright and keep his head still. He was then praised for doing so. In some cases, it might be necessary to prevent serious injury from the behavior. These procedures are covered under emergency procedures in Chapter Ten.

Pica

Pica is a form of self-injury that needs special consideration. Pica, the ingestion of nonedible substances, is a behavior that is occasionally present in persons with autism, and it is a behavior that can be life threatening as well as job threatening. Adults with autism occasionally engage in pica for years, and they have ingested or attempted to ingest such items as laundry detergents, paper clips, paper, bottle caps, metal objects, cigarette butts, and threads torn from shirts, blankets, and sheets.

Modification of pica in integrated community settings involves several components. The strategy needs to be individualized to take into account the needs of the person and the characteristics of the setting. Any given case might use any combination of the following procedures:

1. Staff might limit access to desired items to prevent or minimize the likelihood that pica might occur. For example, if James typically eats cigarette butts, the most effective and economical solution is to keep ashtrays and open trash areas free of cigarette butts. Lyn's case is another example. She likes to drink cleaning fluids, so cleaning fluids are kept in a locked cabinet in her group home. While it is recommended that limiting access to desired nonedibles be done to the fullest extent possible, obviously, in many cases, this is not entirely practical. For example, if an individual shreds cloth for ingestion, it may not be possible to remove all cloth from the environment, as this would involve not only bed linens, but clothing as well.

2. In those cases where limited access to desired items is not feasible, then vigilante supervision may be necessary, particularly if the pica is life threatening. For example, a person who ingests metal objects is at high risk for physical injury. Such an individual needs close supervision when in environments containing metal objects so that ingestion can be prevented.

3. If an individual begins to reach for an inedible object, then the caregiver should intervene at that point, before he or she actually takes the object. Trying to take the object from the individual could result in aggression. For example, if the individual reaches for a paper clip, the caregiver should take the clip first. Any verbal redirection should be as brief as possible, such as, "Put your hands on the (task). This is done to avoid inadvertently reinforcing pica with undue attention.

4. It might be helpful to teach the person to discriminate between edibles and inedibles. The individual can be shown different items and told which are edible and which are not. The person can then be asked to make the discriminations and can be rewarded for making correct discriminations. The fact is, however, that in most cases the individual knows very well what is edible and what is not. Discrimination training cannot hurt, but it is questionable how much it helps.

5. Access to similar, more acceptable items to eat might be helpful. This component involves providing the individual access to foods that are similar in texture to the desired nonedibles. For example, frequent access to celery might result in decreases in pica in an individual who enjoys eating shredded cloth, or crunchy foods might be a satisfying alternative to a person who enjoys eating paper clips. If items similar in texture do not exist, then liberal access to any favorite edibles should be provided.

6. It might be important to provide positive reinforcement for keeping the mouth clear of inedibles. Individuals who engage in pica might do so for sensory stimulation; however, it is also possible that the behavior is maintained by other positive reinforcers. In order to discourage pica, positive reinforcers should be provided on a designated schedule when the individual's mouth is clear. Praise for having a clean, clear mouth might be a sufficient reinforcer, but in some cases it might be necessary to use primary reinforcers. Use of food as a reinforcer for having a clear mouth can be particularly useful, as it also provides the opportunity to enjoy alternate, more acceptable sensory stimuli. A functional analysis of the behavior might indicate what reinforcer is maintaining the behavior, and that reinforcer can be used to encourage a clear mouth.

7. A functional analysis of the behavior might provide information on what reinforcer is maintaining the behavior. If possible, an intervention plan should include a severing of the connection between pica and the reinforcement. For example, if it appears that attention is reinforcing the pica behavior, then the plan should stipulate that when pica occurs, attention should be minimized. Even if the individual needs to be prevented from ingesting the item, social attention should be minimized during the prevention.

8. Instruction may be helpful. In some cases, it might be possible to teach the individual an alternate response to the desired items. For example, if a person eats cigarette butts, it might be possible to teach him to throw cigarette butts in the trash can.

CASE 1

Ricky was an 18-year-old male with autism and a history of severe self-injury, including banging his head and pulling his hair. His verbal expression was limited to two- and three-word phrases. Interpersonal relationships were impaired and generally consisted of either withdrawal or clinging behavior. Review of his records indicated that previous interventions in past programs included medication following aggressive episodes, restraint, and seclusion. Ricky attended a community-based school for adolescents with severe autism, and he lived in a group home in the community where he was supervised by trained residential counselors.

Procedures

Data Collection Data were collected using a 5-minute time block. For each 5-minute period of the day, beginning at 9:00 A.M. and ending at 4:00 P.M., instructors working with Ricky recorded whether or not hitting others or self occurred. Data were also collected once per hour on the antecedents and consequences of each aggressive episode.

Functional Analysis A functional analysis of this behavior indicated that self-injury was usually accompanied by verbal requests for food, suggesting that self-injury served the purpose of obtaining food. Presentation of tasks was also an antecedent to self-injury, suggesting that self-injury served the purpose of escape. Attempts by staff to have Ricky move from one location to another (e.g., from the hall to the room), suggested that self-injury was used as an escape from demands. Since some incidents of self-injury were severe, it was often necessary for staff to physically prevent Ricky from causing injury to others or self. Thus, the possibility was presented that this physical contact was serving as a positive reinforcer.

Intervention Plan The intervention plan had several components. First, since the frequency of self-injurious behavior was so high, that is, it occurred almost continuously, a variable interval 3-minute schedule was implemented. Staff were to provide a positive reinforcer approximately every 3 minutes (plus or minus 1 minute) to Ricky if he exhibited any of the following target behaviors: hands in lap, hands on work materials, hands on leisure material, hands by side. Positive reinforcers offered were food snacks and physical proximity of staff, including allowing Ricky to put his arm around his instructor. Large quantities of favorite foods were presented as reinforcers for targeted acceptable behavior.

A second component was free access to food on request. Any time Ricky asked for food, staff were instructed to immediately provide him with what he requested. The rationale for this liberal policy was that Ricky would learn that verbal requests worked and head banging was not necessary. Third, short tasks were presented in a one-to-one instructional format. If Ricky worked on the task or activity, a positive reinforcer was presented. If Ricky chose not to work on the activity, no attempt was made to force him. Fourth, all deliveries of reinforcers were accompanied by specific praise, and finally, staff were trained to quickly handle self-abusive situations. If Ricky became self-abusive, he was verbally redirected to the task at hand. If self-abuse continued, presenting risk of injury, then Ricky was physically prevented from harming himself or others. He was redirected to the ongoing activity as soon as he was willing to respond to verbal instructions. The instructions provided to staff are as follows:

1. Reinforcers will be provided on a variable interval schedule. Target behaviors are any appropriate, cooperative, non–self-injurious behaviors including walking without physical assistance with hands by side, doing anything with hands but self-abusing, sitting with hands in lap, working on a task or chore, coming to location when asked, staying in assigned location, initiating social interaction or an acceptable activity, engaging in conversation, handing over materials or objects when asked, and riding in van or car without self-abusing.

2. Every 3–5 minutes (plus or minus 5 minutes) Ricky will receive a reinforcer contingent on a cooperative behavior. He will receive the reinforcer while displaying one of the target behaviors. Specific verbal praise will accompany the delivery of the reinforcer. Vary the target behaviors that are being reinforced. For example, if on one occasion he is rewarded for keeping his hands by his side, next time he might be rewarded for working well on a task.

3. Reinforcers to be used include: food or drink reinforcers that Ricky enjoys, such as ice cream, cookies, candy, chicken, popsicles, chips, and pretzels; cold items like a cold water bottle, an ice pack, or leaning up against a cold window; tools that Ricky enjoys holding and manipulating, such as a pair of tongs; and physical contact such as the counselor putting an arm around Ricky, allowing Ricky to put his arm around a staff member, shaking hands, or other forms of physical contact that Ricky might like and that are acceptable to staff.

4. Specific praise should accompany the delivery of the reinforcers. Ricky should be told exactly what he did to earn the reinforcer. His name should be used to get his attention and praise should be given enthusiastically. Reinforcers should be delivered while Ricky is displaying a target behavior, or in the case of a task, immediately after the task is finished. Do not give Ricky a reinforcer within 3 minutes of self-injury, and no reinforcer should be given during self-injury. Reinforcers should not be promised in advance but delivered spontaneously during periods of good behavior. Do not mention reinforcers when Ricky is misbehaving, and do not discuss Ricky's misbehavior with him.

5. Ricky should be praised approximately every 5 minutes for displaying one of the target behaviors. All praise should be specific with exact reference to what Ricky did to earn the praise (e.g., "Good job vacuuming, Ricky," not "Good job.") Praise should not be given

within 3 minutes of uncooperative behavior, but should occur during good behavior.

6. Ricky should have a fairly busy schedule. In the house, at least one task or chore should be scheduled each half hour. A picture schedule should be used so that Ricky can see what his activities are. The picture schedule should include, in the order of occurrence, all tasks, chores, activities, meals, and other events planned for the day. Ricky should be shown the picture schedule before each task or activity so that he can see what is next. After the task, he can return to the picture schedule and indicate completion, either with a tab or by removing the picture. Prior to the next activity, Ricky can be shown the next picture and asked, "What's next?" If he is correct, he should be praised, "Yes, it's time to sweep." If he is incorrect, he should be told, "It's time to sweep."

7. Ricky seems to enjoy using tools to fix things. He should be given the opportunity to do this, especially at home, at least once per day.

8. The prompt hierarchy should be used when presenting familiar tasks.

9. If Ricky asks for something that is on hand, he should be given it. If this is not possible, he should be told why, then redirected to his activity.

10. Ricky should be physically prevented from self-injury only in those instances where he is likely to hurt himself. If physical prevention is needed, this should be done by staff trained in physical management of self-abuse. The only words spoken at that time should be, "You need to keep your hands still." If Ricky is not actually harming himself, the self-injury should be ignored. Staff should avoid eye contact with him during self-injury. In any case, nothing should be said to Ricky about his self-injury.

11. Data on self-injury is to be taken on a 5-minute time block. Severe episodes where injury occurs or where he must be held for more than 5 minutes, should be recorded on ABC forms.

Results

The percentage of 5-minute intervals per day in which Ricky's hands were engaged in acceptable activities (as listed above) are shown in Figure 11.1, starting with baseline (day 1) and continuing for 56 days. The figure shows a gradual and uneven increase in the amount of time that Ricky spent engaged in nonaggressive, noninjurious activities. By day 13, acceptable use of hands was above 90%. After 2 years of intervention, the reinforcement schedule was thinned to a variable interval 15-minute schedule (plus or minus 10 minutes). A follow-up data probe 1 year after this schedule change indicated that Ricky had 99% acceptable use of hands (i.e., no head banging) at his group home and 96.4% at his job. A second follow-up data probe done 2 years after the schedule change revealed the percentage for acceptable use of hands was 98%

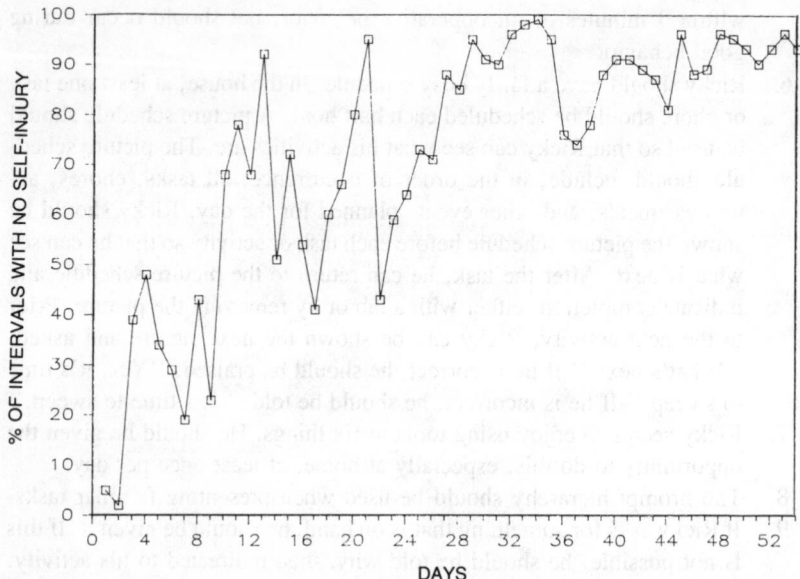

Figure 11.1. Percent of 5-minute intervals in which Ricky had no self-injury. (From Smith, M. [1985]. Managing the aggressive and self-injurious behavior of adults disabled by autism. *Journal of The Association for Persons with Severe Handicaps, 10,* [4], 231; reprinted by permission.)

percent. It is also important to note that at the time of both follow-ups, Ricky was successfully working in a supported employment program with the assistance of a job coach.

CASE 2

Jared was a 23-year-old male untestable by standard measures of intelligence with severe autism and a history of life-threatening pica, including ingestion of paper and metal objects such as paper clips and bottle caps. Jared was nonverbal with a tendency to bite should one attempt to prevent him from putting an item in his mouth. Jared was employed at a department store in the stockroom. During the course of his day, he attempted to ingest paper clips, paper, and plastic.

Procedures

Data Collection A daily frequency count was kept of ingestion of nonedibles, or of attempts to do so. Data were also kept on the antecedents and on the consequences of the incidents. Antecedents were defined as who was with Jared, what was happening prior to the incident, and when and where the incident occurred. Consequences were considered to be whatever events or responses occurred in Jared's environment immediately following the behavior.

Functional Analysis   A functional analysis was done using the anteced-ent and consequence information to determine the purpose of the behavior for Jared. The data indicated that pica behavior may have occurred for any (or all) of the following reasons: sensory stimulation, attention, or task avoidance.

Intervention Plan   The intervention plan implemented included a num-ber of components. First, a list of desired target behaviors was developed. Several of these behaviors were incompatible with pica, such as having a clear mouth, correctly using paper, working on task, eating his own food, keeping hands on work materials, and staying in assigned location (usually, attempts at pica were accompanied by leaving work station to obtain the object).

Any of these desired behaviors were reinforced on a variable interval 15-minute schedule. Since pica occurred frequently, a 15-minute schedule was chosen to provide ample opportunity for reinforcement within the bounds of feasibility at the worksite. A second component was easy access to sensory stimuli similar to the desired object of pica. Jared was given frequent access to stimuli through positive reinforcement and through snacks.

Third, to prevent pica, counselors were alert to the position of Jared's hands at all times. If he began to reach for an inedible object, he was given short verbal instructions to return his hands to his task or to a more acceptable area. If he did not comply immediately, then physical assistance was given. It was important to prevent him from obtaining the object in the first place, because attempts to take it from his mouth had resulted in his biting staff. Fourth, staff were instructed not to respond to pica or attempts at pica. Jared's hands were to be redirected to a more acceptable location (either verbally or physically), and a period of at least 3 minutes was to follow during which there was no praise or discussion. The only exception was if staff were instructing or teaching prior to the attempt, then they were to continue with the instructions after redirection. Jared's attempts to eat nonedibles were not discussed with him in any way, as previous experience had indicated that this type of discussion had resulted in an escalation of pica.

Finally, Jared was given limited access to desired objects. A small vacuum cleaner was kept at the worksite, and Jared's work area was vacuumed before work and several times throughout the day in order to keep the area as clear of paper clips as possible. The intervention instructions provided to staff are as follows:

1. Cooperative behaviors that are incompatible with pica will be rewarded on a variable interval schedule of positive reinforcement. Target behav-iors for reinforcement are any appropriate, cooperative, non–self-inju-rious, nonaggressive behaviors including attempting to communicate ac-ceptably, working on task with the maximum amount of independence, staying in assigned location, keeping hands on work or to self when being instructed, using papers correctly (i.e., not eating paper), eating his own

food (as opposed to food or drink that belongs to others), and keeping his work area clean.

2. Every 15 minutes (plus or minus 10 minutes) Jared should receive a reinforcer contingent on a cooperative behavior, and should receive the reinforcer only while displaying one of the target behaviors. Specific verbal praise will accompany the delivery of the reinforcer.

3. Reinforcers to be used include: food or drink reinforcers such as crunchy foods like granola, granola bars, or any other food or drink that Jared might enjoy; and activity reinforcers such as playing with water in the sink, going for a walk, or other favorite activities. Reinforcers should be alternated to ensure variety and to keep Jared interested and should be delivered while Jared is engaging in the behavior, or in the case of a task, as soon as he finishes. If Jared is destructive, sits on the floor, leaves assigned location, is aggressive, or attempts to eat a nonedible, there should be at least a 10-minute period during which no reinforcer is delivered.

4. Jared should be told why he is getting the reinforcer. Specific praise should accompany the delivery of the reinforcer.

5. If Jared goes off task or displays uncooperative behavior for more than 1 or 2 minutes, then he should be directed back to task using the prompt hierarchy.

6. Staff need to be alert at all times as to the position of Jared's hands in order to prevent pica. If he begins to reach for an inedible object, he should be given verbal instructions to return his hands to his task or to a more acceptable location. If he does not comply immediately, then physical assistance should be given. It is important that he be prevented from obtaining the object in the first place, because attempts to take it from his mouth have resulted in his biting staff.

7. Once his hands have been redirected to a more acceptable location (either verbally or physically), there should be a period of at least 3 minutes during which any praise or discussion is withheld. The only exception to this is if staff are instructing or teaching prior to the attempt, then they should continue with the instructions after redirection. Jared's attempt to eat nonedibles should not be discussed with him in any way.

8. It is important that Jared be praised frequently for having a clear, clean mouth and for keeping his hands in acceptable locations. Furthermore, reinforcers provided under his variable interval schedule should frequently be given for clean mouth and hands in acceptable location. It is also suggested that Jared have easy access to favorites edibles. A snack pouch can be used that contains crunchy items and celery, and Jared can even be given unlimited access to the snack pouch.

9. Staff should be aware that attempting to take objects from Jared's mouth can be dangerous, and in the past has resulted in staff being bitten. Staff

should avoid being in a position where he can bite them. Furthermore, staff should always be situated in such a way that they can move away should he try to bite them.

Results

The total number of incidents of pica per day are shown in Figure 11.2. Days 1–7 are baseline during which time Jared was rewarded for being on task and in his area, but the full plan described was not yet implemented. Intervention data are shown for days 8–41. A significant decrease in pica occurred during this period. Days 42–53 was a period during which new staff did not implement the plan, and instead, staff would lecture him about his pica. An immediate increase in pica was seen. At day 54 the program was again reliably implemented and a subsequent drop in pica occurred. A follow-up probe done 2 years later revealed no incidents of pica in the month probed. Jared remains at risk for pica only if his plan is not reliably implemented.

Considerations

The incidence of pica decreased significantly following a multi-part behavior program that included positive reinforcement for incompatible behavior, alternate sensory stimuli, and limiting, as much as possible, access to nonedi-

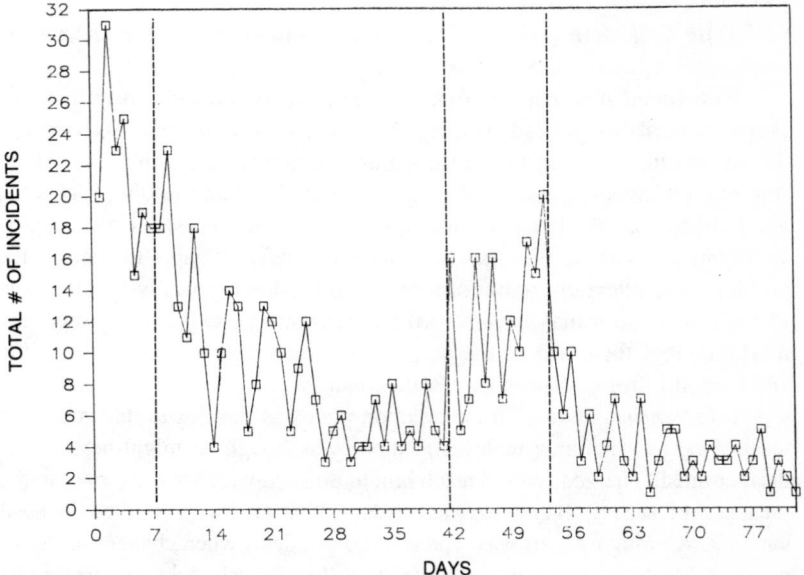

Figure 11.2. Total number of incidents per day for baseline (days 1–6), intervention (days 7–41), no intervention (days 42–53), and intervention (days 54–82). (From Smith, M. [1987]. Treatment of pica in an adult disabled by autism by differential reinforcement of incompatible behavior. *Journal of Behavior Therapy and Experimental Psychiatry, 10,* 287; © 1987 Pergamon Press; reprinted by permission.)

bles. The present program was more effective than its forerunner that simply called for positive reinforcement of other behavior.

Although the behavior had decreased to zero in the follow-up probe, the behavior programming remains in place because of the high medical risks of the pica. It is likely that intensive, ongoing programming may always be necessary in order to keep pica at a low level and prevent self-injury.

CASE 3

Adults with autism who are verbal and have low-average or above-average levels of intelligence may engage in occasional self-injury involving head banging, self-scratching, self-kicking, and self-hitting. Typically, self-injury in this group occurs less often than in nonverbal adults with profound retardation. Case 3 demonstrates management of self-injury in an older man who occasionally banged his head.

Albert was a 48-year-old man with autism and low-average intelligence. He was fully verbal. Under normal conditions, Albert was cooperative and independent both in his group home and at work. However, whenever an unexpected change occurred, Albert became self-injurious. He became red in the face, shook his head, then banged his head.

Procedures

Data Collection The antecedents and consequences of each incident were recorded.

Functional Analysis A functional analysis was done to determine the purposes of Albert's head banging. Several antecedents were noted where Albert was likely to bang his head: an unexpected change in his schedule or routine, a disappointment (such as going to the bank and finding it closed), and failure to receive letters from his parents at expected times. Head banging was typically followed by explanations from staff, attempts to remedy the problem, and attention in the form of comfort. Albert typically left the room to head bang, so it may have served the purpose of escape. It appeared that head banging, then, served the purposes of obtaining comfort and attention and escaping from tasks under certain conditions.

Intervention Plan An intervention plan was developed that sought to teach Albert to continue with his routine even though he might be upset or disappointed. The goal was to teach him to proceed with his work even in the presence of setting events and antecedents that typically resulted in head banging. Although Albert was typically independent, when changes or disappointing situations occurred, he ceased to follow his schedule, and instead he would head bang. The intervention plan provided for increased supervision during designated setting events and antecedents, and the plan sought to teach him to continue with his work or activity despite the disappointment. He was trained on the "that's too bad program," introduced in Chapter Seven. This program taught Albert that even though certain unfortunate events occurred, that's too bad, but life must go on. The instructions given to caregivers are as follows:

1. Staff should be aware that Albert becomes agitated and may head bang if there is a major, unexpected change in his schedule. Examples are canceled doctor appointments or going to a store or bank to find it closed. Also, Albert can become self-injurious if his parents are out of town and he does not receive a letter when he expects one.
2. If Albert brings up a problem or if he appears agitated (such as becoming red in the face and shaking his head or his hands), the counselor should help identify the problem and assist him with a solution if possible. If there is no solution and Albert appears agitated, the counselor should say sympathetically, "Albert, that's too bad. Are you upset about (name the problem, if known)?" If Albert says "yes," the counselor should say, "I can understand how you would feel, but now it's time to (state name of ongoing activity or task)." Albert can be encouraged to say, "that's too bad."
3. If Albert appears agitated he should be closely supervised. Staff should stay with him and give him gentle instructions to proceed with his scheduled activity. Staff should remain with him, giving gentle instructions, until he no longer appears agitated and remains on task independently.

Results

Before the intervention plan was implemented, Albert was having an incident of self-injury about once a week. Following implementation of the plan, incidents decreased to about one every 6–12 months. An interesting aspect of the results is that Albert came to self-manage his own behavior. Initially, staff would need to stay with Albert for up to 2 hours after a disappointing event, gently redirecting him to task with the "that's too bad" approach. After several months, Albert would take care of the problem himself. After a disappointment, he would say, "that's too bad," and then would proceed with his ongoing activity. After about 6 months of "that's too bad" training, Albert wrote the following note to a supervisor.

> Dear Doreen, Thank you for the brownies. They were very good. Jack ate all my brownies. That's too bad. Love, Albert.

CASE 4

Wesley was a 22-year-old man with severe autism and a history of severe self-injury, including head banging, ear banging, self-kicking, and self-pinching. Wesley could speak in short phrases or sentences, and usually he used language exclusively to make requests. Prior to his entry into an integrated community program attempts to modify his self-injury included electric shock.

Procedures

Data Collection   Initially, Wesley's self-injury occurred up to 400 times per day. Therefore, ABC data could not be collected on each incident. The number of incidents per day was recorded, and ABC data were collected on a sample basis.

Functional Analysis   Analysis of the data suggested that self-injury served several functions for Wesley. He would self-injure during the following circumstances: after being on task for several minutes, when his job coach or counselor walked away, or when his verbal requests were not met. Wesley had a tendency to become attached to certain items such as bandages and hats. If he was denied access to these items, he would self-injure. He would also engage in self-injury during waiting situations or changes in routine. Additionally, Wesley often ruminated, and if asked to clear his mouth he would self-injure. He often kept lint balls in his hands, and attempts to have him clear his hands resulted in self-injury.

Consequences to self-injury were attention and verbal reprimands. Occasionally, staff would give him the desired item, such as the bandage or hat in order to get him to cease. If Wesley self-injured after staff made a request, staff would often abandon any follow-through efforts on the request. The functions of self-injury then appeared to be: to escape from tasks, to escape from demands, to increase attention, to have verbal interaction or physical interaction and to have demands met.

It was also noted that whenever Wesley would walk by a table or other hard surface, he would bang his elbow against it. This behavior continued even after staff no longer responded to this form of self-injury with either physical or verbal intervention. It is possible, then, that the self-injury occasionally served the purpose of sensory stimulation.

Intervention Plan   An intervention plan was developed that sought to replace the many functions of self-injury and to provide motivation for more cooperation with daily routine and requests. Self-injury was severe, so the plan also needed to include a component on preventing tissue damage from self-injury.

Wesley's plan contained many components that were similar to Ricky's plan. Wesley's plan included alternate sensory stimuli and a picture schedule that clarified demands and signaled when favorite events would occur. The plan also provided specific instructions to staff on how to deal with antecedents to self-injury, such as removal of lint balls or clearing the mouth of regurgitated food. Finally, the plan gave detailed information on how to prevent tissue damage. The instructions to staff are as follows:

1. A daily pictorial, captioned activity schedule should be posted in Wesley's house. Two schedules should be posted, one in the living room (which displays pictures representing major activities, chores, self-care activities, meals, and bedtime in order of occurrence), and one in the bedroom (which displays the bedtime routine and wake-up routine). The picture schedule for a given day should be posted prior to the start of Wesley's day. Prior to each activity, Wesley should be shown the picture on the schedule and should be told, "Wesley, now it is time to (activity or task)." After completing the activity, Wesley should return to the picture schedule, turn over the picture of the completed activity, and move on to the next picture. Wesley should be praised for following his schedule.

2. Cooperative behavior should be rewarded on a variable interval 20-minute schedule of positive reinforcement. Target behaviors for reinforcement are any on task behavior, cooperative behavior, or any acceptable behavior that is incompatible with aggression or self-injury. These behaviors include but are not limited to the following: working on task with the maximum amount of independence, having hands on work materials or leisure materials, having hands on lap during leisure without self-injury, walking through a room keeping arms at side (i.e., not banging into objects), having a clear mouth, eating his meals with his arms/hands used for eating or resting on the table, waiting in assigned location independently if counselor has to leave briefly, attending to and following picture schedule, having clear skin (i.e., no marks from self-injury).

3. Every 20 minutes (plus or minus 10 minutes) Wesley should receive a reinforcer contingent on a cooperative behavior. He should receive the reinforcer while displaying one of the target behaviors, and specific verbal praise should accompany the delivery of the reinforcer. The target behaviors that are being reinforced should be varied. For example, if on one occasion he is rewarded for keeping his feet on the floor, next time he might be rewarded for working well on a task.

4. Reinforcers to be used include tactile reinforcers such as smooth stones, silky scarves, fuzzy cards, rubber balls, clay, cotton, feathers, sandpaper, fishnet, yarn, sponges, and pine cones. The counselor should encourage Wesley to hold and feel the object for about 5 minutes. Lotion, after shave, or cologne can also be used to spread on the skin, and activity reinforcers can be provided, such as drawing, playing with clay, time with airplane picture, soaking hands in water or other water-related activities. Reinforcers should be alternated to ensure variety, with tactile or lotion reinforcers being used at least once within each hour period. There should be a minimum of 5 minutes of cooperative, noninjurious behavior before a reinforcer is delivered.

5.   Wesley should be told why he is getting the reinforcer, and all praise should be specific with exact references to what Wesley did to earn the reinforcer or praise. Wesley should especially be praised for any independence shown on tasks or activities and for any work that he does for which he did not wait to be prompted. If Wesley switches to a self-injurious behavior while he is being praised, the praise should be cut off and conversation should be changed to another topic. Wesley should not be praised while self-injuring or within 5 minutes of self-injuring, yelling, or picking his fingers.

6.   Prior to self-injury, Wesley will sometimes attempt to communicate his displeasure in more acceptable ways. Staff should be alert to his attempts at communication and should provide immediate response or assistance when possible to prevent escalation to self-injury.

7.   Wesley should have a box with his name and picture on it to hold a variety of favorite objects and activities. These objects can include pictures, cards, games, markers, papers, magazines, music, a radio, stickers, model airplanes, and other tactile reinforcers. A picture of this box should be included on Wesley's picture schedule following about 1 hour of work task activities.

8.   Wesley must clear his hands of all lint balls before doing tasks. The prompt hierarchy should be used to get him to clear his hands. During leisure time when he has no assigned tasks, lint balls should be ignored.

9.   Wesley should be allowed to have one mint after dinner. He must first complete dinner, clear his mouth, brush his teeth, and then he may have a mint.

10.   Wesley's mouth should be checked hourly to see if it is clear. The prompt hierarchy should be used to clear his mouth, and he should be praised when his mouth is kept clear independently.

11.   All praise guidelines should apply to mealtime. When Wesley throws his food in the trash, this act is considered termination of the meal, and the counselor should proceed with the next activity on the schedule.

12.   Wesley needs to be prevented from injuring himself. However, staff's attempts to prevent injury should be as low key and subtle as possible, and every attempt should be made to avoid giving him undue attention during self-injury. Wesley's counselor should attempt to prevent arm and elbow banging by walking between Wesley and any object he might normally bang. For example, if there is a table that he might bang on, the counselor should walk between Wesley and the table. The counselor should also remind Wesley of where to keep his arms while walking. If Wesley normally bangs on certain objects or furniture while on task, the counselor should be positioned to prevent banging. If the counselor sees Wesley about to ear bang or arm bang against a hard surface, he should attempt to physically prevent banging. If possible, Wesley should be

physically redirected to task. If Wesley is engaging in any behavior that could result in injury, and if he does not respond to verbal redirection, he should be physically prevented from causing injury and redirected back to task.

13. Staff should not discuss Wesley's self-injury with him at all. The only conversation that should be allowed during or immediately after self-injury is a verbal redirection to task. Wesley should be given specific instructions on where to keep his arms and legs prior to situations where banging and other self-injurious behavior occur. Situations where self-injury often occurs include walking to the table for a meal or activity, entering a car, finishing a task, when the counselor turns away, or walking to another room or across the room. The counselor should remind him of what to do prior to any of these situations.

Results

Prior to implementation of the behavior program, Wesley had as many as 400 incidents of self-injury per day. After rigorous implementation of the plan, Wesley averaged about six incidents per week, and his incidents were much less severe than in the past, consisting primarily of light taps to the side of his head. Wesley has been able to maintain his residence in a group home and a job in a supported employment program as a worker for a county department of transportation.

SUMMARY

Providing services to persons with self-injury is a huge responsibility. Not only are staff and/or family responsible for the general care of the individual, they also become responsible for the safety of that individual. This responsibility can be unrelenting, because in a sense, the person's own worst enemy is him- or herself. The person becomes a threat to his or her own well being. The management of self-injury and prevention of harm is difficult; however, it is far from impossible. Functions for self-injury have been described, and a careful functional analysis can reveal suggestions for a variety of purposes of the behavior, even in the most difficult cases. In fact, the higher the frequency, the more purposes self-injury typically serves.

Once functions are identified, intervention strategies easily fall into place. Strategies can be designed to meet many kinds of needs. Even the evasive function of sensory stimulation can be handled by providing alternate sensory stimuli. Despite the provision of rewards for cooperative behavior and strategies that seek to meet all of the individual's purposes and desires, self-injury still may occur. However, the rate should be greatly reduced as well as the severity. The remaining incidents can be managed by trained caregivers in such a way that the individual does not cause harm. Caregivers can be trained to block or otherwise prevent injury, so even though the behavior may exist at some level, there is no need for the behavior to overcome the environment. Instead, the environment can overcome the behavior.

REFERENCES

Baumeister, A., & Baumeister, A. (1978). Suppression of repetitive self-injurious behavior by contingent inhalation of aromatic ammonia. *Journal of Autism and Childhood Schizophrenia, 8*(1), 71–77.

Berkman, K., & Meyer, L. (1988). Alternative strategies and multiple outcomes in the remediation of severe self-injury: Going "all out" nonaversively. *Journal of The Association of Persons with Severe Handicaps, 13*(2), 76–86.

Burke, M., Burke, D., & Forehand, R. (1985). Interpersonal antecedents of self-injurious behavior in retarded children. *Education and Training of the Mentally Retarded, 20,* 204–208.

Carr, E.G. (1977). The motivation of self-injurious behavior: A review of some hypotheses. *Psychological Bulletin, 84*(4), 800–816.

Carr, E., & Durand, V. (1985). Reducing behavior problems through functional communication training. *Journal of Applied Behavior Analysis, 18,* 111–126.

Dorsey, M., Iwata, B., Ong, P., & McSween, T. (1980). Treatment of self-injurious behavior using a water mist: Initial response suppression and generalization. *Journal of Applied Behavior Analysis, 13,* 343–353.

Favell, J., McGimsey, J., & Jones, M. (1978). The use of physical restraint in the treatment of self-injury and as positive reinforcement. *Journal of Applied Behavior Analysis, 11,* 225–241.

Favell, J., McGimsey, J., & Schell, R. (1982). Treatment of self-injury by providing alternate sensory activities. *Analysis and Intervention in Developmental Disabilities, 2,* 83–104.

Iwata, B., Dorsey, M., Slifer, K., Bauman, K., & Richman, G. (1982). Toward a functional analysis of self-injury. *Analysis and Intervention in Developmental Disabilities, 2,* 3–20.

Juhrs, P., & Smith, M. (1989). Community based employment for persons with autism. In P. Wehman & J. Kregel (Eds.), *Supported employment and transition: Focus on excellence* (pp. 163–175). New York: Human Sciences Press.

Lovaas, O., Freitag, G., Gold, V., & Kassorla, I. (1965). Experimental studies in childhood schizophrenia: Analysis of self-destructive behavior. *Journal of Experimental Child Psychology, 2,* 67–84.

Luiselli, J.K. (1986). Modification of self-injurious behavior: An analysis of the use of contingently applied protective equipment. *Behavior Modification, 10*(2), 191–204.

Mace, F., & Knight, D. (1986). Functional analysis and treatment of pica. *Journal of Applied Behavior Analysis, 19,* 411–416.

Romanczyk, R., & Goren, E. (1975). Severe self-injurious behavior: The problem of clinical control. *Journal of Consulting and Clinical Psychology, 43,* 730–739.

Singh, N., & Bakker, L. (1984). Suppression of pica by overcorrection and physical restraint. *Journal of Autism and Developmental Disorders, 14,* 331–341.

Singh, N., & Winton, A. (1984). Effects of a screening procedure on pica and collateral behaviors. *Journal of Behavior Therapy and Experimental Psychiatry, 15,* 59–65.

Smith, M. (1987). Treatment of pica in an adult disabled by autism by differential reinforcement of incompatible behavior. *Journal of Behavior Therapy and Experimental Psychiatry, 10,* 285–288.

Tanner, B., & Zeiler, M. (1975). Punishment of self-injurious behavior using aromatic ammonia as the aversive stimulus. *Journal of Applied Behavior Analysis, 8,* 53–57.

Taylor, C., & Chamove, A. (1986). Vibratory or visual stimulation reduces self-injury. *Australia and New Zealand Journal of Developmental Disabilities, 12*(4), 243–248.

Willis, T., & LaVigna, G. (1988, May). *Non-aversive treatment of severe self-injury.* Paper presented to the annual convention of the Association for Behavioral Analysis, Philadelphia, PA.

Yeakel, M., Salisbury, L., Greer, S., & Marcus L. (1970). An appliance for autoinduced adverse control of self-injurious behavior. *Journal of Experimental Child Psychology, 10,* 159–169.

Chapter Twelve

Decelerating Destructive Behaviors

Some people with autism have destructive behaviors resulting in damage to property and possessions. Destruction of property and possessions can occur in a variety of forms, and although the form is not as important as the function, it is necessary to pinpoint the behavior with precision.

Relatively small personal possessions can be easily destroyed. Some individuals with autism will rip their clothes, tear paper, break dishes, and destroy lamps as well as break household appliances such as radios and stereos. Larger property can also be destroyed: furniture can be thrown and overturned; decorations such as wall hangings, paintings, and draperies can be torn down; walls and doors can be damaged by punches and kicks, and also by objects thrown; and windows can be smashed by direct contact or thrown objects. Occasionally property destruction can extend beyond the individual's home. There have been cases of individuals leaving their home, walking up the street, and destroying newspapers belonging to neighbors, or throwing chairs at passing cars when not well supervised.

Property destruction is not a behavior that only people with autism display, and conversely, not all people with autism destroy property. In fact, many individuals with autism are exceedingly careful with their possessions, as well as the possessions of others. However, when an individual with autism does have a destructive behavior, an intervention plan is a must since property destruction can threaten community and job adjustment. The purpose of this chapter is to explore strategies for decelerating destructive behaviors in people with autism.

PINPOINT AND MEASURE THE BEHAVIOR

Property destruction is generally an obvious behavior. Broken clocks, torn clothing, damaged furniture, and ripped drapes are all observable and measur-

215

able. Property destruction can be measured by the actual behavior that causes the destruction, or by its effects, for example, the number of watches broken. In some cases, records might be useful on both the behavior and its effects.

Tally

A tally can be kept by counting each act of property destruction. A tally provides a good measure of frequency, but it does not necessarily provide information on the severity of the incident. If property destruction occurs less than 10 times per day, a tally is probably a convenient measure.

Time Block

For high frequency property destruction, a time block might be necessary. If property destruction occurs more than 10 times per day, caregivers might need to use this type of procedure.

Structured Diary

A structured diary or a regular diary will be necessary in order to obtain information on antecedents and consequences of property destruction. If the behavior occurs more than about five times per day, a structured diary might need to be done on a time sample basis.

Record of Effects

Caregivers might want to keep data on the effects of property destruction. This might involve a count of the number of pieces of property that are destroyed. This type of data is useful when the behavior is not actually observed. For example, an individual might tear his or her clothes in private making it impossible to determine how many clothes-tearing incidents resulted in the clothes being ripped. It is possible, however, to count the number of ripped items.

FUNCTIONS OF PROPERTY DESTRUCTION

In many respects, property destruction can occur for the same reasons that aggression occurs, and in fact, in some cases property destruction occurs along with aggression. However, it is still necessary to explore functions that destructive behavior can serve, either independently or along with other problem behaviors.

Attention

It is possible for property destruction to serve the purpose of obtaining attention from others. Attention is a likely candidate when property destruction occurs in austere environments or in environments that lack structure and activity. Since destructive behavior in such environments almost always results in attention and activity, these events must be considered as possible purposes for the destruction itself. For nonverbal individuals, attention usually comes in the form of immediate feedback and increased staff activity of which the individual is the center of attention. For verbal individuals, attention can come in the form of questioning, reprimands, counseling, and even comforting following apologies for the property destruction.

Escape

Destructive behavior can be an effective means to escape from a task. If an individual is given a vacuum and is told to vacuum, then breaking the vacuum is an effective way to terminate the activity. In school situations, if an individual is presented with work materials, breaking those materials can be an efficient way to end the activity.

Restitution

Oftentimes, people who destroy property are told to clean up the mess. It is possible that cleaning is a preferred activity. If this is true, then for these individuals, destroying property serves the purpose of providing cleaning activities. A related reason is the possibility that the restitution often required after the destructive behavior can be rewarding. Martha is a young woman who occasionally broke items belonging to her roommates. Following her behavior, she would be taken shopping to replace the broken items. Martha's favorite activity was shopping. Property destruction increased as Martha discovered her new method for scheduling shopping trips.

Obtaining Assistance

Property destruction occasionally occurs when the individual is having difficulty with a task. Destroying the materials is often a way to obtain assistance from staff. Glenda's case is an example. When she had difficulty with a task at work, she would begin to destroy the task materials or tools. Then her job coach would rush over, ask what was wrong, and provide assistance. Glenda had learned that destroying property was an effective way to get assistance.

Self-Stimulation

The function of property destruction might also be self-stimulation. Although the behavior might not be repetitive and rapid, such as hand flapping or finger flicking, property destruction can still serve the purpose of creating stimulation. Case 3 presented in Chapter Eight concerned an individual who shredded clothing in order to have strings to handle and chew. Ripping paper occasionally serves a self-stimulatory function, as does dismantling electronic items, or stuffing of toilets.

It is not always possible to determine the exact function of the destructive behavior, however, by examining the antecedents and consequences, good guesses can be made. It can be valuable to simply examine the consequences, then assumptions can be made about those consequences that are maintaining the behavior. Intervention strategies can then be selected to teach the individual more acceptable ways of meeting his or her needs. If necessary, motivation can be provided for taking better care of property and engaging in more acceptable behaviors.

STRATEGIES FOR REDUCING PROPERTY DESTRUCTION

Many of the same strategies that are useful for management of other behavior problems are useful for reducing property destruction. The deciding factor in selection of strategies is not only the target behavior, but the functions that the behavior serves. Since property destruction can serve the same functions as aggression, self-injury, and even self-stimulation, the solutions to these behavior will have many strategies in common.

Destructive behavior, however, does have some distinguishing characteristics that will require specialized strategies. Property destruction, by definition, is a class of behaviors that results in property being destroyed. Therefore, any intervention plan for destructive behavior will have to include an element that covers prevention of property destruction, as well as instructional or motivational components.

Manipulation of Setting Events and Antecedents

Property destruction is often associated with certain setting events or antecedents, and these events can vary from one individual to the next. An intervention plan might include a component that seeks to eliminate or reduce certain setting events or antecedents. Those events that lend themselves to reduction or elimination would include circumstances such as long waiting periods, unclear expectations, disorganization, harsh interactions with staff, and difficult tasks. If events such as these are associated with property destruction, then an intervention plan can call for elimination or reduction of such events.

Setting events and antecedents that cannot be eliminated or reduced are those that are out of the control of staff. For example, property destruction may tend to occur during thunderstorms, and obviously, staff cannot halt thunderstorms. If setting events and antecedents cannot be controlled, then a strategy based on control of these events cannot be used. Other strategies will be necessary. Similarly, setting events or antecedents might also be important features of an individuals' environment, and in those cases, reduction of events would not be an appropriate strategy. For example, an individual might destroy property whenever a task is presented. Eliminating tasks would not be the strategy of choice.

Setting events or antecedents can be reduced or eliminated when adjustment to such events is not an integral part of the individual's goals. For example, if waiting in long lines is an antecedent for destructive behavior in stores, it might be best to simply take the individual to stores without lines. Later, as the individual's behavior improves, then caregivers can work on waiting behavior.

Scheduling

Destructive behavior might serve the purpose of creating interesting activities for the individual. Destroying the property itself might be interesting, or the clean-up or restitution that follows might be appealing to the individual with autism. When property destruction serves this function, it typically suggests that there is an absence of activity in that individual's schedule. In such cases, scheduling more activity might be a strategy of choice. Although these individuals with autism do not need to be kept occupied every minute of the day, there is often a minimum requirement of activity in order to prevent behavior problems such as property destruction that might result from too much free time.

If lack of activity increases the likelihood of property destruction, then the behavior plan should specify how often activities should be presented, and how much unstructured time should be allowed. The plan might also specify the types of activities to be included. It is often useful to alternate work and less preferred activities with favorite activities. Property destruction might also be a way to escape from tasks. If the functional analysis suggests that property destruction is serving that purpose, then it might be helpful to schedule more frequent breaks.

Self-Management

Self-management procedures can be useful in reducing or eliminating destructive behavior. As discussed in Chapter Seven, there are a variety of self-management procedures, and any of these procedures could conceivably be used to help with property destruction. The reader is referred to Chapter Seven for instructions on implementing these procedures.

Asking for Assistance   If the property destruction occurs when the individual is having difficulty with a task, it might be important to teach the person how to ask for help.

Self-Disclosure   Property destruction sometimes occurs when the individual has had some kind of conflict or disappointment in scheduling or with other people. For example, an individual might expect to be taken out to dinner, and when the plan is canceled, the individual might claim not to mind, then go to the bedroom and rip clothes. Where property destruction is associated with problems, then the self-disclosure program might be useful. Teaching individuals to seek help with their problems can prevent destructive behavior as a way of getting attention and sympathy.

That's Too Bad Occasionally property destruction occurs when there are disappointments or events over which staff have no control. In those cases, the individual needs to learn to carry on with the schedule even though there might have been a disappointment. The "that's too bad" program can be a useful tool to teach the individual to take disappointments in stride.

Stop Training Just as some individuals can learn to stop themselves from self-injury or self-stimulation, they can also be taught to stop themselves from destroying property. In some cases, stop training can be a valuable way to teach individuals not to destroy property.

Self-Monitoring and Self-Evaluation Teaching individuals to monitor and evaluate their own behavior has been useful in the management of property destruction. The individual might have a checklist of one to six items of acceptable behaviors that are expected. At designated intervals, the individual might record whether or not he or she was successful with each item.

In property destruction cases, a checklist item might state, "Respects property," or "Correct use of property." The individual is then taught specifically what the item means. In cases where property destruction involves several items, a checklist that separately lists the types of property involved might be useful.

Social Skills Training

Training in specific social skills can be an important strategy in the prevention of property destruction. Inadequate social skills might cause an individual with autism to resort to destructive behavior to have his or her needs met. An individual might be criticized at work, and as a result tear his or her clothes, or an individual might be bothered by a stranger on the bus, and go home and throw a clock. Teaching specific social skills can provide these people more acceptable ways of handling difficult situations. Teaching a person with autism how to accept constructive criticism provides a better response than clothes tearing; likewise teaching an individual to walk away from an annoying stranger on the bus or to seek help provides a better response than throwing a clock.

Alternate Sensory Stimuli

If the destructive behavior serves the purpose of providing stimulation, then it might be necessary to provide alternate, more acceptable, sensory stimuli. Often this strategy involves providing the objects that the individual likes destroying; however, the objects would obviously be discards without value. For example, an individual might enjoy tearing papers, so providing periodic access to unimportant papers to tear might prevent tearing of important documents. Similarly, providing authorized water play or water activities periodically can prevent toilet stuffing. Case 3 in Chapter Eight provides an example of providing discarded fabric to a young man who enjoys shredding fabrics.

Rewards for Respecting Property

It might be necessary to provide rewards for correct use of property. Whereas most of us find a clock merely useful for telling time, a person with autism might have for years used clocks for throwing. Although it is possible to teach people better ways to achieve their needs, it still may be necessary to provide motivation to handle property with care that for years was handled without care.

If the individual is using destructive behavior to escape from tasks, then a reward schedule might be necessary to provide incentive to do the task. For example, if an individual regularly throws tools when presented with a task, he or she might need motivation in order to do the task. If well motivated to do the task, then throwing tools as a means of escape would not be necessary. Rewards might be provided directly. Schedules of reinforcement might be necessary to provide concrete rewards for correct use of property, or rewards might be mediated through a point system or checklist system. "Correct use of property" might be one item on a checklist for which the person can receive a point. Points might be rewarded with praise or with tangible rewards. Issues involved in determining reinforcement schedules are similar as for any other behavior and are discussed in detail in Chapter Four.

Limit Setting

Sometimes the property destroyed belongs to someone other than the destroyer. In those cases, it is clear that the property must be replaced. However, the issue of replacement also arises when the individual destroys his or her own property. Obviously, some items must be replaced. For example, if the individual destroys a coat, then the coat must be replaced; if an individual rips a shoe, then the shoe must be repaired or replaced.

For some items, replacement is optional, and in those cases, limits can be set. If an individual has a tendency to break clocks, one form of intervention might be to limit the number of clocks that can be purchased each week or month.

Physical Prevention

As well as educational and motivational aspects of the behavior plan, it is also important to include a preventive component. Sometimes the individual displays behavioral signs that indicate property destruction might take place. The caregiver should compile a list of possible behavioral signs. Behavioral signs in verbal individuals might include threats, shouting, or refusal to follow directions. Behavioral signs in nonverbal individuals might include head shaking, refusal to follow direction, loud noises, foot stomping, self-injury, or aggression.

Certain environmental events, either antecedents or setting events, might be associated with property destruction. Environmental events can range for different individuals, but might include unexpected changes, unexpected cancellations, disturbances between others in the environment, or absence or presence of certain staff. The intervention plan should include a list of these events as well. The plan should also include a component that states that when the behavioral or environmental signs are present, then access to the property at risk should be limited. For example, Martin occasionally throws objects such as staplers, glasses, dishes, and lamps. However, there are signs that he might throw such objects. Staff should compile a list of such signs, and when any environmental or behavioral signs are present, then staff should temporarily remove heavy objects from his environment.

Long-term removal of certain items might be necessary in difficult cases. For example, an individual might have a long history of breaking dishes. In such a case, it might be best to simply keep plastic dishes in the home. Another individual might have a history of setting fires, so limited access or no access to matches might be prudent; or an individual might have a history of damaging floors with an iron, therefore unsupervised access to irons should be eliminated. In extreme cases, it might be necessary to make structural modifications to the residence in order to prevent property destruction or injury. For example, if an individual has a history of punching out windows, then plexiglas might be necessary. If it is not possible to remove items during high risk times, then it would be necessary to increase supervision at those times. For example, some individuals, under certain circumstances, might punch or kick holes in walls. In such cases, increased supervision would be mandatory when signs of property destruction are present.

Extinction

As with aggression, extinction must be included in the intervention plan. Due to the nature of property destruction, caregivers might be limited in their ability to totally put the behavior on extinction. However, to the greatest extent possible, extinction must be in place, and caregivers must minimize any possible payoff for the behavior. Several procedures can maximize extinction while minimizing the possibility of property damage and injury.

Give Specific Verbal Instructions If the individual is about to destroy property, and if there is time, the caregiver should tell the individual exactly what he or she should be doing. For example, if the individual is about to throw a chair, the caregiver should say, "Put the chair down."

Prevent Damage and Injury If there is not time, and if damage or injury might result from the individual's actions, the caregiver should try to physically prevent property destruction. Any caregiver who might need to intervene should be trained in such procedures.

Say Little Else During the incident, only necessary verbal instructions should be given. Nothing else should be said. There should be no lectures, promises, threats, or other discussion about the behavior.

Redirect as Soon as Possible As soon as the individual is willing to respond to verbal instructions, he or she should be directed back to the ongoing activity. There should be no further discussion of the incident. It is important that the individual be directed back to the ongoing activity. The individual should not clean the mess at that time. The best way to ensure extinction (i.e., breaking the connection between the property destruction and its payoff) is to stay strictly with the ongoing routine. There are several reasons for this. First, cleaning the mess might actually encourage property destruction. If the property destruction serves the purpose of escape from a task or activity, then having the individual clean the mess provides him or her with an escape from the activity.

Jim's case is an example of destructive behavior used for escape. Jim tears papers during math class. Instead of proceeding with math, he is told to clean up the mess. First, Jim learns that the way to get out of math is to tear papers because instead of doing math, he gets to clean up. By simply redirecting him to the math after he tears papers, he learns that tearing paper will not provide a way out of math.

Second, cleaning the mess might actually be a favorite activity, thus, it would serve as a positive reinforcer for property destruction. The individual learns that by destroying property he or she is allowed to clean, a favorite pasttime. Finally, some adults with autism will merely incorporate the cleaning up into the routine of property damage. For example, Jake smashes dishes, then automatically gets the broom to clean up the mess. Having to clean the mess does not discourage him from doing it again. Cleaning the mess has become part of the property damage routine for him.

Beware of Restitution Restitution seems to be a logical consequence of property destruction. If someone breaks something, he or she should replace it, but a major problem with restitution is that it might actually encourage property destruction. The individual might enjoy the act of restitution, thus the restitution itself might be rewarding. The reader is referred to Martha's case, discussed earlier in this chapter, for a good example of this problem.

When restitution is necessary in order to be fair to others, it is best not to directly involve the individual who did the damage. Caregivers should quietly take care of the restitution, not to let the individual off the hook, but to avoid the possibility of rewarding the behavior of property destruction.

As with any behavior problem, there may be many functions, and extinction might be difficult and incomplete. Extinction can be maximized, however, by avoiding discussion of the incident and proceeding with the schedule as quickly as possible. The only exception to such a rigid implementation of the extinction procedure would be cases in which the behavior is new, or the behavior is accidental. If an individual accidentally spills milk, of course there is no problem with cleaning the mess; or if an individual breaks something purposefully, and has never done such a thing before, then having him or her replace the item might be beneficial. However, if after several incidents of having the individual repair the damage, replace the item, or clean the mess, and if the behavior escalates, then it might be that restitution is encouraging the behavior. At that point a functional analysis should be done and extinction procedures considered.

CASE 1

Fred was a 24-year-old male with autism and with an IQ of 52 as measured by the WAIS—R. He had been living in a group residence for developmentally disabled adults for 3 years. For 16 years, Fred frequently tore his clothes.

Fred was on a behavior management program that provided a structured schedule, a written schedule for his use, and rewards for cooperative behavior. His behavior was evaluated hourly on a checklist format. If he received 90% of his points each week for specific target behaviors, he was rewarded with a favorite activity. Although his behavior management plan was successful in reducing aggression and other problem behaviors, the clothes tearing remained a problem.

Procedures

The stop training self-management strategy was implemented. This procedure is described in detail in Chapter Seven. Two practice sessions were held each evening in Fred's residence to teach him to stop himself from tearing his clothing. Fred was first instructed to begin to tear his shirt. As his hand approached his shirt, the counselor said firmly, "Stop! Hands down," and modeled the appropriate behavior of dropping hands to side. Fred was immediately praised when he stopped himself. He was told, "Good, you stopped yourself. You put your hands down." These practice sessions were repeated three times in a row, twice per evening.

Positive reinforcers were also given for intact clothing. If his pajamas were not torn in the morning, he was given a favorite food (yogurt), along with praise. If a nighttime inspection revealed no tears in his clothing, he was given a bowl of ice cream.

Results

During the baseline period of 2 weeks, Fred had four instances of clothes tearing. However, during the period prior to that, Fred had destroyed most of his wardrobe. At the time that stop training was started, he had only one pair of pants left. During the intervention period of 20 weeks, there was a total of only two instances of clothes tearing. Incident reports revealed a qualitative difference in clothes tearing. Before intervention, tearing was extensive and it was not unusual for Fred to rip apart a pair of blue jeans. During intervention the two incidents involved two small tears without destruction of the item.

Other Destructive Behavior

Fred has other forms of destructive behavior. He enjoys carrying around a portable transistor radio. However, he began destroying the radio, and then when he does not have his radio functioning, he cries and becomes aggressive.

In order to prevent the problems that occurred when his radio was broken, it was replaced each time. This strategy became expensive. During one month the radio was replaced three times. A very simple procedure was implemented that eliminated the problem. Fred was told that he could buy as many as two radios each month. After Fred was given this set limit, there were no further instances of radio breaking.

CASE 2

Evan was a 24-year-old man with severe autism and no verbal language skills. He had a severe problem with property destruction such as throwing shoes, heavy objects, and lamps, and regularly breaking windows, lamps, and other household items.

Procedures

Data Collection A structured diary form was filled out for each incident of property destruction. The structured diary included information on the antecedents of the behavior, the behavior itself, and the consequences of the behavior.

Functional Analysis A functional analysis suggested that property destruction served at least two functions for Evan—attention and creating activity. Property destruction often followed periods of no activity, suggesting that it served the purpose of creating activities that were preferable to doing nothing. After destructive behavior, Evan received a great deal of attention as staff attempted to calm him down. Due to the severity of the outbursts, additional staff were often called to assist; often he was required to clean up the mess, which provided even more activity.

Intervention Plan The goal of Evan's intervention plan was to eliminate the need for him to destroy property. In order to meet that goal, several strategies were implemented. Changes were necessary in the original plan, due to lack of improvement.

Rewards for Cooperative Behavior Evan was placed on a variable interval 15-minute schedule of reinforcement (VI 15). On this schedule, he was rewarded about every 15 minutes for cooperative behavior. Rewards included favorite nutritious foods and drinks, physical affection such as back rubs and pats on the back, and access to favorite objects. Favorite activities were also used as rewards, such as riding his bike, twirling in the yard, and running and jumping.

Frequent Praise Since the functional analysis suggested that attention was a factor in property destruction, Evan's intervention plan called for praise every 5 minutes for cooperative behavior.

Busy Schedule Evan was given a structured, busy schedule. His schedule included at least one activity every half hour. Also, since the period following dinner was an antecedent for property destruction, his schedule called for an activity to be scheduled immediately after dinner.

Picture Schedule A picture schedule of Evan's daily chores and activities was posted in his residence. Staff used the picture schedule to show him the upcoming activities.

Limited Access to Breakable Objects Evan was likely to throw heavy and dangerous objects such as ashtrays, knives, scissors, dishes, and glasses. His plan called for close supervision when around such objects, and also instructed staff not to leave these objects lying around. Additionally, only plastic plates were kept in the home.

Extinction Any episode of property destruction was to be followed with instructions directing him to the previously scheduled activity. He was not asked to clean up the mess.

Modifications to Plan

Evan's original plan included a reward every 30 minutes. His first plan did not address his schedule, and his behavior did not improve under this original plan; therefore a new functional analysis was done. The reward schedule was changed to a reward every 15 minutes. At that time, the busy schedule was included in the plan, along with an activity after dinner.

Results

The results of Evan's intervention plan are shown in Figure 12.1. The graph shows the total number of incidents of property destruction per month for the month prior to intervention, and for the following 40 months. Evan did not improve during the original plan that called for rewards approximately every 30 minutes, so the plan was changed. A VI 15-minute schedule of reinforcement was implemented, as well as a more active schedule. Under this plan, the behavior was reduced to zero.

Since Evan did so well for several months, the reinforcement schedule was changed back to a VI 30-minute schedule. This proved disastrous since

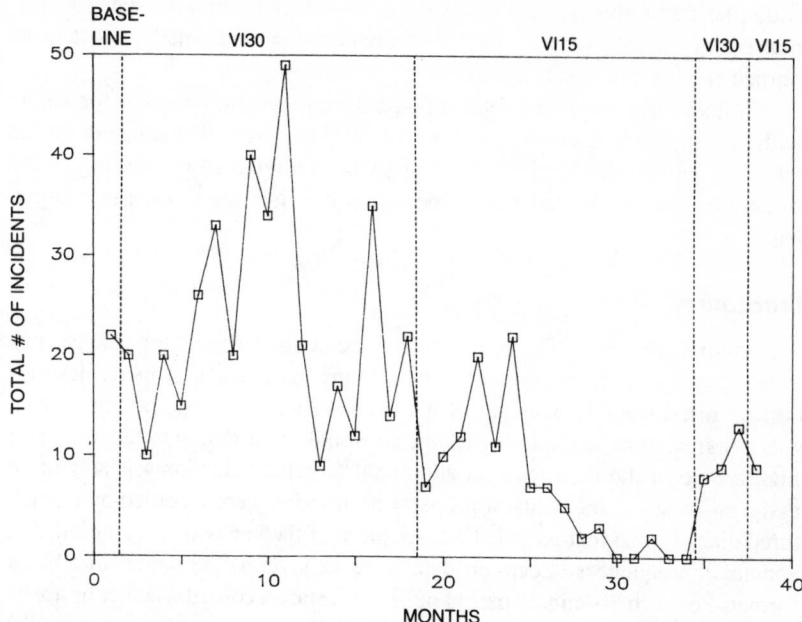

Figure 12.1. Total number of incidents of property destruction by Evan during baseline and each phase of intervention.

Evan had an increase in property destruction; thus the schedule was changed back to a VI 15-minute schedule. A follow-up probe done 18 months later revealed no incidents of property destruction for the 3 months probed. Inspection of the data over a 3 year follow-up period revealed that property destruction occurred about once every 4 months, and primarily occurred during periods where unstable staff did not reliably implement the behavior plan.

The critical elements of Evan's intervention plan appear to be the structured, full schedule of activities, and the VI 15-minute reinforcement schedule. Additionally, the extinction component ensures that when property is destroyed, staff do not provide any payoff in the form of undue attention or excitement.

CASE 3

Sidney was a 24-year-old man with severe autism. His intelligence was in the low-average range as measured by standardized measures of intelligence. Sidney had good verbal skills, but generally spoke in short sentences with abnormal rhythm. He also had a history of severe destructive behavior. For example, he threw furniture into walls, damaging both the furniture and the walls; he threw objects such as ashtrays and staplers; he knocked over furniture and kicked holes in walls and doors; he started small fires; and he burned the tile floor with a hot iron.

Sidney was employed in a supported employment program for adults with autism, but lost several positions because of destructive behavior on the job. The job that he has held for 2 years is in a retail store working in the stockroom. He works under the supervision of a job coach, on a one-to-one basis.

Procedures

Data Collection The most obvious behavior targeted for change was Sidney's property destruction. However, many instances of property destruction occurred when he was out of his assigned location. For example, if he was assigned to be in the living room, he would often run up to his room and kick a hole in the door. So, an additional targeted behavior was staying in assigned location. Incidents of property destruction were recorded on a structured diary format that included a description of the behavior, its antecedents, and its consequences. Location data were kept on a 30-minute time block format. For each 30-minute period of his day, staff recorded whether or not he had remained in his assigned location.

Functional Analysis Sidney's property destruction was often associated with lack of a structured schedule, inconsistent staff, inconsistent management, and lack of favorite activities in his schedule. Also, the opportunity to engage in property destruction was an antecedent. In other words, if he had access to matches, it was likely he would start a fire. If he was denied his way, and a heavy object was nearby, he would throw it.

The functions of Sidney's property destruction appeared to be increased staff attention and escape from assigned tasks. Outbursts of property destruction often resulted in additional staff being assigned, so change in staff and additional staff might also have served to reward the behavior.

Intervention Plan The goal of Sidney's intervention plan was to eliminate the need and opportunity for him to destroy property. An intervention plan was designed that sought to decrease the opportunities for property destruction and provide motivation for respecting property. Initially, a variable interval 15-minute reinforcement schedule was tried. This schedule was in effect for approximately 2 years. Progress was uneven, so a new plan was developed. The goal of the new plan was to provide Sidney with a very structured schedule that included interesting activities, ample attention, and little opportunity for property destruction.

Structured Written Schedule A daily written schedule was compiled for Sidney. Since he could read, the schedule was posted on cards. He was taken to the schedule before each activity. He read the card, completed the activity, then returned to the schedule where he turned the completed card over, and read the next card. This process was followed throughout all waking hours in his residence.

Sidney's schedule was very active and included at least one activity every 15 minutes unless a scheduled activity took longer than 15 minutes. Sidney's schedule included chores and tasks, as well as many outings and other activities that he enjoyed. Instructions for each activity included the location in which he was to do the activity.

Rewards for Cooperative Behavior   Sidney was placed on a report card. Each half hour he was rated on keeping his hands and feet to himself, staying in assigned location, and respecting property. If he earned all of his points during the half hour, he was allowed to choose from a variety of reinforcers.

Limited Access to Dangerous Items   Matches, lighters, knives, razors, and irons were locked away. He was allowed to use these items under very close supervision.

Supervision   Because of Sidney's serious destructive behavior, he was supervised under a one-to-one staff/client ratio. He received continuous supervision, and staff were aware of his whereabouts at all times. However, he was allowed private time in his room and in the bathroom.

Nighttime Behavior   Sidney occasionally left his room at night and destroyed property. A system was devised so that if he opened his door at night, staff were alerted and could monitor his activities. Bathroom use was allowed, otherwise, Sidney was redirected back to bed. Sidney was given a special reinforcer in the morning if he stayed in his room all night except for bathroom visits. The instructions to staff for implementing Sidney's plan are as follows:

1.   Sidney is to be rated on a report card each half hour on each of the following behaviors: <u>Hands and feet to self</u>, he will not hit or kick others; <u>Remains in assigned location</u>, he will stay in the room or area to which he has been assigned; <u>Respects property</u>, he is to use property according to its intended use, and he will not destroy it. If he has displayed the desired behavior, he will earn 1 point and be told exactly why. If he has not displayed the desired behavior, he is given a zero and told why. If Sidney earns all of his points, he should be allowed to choose one of the following reinforcers: activity reinforcers such as going for walks and preparing meals; food or drink reinforcers such as small amounts of nutritious and favorite foods including pretzels, juice, chicken nuggets, saltines, ice cream, and pop tarts; and music. Reinforcers should be alternated to ensure variety, and keep him interested.

2.   Sidney should be told why he is getting the reinforcer. Specific praise should accompany delivery of the reinforcer and refer to successful performance on the report card. Sidney should especially be praised for any independence in leisure activities, for staying in his assigned location, and for following through on his tasks. Sidney should not be praised

while he is out of his assigned area nor within 20 minutes of aggression or property destruction.
3. Sidney should have a daily schedule of all of his chores, activities, and events of his day. The schedule should include at least one activity every 15 minutes, unless a particular activity takes longer than 15 minutes. Each event should be written on an index card, and the index card should be posted on the bulletin board. Prior to each event on the schedule, Sidney should be directed to look at the schedule. After completing each event, he should be directed back to the schedule to see what is next.
4. Prior to each leisure period, Sidney should be told exactly what to do during leisure time and where to do it. Sidney can help decide how he will spend his leisure time, and this will be written into his schedule. Sidney can work with staff to develop his schedule for the afternoon and evening. This should be done when he returns home from work.
5. In order to encourage Sidney to stay in his room at night, prior to bedtime a nighttime schedule should be written with him that designates in-room activities. He will be told that these are the activities he can do if he wakes up, and he should do them in his room. A system should be set up so that counselors can hear if Sidney leaves his room at night. If he does, he should be directed back to his room (unless he is going to use the bathroom). If Sidney has stayed in his room all night (other than bathroom use), he should be given chocolate ice cream in the morning and told that it is because he stayed in his room all night.
6. All matches, lighters, knives, and razors should be kept from Sidney except under supervised conditions. Heavy items such as heavy glass ash trays must also be kept out of his reach as he may throw them.
7. The guidelines for emergency management of aggression or property destruction should be in effect for Sidney.
8. Report card data will be kept for Sidney, and any incidents of aggression or property destruction should be recorded on ABC forms.

Results

When Sidney has inconsistent staffing and inconsistent implementation of his intervention plan, property destruction occurs several times per week. When his intervention plan is fully implemented on a consistent basis, property destruction is virtually nonexistent. Sidney has maintained a job for 2 years in the stockroom of a department store, and has had no incidents of property destruction at work.

CASE 4

Roberta was a 25-year-old woman with autism and low-average intelligence. She was verbal and had fair communication skills. Roberta lived in a group apartment with three other young women with autism and had a job in a supported employment program working in the stockroom of a drug store. She worked both in the stockroom and out on the floor stocking shelves.

Roberta had a history of destructive behavior. She hoarded and destroyed property, and although her destructive behavior was relatively minor compared to the other cases presented, the frequency was high. On occasion, she had taken her housemate's shampoo and mixed it with conditioner. She had overused detergents; for example, she emptied an entire can of cleanser into the toilet when cleaning it, and she poured half a box of laundry powder into the washing machine.

Roberta had other forms of misuse or destruction including going into the residential counselor's room and taking her property, taking her roommate's property, especially toiletries, attempting to wear dirty clothes, or wetting her clothes and then drying them with a hairdryer. Roberta's misuse of property also extended to food. She had several instances of throwing out good food, eating moldy food, and putting fruit into the toilet. On at least two occasions she poured detergent into her roommate's drink.

Procedures

Data Collection Roberta had a number of behaviors that resulted in misuse of property, unauthorized use of property, or property destruction. A very specific list of target behaviors was developed. This list specified acceptable use of the property in question. Antecedent and consequence data were kept for each behavior on the list.

Functional Analysis Roberta's misuse of property in some instances seemed to be due to a lack of firm structure regarding correct use of the property. The behavior also had the appearance of being self-stimulatory. That is, it appeared to be ritualistic and seemed to serve no obvious function in terms of an obvious payoff. The behaviors were done in private and she did her best to avoid calling attention to them, therefore, it did not appear that the purpose was attention. Also, she was cooperative about her assigned tasks, and the misuse of property did not appear to be related to a desire to escape tasks.

Intervention Plan Since obvious functions could not be pinpointed, the focus of intervention was to provide instruction on correct use of property, to provide limits on its misuse, and to provide motivation for correct use. The plan had several components.

Instructions on Correct Use of Property A specific list of correct behaviors was developed. This list explained exactly how the target items were to be handled.

Rewards for Correct Use Roberta was rewarded for each correct use of property, that is, for each item on her list. Coins (nickels and pennies) were chosen as reinforcers because Roberta loved collecting coins. (In fact, on one occasion she was discovered with $60 in coins in her purse).

Limited Access   Roberta's access to certain items was limited as much as possible. For example, valuables were kept locked up. However, Roberta's job in the drug store was of concern because of her tendency to take others' shampoo and toiletries. She was not permitted to take a purse into work because of the great likelihood she would steal toiletries from the drug store. Roberta was also closely monitored when around someone else's food because of her tendency to contaminate drinks with detergent.

Roberta hoarded items as well. At one point she had 100 bars of soap under her bed. Hoarding was a problem because items she hoarded were often taken from her housemates or shoplifted. Therefore, limits were set on the number of consumables (toiletries) that she could have at any one time.

Structured Activities   Roberta was capable of spending several hours per day unsupervised in her apartment. The only concern was that during this unsupervised time she would take or contaminate her housemate's possessions. When left alone, Roberta was given a structured assignment of activities and tasks. When provided with such a structure, she was much less likely to disturb the belongings of others.

The instructions to staff for implementing Roberta's plan are as follows:

1. Roberta will have a list of items on a checklist. She can earn either 1 cent or 5 cents for each item each day. These items and their value are as follows: wears prepared clothes (5 cents); uses hair dryer appropriately (5 cents); uses correct amount of bleach/laundry soap, shampoo, and cleanser (5 cents); uses food properly (keeps food out of toilet, does not eat moldy food, does not throw out unspoiled food) (5 cents); stays out of counselor's room (5 cents); uses only own property such as shampoo/conditioner, toilet paper, sanitary napkins, toothpaste/toothbrush, mouthwash, washcloth/towel, soap, comb/brush, thermostat (1 cent); follows budget (5 cents); brushes teeth as scheduled (5 cents); and puts dirty clothes directly into laundry bag (5 cents).

2. Roberta will receive feedback for each specific item immediately after she uses that particular item appropriately. If she has been successful, the residential counselor will award her the amount of money that she earned. This money will be entered on her chart, and the counselor will praise her. If Roberta was not successful, the counselor will enter a zero on the chart and briefly tell her why she was not successful.

3. At the end of the day the residential counselor will review the general rules with Roberta (i.e., staying out of the counselor's room). The counselor will praise her and award Roberta 5 cents if she has been successful, or the counselor will enter a zero if Roberta was not successful. The daily amount that Roberta earned will then be totaled and she will be praised for what she has earned.

4. Each evening before bedtime Roberta and the counselor will select the clothes that she is to wear the next day. The residential counselor will record 5 cents on her chart the next day if she wears the designated clothes.

5. The residential counselor will limit the amount of consumables that Roberta has at any given time. As a general rule she should have no more than two bottles or boxes of the consumables, one for current use and one for use when the other runs out. Only when Roberta uses one of the bottles or boxes may she purchase another. For monitoring purposes, Roberta should have her own shelf for storing her items. If she uses another resident's item, she will replace exactly what she used. The residential counselors must pay close attention to the amounts of consumables that Roberta has and uses to avoid giving her money when she has not earned it.

6. If Roberta earns all the possible money in a given week she will be given a bonus to bring that amount up to the next highest dollar, which would be $4.00.

Modifications to Plan

The list provided is Roberta's final list. At the outset of the intervention plan, there were fewer items. As new problems cropped up over the years, new items were added to the list. For example, the food item is a late addition, as well as the item for putting dirty clothes into a laundry bag. Items were added only after a new problem occurred and stayed. Over the course of 5 years, the total number of items increased from 8 to 11.

Results

Roberta's behavior showed a significant improvement following intervention. The few times that new items were added to the list, improvements were noted on those behaviors as well. The years of vigilance over her behaviors and consistent rewarding of more acceptable behaviors has enabled Roberta to work successfully at several retail stores over the years. She currently works at a drug store under the supervision of a job coach, and has held this job for 2 years. She is well liked by her employer and co-workers. Roberta works with shampoo, soap, cleaners, and all the consumables that she has had trouble with in the past. Her past behavior of stealing such items, and ruining them by contamination, has not occurred at all at her current job.

SUMMARY

Property destruction can jeopardize both job and residential placements. Property destruction can even result in legal difficulties. Breaking windows, throwing chairs at cars, and smashing property are not always restricted to the individual's belongings. These behaviors can occur with others' belongings as well. Property destruction must be taken seriously. However, destructive behavior does not preclude good community adjustment for persons with autism. An intervention plan that is based on a complete functional analysis can eliminate the need for property destruction, and in cases in which property destruction still occurs, preventive measures, limit setting, and careful monitoring and supervision can close the gap between addressing functions and eliminating the behavior.

Often, the caregiver's initial responses to property destruction inadvertently reward the behavior. It is mandatory in cases of property destruction that well designed intervention plans be faithfully implemented. All caregivers must know how to prevent the behavior, how to meet the needs of the individual, how to teach more acceptable behaviors, and how to respond should the behavior occur. A united, consistent effort can pay off in good adjustment despite a long history of property destruction.

Chapter Thirteen

PROVIDING SUPPORT SERVICES

People with autism live and work in the community as successfully as people without autism. They hold jobs, live in houses or apartments, go to restaurants, enjoy movies, shop, bowl, swim, and participate in the myriad of other activities enjoyed by their neighbors without autism.

People with autism also have needs similar to those without autism. They need to visit the dentist, doctor, and other specialists, such as speech and language specialists, neurologists, psychiatrists, or occupational therapists. Some people with autism also benefit from therapy. Some need individual psychotherapy, or they find art therapy or music therapy helpful. In order to actively participate in the community, many people with autism need some form of support services. They might need residential counselors, job coaches, or the support of an agency that coordinates and provides such services. The purpose of this chapter is to review some of the support services that a person with autism might need in order to be a productive worker and good neighbor. This chapter does not seek to provide a comprehensive explanation of each type of support service, instead it highlights key issues with a focus on those issues that affect behavioral adjustment.

IDENTIFICATION OF SUPPORT SERVICES

Support services are typically identified by an interdisciplinary team of professionals. Educational agencies usually organize such teams for school-age children, and service providers for adults with autism also organize interdisciplinary teams. The interdisciplinary team consists of the individual with autism, parents or advocates, teachers, caregivers, the case manager, and professionals in the field. Depending on the needs of the individual, professional membership might include a psychologist, a physician, a speech and

I would like to acknowledge several people who contributed to this chapter with the knowledge they have gained from providing support services to people with autism: Iris Littig, M.S.W., Aimee Causey, Alan Dechter, D.D.S., and Maureen Lynch-Makarechi.

language therapist, a nutritionist, or an occupational therapist. Other disciplines who have been involved or might be involved with the individual would also be represented.

Support services for persons with autism are arranged by parents, advocates, caregivers, or an interdisciplinary team, and are planned according to the needs of the individual. Some services such as dental and medical that are provided readily and easily to nonhandicapped people might require special adaptations or considerations when the person has autism. Other services might need to be designed specifically for the needs of that person. Examples would be the use of specially trained job coaches.

BEHAVIOR MANAGEMENT CONSULTATION

Many people with autism have pervasive needs in the areas of social adjustment and self-management. As presented, severe problems can include self-injury, aggression, and property destruction, and less severe problems can include excessive self-stimulation, less serious forms of property destruction, noncompliance, and screaming. Social skills deficits can also occur in varying degrees.

Behavior management consultation can be a critical component in helping people with autism overcome their behavior problems and achieve good adjustment to home, school, and work. Behavior management consultation can also help achieve adjustment despite the continued presence of behavior problems, and it can encourage cooperation so that the individual with autism benefits from a variety of other support services.

Participants

A psychologist who is an expert in behavior management and an expert in autism serves as the behavioral consultant to develop goals and an intervention plan in consultation with caregivers. Primary caregivers, such as teachers, parents, job coaches, or residential counselors meet with the behavioral consultant to pinpoint goals and develop plans. Supervisors as well as direct care people should be present.

Behavior change is a team effort. The behavioral consultant can be considered both a leader and member of the team. This professional has expertise on process, and the team has expertise on the individual with autism. These two fields of knowledge need to be combined to develop a practical, effective plan.

The behavioral consultant, in order to be effective, must develop some expertise concerning the individual being served. This process involves observing the individual in his or her natural environment. If the individual is in a school, the behavioral consultant must make several visits to the school. If the individual works, the consultant must make several visits to the job site, and if the home is the primary setting, then the consultant must observe in the home.

For the caregivers to be more effective, they must develop some expertise in behavior management. The caregivers must be taught basic training in the principles of behavior management, and how these principles apply to autism. Once the behavioral consultant gains sufficient knowledge about the individual with autism, and the team acquires knowledge about behavior management, then the process can begin.

Process

The process for developing the behavior intervention plan has been explained in detail in Chapters Three and Four. Goals are pinpointed, data are collected, and strategies are developed. Caregivers are then trained, and the plan is implemented. Caregivers continue to take data and review progress with the behavioral consultant.

Follow-Up

Behavior change is a long-term process and the psychologist needs to be involved throughout. Successful behavioral consultation is highly dependent on follow-up. Development of the plan is an early stage in the process. Caregivers need thorough training under the supervision of the behavioral consultant. Data need to be carefully reviewed, and if changes need to be made, staff must be retrained accordingly. The behavioral consultant needs to be available to review data, to observe implementation of the plan, to troubleshoot, and to help make decisions regarding any necessary changes.

PSYCHOTHERAPY

Many of the more distressing behavior problems that an individual with autism has will need to be addressed on an ongoing basis by caregivers. Strategies for caregivers are the focus of this book, however, these strategies do not eliminate the usefulness of counseling for the individual by a trained psychotherapist.

Who Can Benefit

Benefits can be realized by individuals with autism who have some language skills. It is not necessary for language to be fluent, and in some cases, it is not even necessary for the individual to speak in complete sentences. However, the individual should have some verbal language skills in order to be considered for counseling.

Potential Benefits

Psychological counseling can have important benefits for an individual with autism. These benefits are discussed below.

Repository of Information People with autism, particularly as they grow older, may have high turnover in their caregivers. This is particularly true if they live in group homes, or if they have been in some other placement out of the parent's home. A psychotherapist who sees the individual on a long-term basis can serve as a repository of the history of the individual.

Individuals with autism often cannot express what is wrong when having a problem. Sometimes, the key to understanding what is wrong involves knowing some past event. The therapist becomes the valuable link between the individual's past and present and can then help current caregivers, or parents, understand problems as they arise in light of the individual's history. The case of Zelda provides a good example of the usefulness of the therapist as a historian. Zelda began having some difficulty in her group home, and thus her crying and self-scratching increased. When talking with her therapist, Zelda could not explain her behavior; however, she did mention that her group home counselor had said that she was tired. This seemingly innocent remark had become an antecedent to Zelda's problem behaviors, and the therapist could explain why.

Zelda had a group home counselor who after complaining that she was tired, quit her job as counselor. Zelda is fearful of counselors leaving and associated her current counselor's complaint about being tired with the past counselor who had quit after voicing such a complaint. Zelda, in other words, was fearful that her current counselor might quit. In this case, the counselor's complaint was an innocent remark, and the therapist explained this to Zelda. The therapist's knowledge of Zelda's history made it possible to identify a seemingly innocent remark as an antecedent to Zelda's problem behaviors. Without the therapist's knowledge of the past incident, Zelda's current reaction to the group home counselor's remark would not have made sense.

As a historian, the therapist can also be alert to patterns of reemerging behavior that caregivers might not have the background information to notice. If the therapist can notice a cycle of behavior problems emerging, then the therapist, the psychologist, and the caregivers can take steps to identify antecedent and setting events, to examine the consequences, and to remedy the situation.

Affirm Control People with autism often have little control over their environment. Major and minor decisions might be made for them. The therapist can help caregivers find ways to allow the individual to have some control over situations. Therapists often achieve this expansion of control by giving the individual assignments or activities to do in certain situations. Encouraging individuals to self-record, to use calendars to keep track of certain events, and to notify caregivers when these events approach are examples. Asking individuals to help with the care of others who need assistance can reduce attention-seeking behaviors that occur out of rivalry.

Establish Limits Therapists help provide an affirmation of control by the individual. They can also teach him or her limits. Therapists can teach individuals with autism appropriate expressions of feelings by developing their vocabularies with which to express their feelings. Therapists can also teach limits to less acceptable forms of expression. For example, a therapist was instrumental in teaching Linda, a young woman with autism, to tell others when she felt sad. At the same time, Linda was taught that crying is also acceptable when she is sad, but only at home, not at work.

Modeling Behavior Therapists play an important role in serving as role models for individuals with autism. People with autism can learn by watching others, thus the therapist serves as a model of how to establish and maintain relationships with others.

Therapist/Client Relationship The one-to-one relationship that develops between the therapist and the individual is one of the greatest benefits of therapy. People with autism have difficulty establishing and maintaining relationships with others, and they often lose those people with whom they have established a friendship. Teachers, group home counselors, and job coaches come and go. The therapist can provide a stable source of friendship throughout the individual's life.

Role as Advocate

The therapist can serve as a valuable advocate for the individual with autism, and often is the first to discover when care is deteriorating. For example, the therapist might be the first to note that the new counselor in the group home is denying the individual privileges that past counselors always allowed, or the therapist might be the one to note that additional services are needed. Since the individual with autism might not be capable of expressing needs or problems effectively, the therapist can serve as an interpreter between the individual and the caregiver. The therapist, serving as advocate, can then press for additional services or changes as needed.

Planning Activities

The therapist can often be a valuable source of recommendations regarding planning of activities for the individual with autism. Over a period of time, the therapist learns the individual's likes and dislikes and can provide this information to caregivers. One interesting example is the case of Melvin. Melvin feared heights and hated elevators. Elevator rides were a source of stress for Melvin and often served as an antecedent for self-injury or aggression. Melvin's new group home counselor was not aware of this problem and innocently planned an elevator ride to the top of a high building as an activity. Fortunately, the therapist was able to intervene and explain Melvin's fear to the counselor.

Applying Behavior Management Principles

The psychotherapist must be familiar with the principles of behavior management and how these principles apply to people with autism. A therapist who is not knowledgeable about autism and the principles of behavior can do more harm than good. There are several important principles that the therapist needs to respect.

Principle of Positive Reinforcement The therapist can serve as an important source of positive reinforcement for acceptable behavior. As such, the therapist becomes a valuable part of the individual's behavior management plan. The therapist can reinforce acceptable behavior by noting and complementing such behavior as observed in the session. If the therapist receives reports of behavioral progress from the individual or caregivers, then such progress can also be complimented.

Principle of Extinction The danger of therapy lies in the therapist's disregard for the principle of extinction. Traditional therapy often involves the therapist discussing problems at great length with the client. When the client is a person with autism, discussing problems can often inadvertently reward the behavior. The individual learns that hitting is a good way to get attention from the caregiver and then prolonged discussion with the therapist. Just as caregivers must put the behavior on extinction, and not inadvertently reinforce it with attention, so must the therapist. The therapist must teach the individual acceptable alternatives to misbehavior, without attention to the misbehavior itself. This is a difficult task, and probably explains why there are not many people who can effectively conduct therapy with people with autism.

Therapists must also be wary of inadvertently rewarding problem behaviors by the suggestions that they make. Often, suggestions that are valid for people without autism can worsen behaviors of people with autism. Martha's case, presented in Chapter Twelve, provides an example. Martha occasionally destroyed property. This problem escalated when she began destroying her roommate's property almost on a daily basis. She broke her roommate's clock, broke one of her dishes, and tore some of her clothes. The increase in destructive behavior was puzzling. Then, the residential counselor mentioned that the therapist had suggested that each time Martha destroyed her roommate's property, she should apologize, then go shopping to replace the item. A functional analysis revealed that shopping was a favorite activity of Martha's, and she had learned that by destroying property she would get to go shopping.

Therapists can be a powerful source of positive reinforcement. When they use the principles of extinction and positive reinforcement consistently in their work, they can be a valuable addition to the behavior management plan.

The Therapist and the Family

The therapist can provide a valuable connection among the client, the family, and service providers. A therapist who understands autism, and who has experience with the service delivery system, can function in several valuable ways.

Turnover   Individuals with autism who live in group homes or who are in day placements often experience continual turnover of staff. This turnover can be a source of great stress for the family. The therapist, as a stable person, can help the family deal with the reality of turnover in their child's life.

Limitations   The therapist can help the family deal with the limitations imposed by their child's handicap. Families may have unrealistic expectations about what their child can achieve.

Priorities   The therapist can assist the family in focusing on priority issues. In many cases the family and therapist serve a critical role as advocate to ensure quality of services. The therapist can help the family determine the issues that are worth dealing with and those that are not as important.

The Therapist and the Caregiver

The therapist can be a valuable resource for the caregiver, whether the caregiver is the family or a service provider. Individuals with autism will often learn to relate well to their therapists, and as a result, the therapist becomes a source of information to the primary provider concerning the individual. The therapist can often determine setting events and antecedents that are not readily detectable by caregivers. The therapist must keep in close contact with the caregiver and must be informed of any changes in staff, responsibilities, or placements.

Goals of the Therapist

Therapists need to work on goals that are consistent with the individual's autism. If the therapy goal is to make the individual "normal," then therapy will be a frustrating experience for all concerned. The therapist must accept the individual's limitations and develop goals that are realistic.

ART AND MUSIC THERAPY

Both art and music therapy can be beneficial to people with autism. These benefits are discussed below.

Potential Benefits

Communication Since people with autism often have impaired communication skills, it can be difficult for them to express themselves through spoken language. Art and music therapy both provide other means of communication for the individual. Art and music therapists who are familiar with autism can use their therapy as a means of promoting and interpreting communication.

Therapist/Client Relationship Art and music therapists can use their activities as a means of developing relationships with their clients with autism. People with autism often have few good relationships because of their social skills deficits. Art and music therapy can be valuable sources of positive relationships.

Recreational Skills Art and music therapy can serve as a good source of recreational skills. Activities and skills used in art and music therapy can serve as good leisure skills as well, and in some cases, individuals can generalize these skills outside the therapy setting.

Applying Behavior Management Principles

Art and music therapists must practice good behavior management when working with their clients with autism. If the individuals are on a behavior management plan, then it might be necessary for the therapist to implement the plan through the therapy session. The therapist must also be adept at strengthening positive behaviors while not inadvertently rewarding problem behaviors that may occur during the session.

Art and music therapists should be knowledgeable about autism and about how to communicate with people with autism. They must be able to combine their knowledge of autism with their knowledge of behavior management and integrate these principles into their therapy sessions.

PSYCHIATRIC THERAPY

Individuals with autism might be under the care of a psychiatrist, receiving psychotropic medication and/or therapy. The psychiatrist can be a valuable member of the individual's interdisciplinary team. There are several issues that need to be addressed in order to make maximum benefit of psychiatric services.

Medication

If psychotropic medication is prescribed, it must be done in conjunction with a behavior management plan. Using drugs as the sole means of controlling behavior can be a dangerous practice, so the psychiatrist needs to work closely with the behavior management consultant when making decisions about medication increases or decreases. Caregivers also need to work with the psychiatrist to keep medication doses as low as possible, and to eliminate medication as quickly as possible.

Approval

Many service providers have standards for psychotropic medication. Such medication might need to be approved by a behavior management committee and a human rights committee. The psychiatrist needs to be informed of approval procedures and be willing to work within such a framework.

Therapy

A psychiatrist who understands autism and the principles of behavior can be a valuable source of therapy. Many of the benefits and considerations discussed in the section on psychological therapy would apply to psychiatric therapy as well. Psychiatrists might use play, music, or art therapy, especially with young children. Such therapy can be beneficial when the principles of behavior are respected and when it is part of a comprehensive intervention plan.

Emergencies

Psychiatrists can serve an important role in behavioral emergencies. Occasionally, even under well run behavior intervention plans, an individual with autism might become excessively violent or self-injurious and be a danger to themselves or others. The caregiver might need to consult a psychiatrist in an emergency situation for immediate, intensive treatment. The psychiatrist might determine that medication or even hospitalization, in extreme cases, is necessary.

SPEECH AND LANGUAGE THERAPY

Since autism is a disorder of communication, speech and language instruction can be a critical support service. The usefulness of this service is highly dependent on the expertise of the speech and language therapist. Several issues should be considered when providing speech and language services to individuals with autism who have severe communication deficits.

Best Practices

Each month numerous studies are published on developing language in persons with autism. It is beyond the scope of this book to survey such practices. Suffice it to say that these studies are becoming increasingly well documented in the literature, and the speech and language therapist should be knowledgeable about current practices. Several key points are worthy of note.

Integrated   Speech and language services should be well integrated into the individual's day and evening settings. Generalizing from a self-contained session with a therapist to the real world can be difficult. To avoid problems, the service itself should be well integrated into the natural setting.

Functional   Speech and language instruction should be functional. Since many people with autism have no speech or very limited speech, they have a great deal of difficulty in situations that require language to be either learned or used. To increase the likelihood of cooperation and learning, instruction for these individuals should be immediately functional for them.

Activity Based   Language services for people with autism who have little or no speech should for the most part revolve around meaningful activities. Teaching language through actual events and objects is likely to be more effective than teaching through pictures. Individuals with autism are more likely to learn language when it is used in the course of meaningful activities, than when it is presented out of context of functional activity.

Avoid Excessive Demands   Unrealistic demands can actually discourage language. When individuals with autism who have severe language impairment are pressed to speak, or to speak in more complete sentences, the result can be no speech, or worse, behavior problems. Speech and language goals need to respect the individual's current level.

Jake's case provides an example of the problem of excessive demands. Jake rarely spoke, although he was capable of speaking in short phrases. Often, he used head banging to make his needs known. Speech and language goals were targeted to teach him to speak in complete sentences. When he spoke in short phrases, he was prompted to speak in complete sentences. Such prompting resulted in screaming and head banging. A more reasonable speech goal would have been speech in one or two-word phrases. Pressing Jake beyond that point became counter-productive.

Focus on Communication, Not Convention   Related to the discussion of goals is the need to focus on functional communication without making demands based solely on style. Often, speech goals focus on social convention and not communication. Again, speaking in complete sentences is a case in point. For some people, communicating with gestures or with one word would be progress enough. To require social conventions, such as complete sentences, does not really focus on communication. In cases where individuals are pressed beyond functional communication into social convention, the language is often rote and repetitive.

Speech and language goals that focus on functional communication can be an important part of a behavior intervention plan. Conversely, goals that are excessively demanding and press social convention over functional communication can actually discourage language development and create behavior problems.

Many people with autism have fairly good communication skills. Their communication deficits might primarily be deficits of style and convention. In those cases, a focus on convention is appropriate.

Coordination with Behavior Intervention Plan

The speech and language goals can coordinate in a valuable way with the behavior intervention plan. People with some speech can often be taught to use language rather than misbehavior as a means of achieving their goals. Teaching individuals to ask for help, to say "no," to ask for a break, or to ask for items that they want can help to significantly reduce behavior problems. Similarly, speech and language goals can help individuals with no verbal speech. Language goals that focus on speech development as well as sign, communication books, or boards can give people alternatives to self-injury and aggression as a means of communicating.

Consultants to Caregivers

Speech and language therapists can achieve communication gains by working directly with individuals with autism. However, more pervasive gains can be realized when they serve as consultants to caregivers. The speech and language specialist can teach caregivers to incorporate language goals and instruction throughout the course of the individual's life. This approach maximizes generalization by providing a pervasive approach to speech and language instruction. Like the behavior management program, speech and language training can be all-encompassing.

OCCUPATIONAL THERAPY

Some individuals with autism have postural, muscular, or other physical deficits that dictate the need for an occupational therapist. Occupational therapists use purposeful, functional activities to promote independence in the activities of daily living, and they can introduce small changes into the individual's life that provide large payoffs in terms of adjustment, comfort, and health. It is beyond the scope of this book to give comprehensive coverage to occupational therapy; however, some possible uses and benefits of occupational therapy for individuals with autism are suggested.

Focus on Function

The focus on function provided by occupational therapists makes them a valuable support service. Occupational therapists can assess an individual at home and work as he or she performs activities of daily living including self-care tasks, such as grooming and dressing; leisure activities, such as bowling and swimming; and work activities. Recommendations for improved functioning are made based on the activities of daily living in which the individual with autism routinely engages.

Support Functional Activities

The goal of the occupational therapist is to assist the individual in achieving maximum potential functioning in the activities of daily living. The occupational therapist will focus on promoting function, preventing injury, and achieving postural gains as the individual performs functional activities.

For example, Mildred works at a convenience store during the day where she sweeps, fills the ice machine, and stocks shelves. The occupational therapy goals involve helping Mildred achieve maximum function while reducing her chances of injury as she performs her tasks. The occupational therapist noticed that Mildred was frequently bent over while loading the ice machine. The therapist was concerned about the effects of posturing and the strain on Mildred's back, so the therapist recommended teaching Mildred to do the task in a kneeling position with a knee pad to make it more comfortable for Mildred.

Occupational therapy goals are not independent of Mildred's vocational goals; rather, the occupational therapy goals seek to enhance the vocational goals in a very functional way. Occupational therapists can be a valuable resource by supporting the implementation of existing goals.

Respond to Changes in Activities

Since physical demands made on an individual can change radically when activities of daily living change, the occupational therapist must revise goals accordingly. Jerry's case provides a good example of the need for flexibility. Jerry worked in a store, and his job required a lot of stooping and bending. The occupational therapist had recommended an exercise program that provided opportunity for extension, to counteract the effects of continual stooping. Jerry left his store job and obtained a job in a stockroom. His new job required little stooping, but a great deal of reaching. He no longer needed the prescribed exercise program since his new job provided plenty of opportunity for extension activities. The occupational therapist immediately reduced the extension exercises to take into account his new activities.

Suggest Appropriate Jobs

The occupational therapist can make valuable suggestions about the type of job an individual with autism should select based on the physical characteristics of the individual, their stamina, and their endurance. The occupational therapist can assess the individual's functioning in these areas and compare the levels with the requirements of potential jobs. The therapist assesses both the individual with autism and the job site in order to provide recommendations on the job/worker match.

Adaptations to Job Site

In many cases, an individual with autism might already have a job or placement. The occupational therapist can assess the placement, and make suggestions to improve functioning in that placement. The occupational therapist can make suggestions on order of tasks, types of tasks, and modifications to the environment that can promote functioning and prevent injury. For example, if an individual has a job with a mixture of types of tasks, the occupational therapist might suggest the sequence of tasks. The therapist might suggest that stooping tasks be alternated with reaching tasks.

The therapist might comment on a variety of physical aspects in the environment. Mildred's case presented earlier in this chapter provides a good example. By introducing a knee pad to the job site, the occupational therapist enhanced functioning and prevented undue stress on Mildred's back. An occupational therapist visiting a classroom for adolescents with autism noted that the beanbag chairs in use were promoting poor posture and were accentuating deficits. The therapist suggested another type of chair that was equally comfortable but that promoted good posture.

Prescribe Exercise Programs

An occupational therapist might prescribe and conduct exercise programs to help promote better functioning. In the case of children, exercises might be used to improve functioning; for adults, exercise might be used to promote specific goals related to activities of daily living.

Focus on Consultation

To optimize the benefits of the occupational therapist, heavy emphasis should be placed on consultation with caregivers—parents, teachers, job coaches, and any others who supervise the activities of daily living. Gains can be realized by the occupational therapist providing services directly to the individual with autism. However, if the therapist can provide suggestions to caregivers, then benefits can be maintained throughout all activities of daily living. The more integrated the service into the daily routine, the greater the gains.

Coordinate with Existing Behavior Programs

Some individuals with autism might have specific behavior plans. Picture schedules, schedules of reinforcement, or other strategies might be in place to encourage cooperation across tasks and settings. The occupational therapist should integrate any existing behavior program into the delivery of occupational therapy. An individual who is on a schedule of positive reinforcement that calls for reinforcers every 15 minutes will probably be more likely to cooperate with the occupational therapist if the reinforcers are also given during therapy. For example, if the occupational therapist is having a session with Bart, who is normally rewarded about every 15 minutes for cooperative behavior, then the therapist should also reward Bart for acceptable behavior about every 15 minutes. Additionally, if the occupational therapist targets specific ways of functioning, then the caregivers can reinforce those behaviors on existing schedules throughout the course of the day. For example, when Mildred kneeled to fill the ice machine rather than bent over, kneeling would be praised or otherwise rewarded.

MEDICAL SERVICES

Providing medical services to people with severe autism can require patience and expertise that go beyond standard patient care. Long waits, crowded waiting rooms, and abruptly administered procedures can spell behavioral disaster for an individual with autism. People without any speech are at an especially high risk since they might not understand what is happening.

A physician does not have to be a specialist in autism to provide medical services to a person with autism. However, the physician does need to have a willingness to work with the caregivers to ensure a successful visit. The physician might need to agree to certain strategies that are not standard office practice. These are covered briefly. These modifications are not needed for all individuals with autism.

Establishing Cooperation

Short Waits Some people with autism have difficulty with waiting situations. Shortened waits can make the visit more pleasant for all concerned. Scheduling the first visit of the morning can be a practical way to eliminate long waits.

Specific Instructions and Explanations People with autism might have difficulty speaking, but one should never underestimate their ability to understand. The caregiver or physician should carefully explain as much as possible about the visit and the procedures that will be used. Specific instructions and explanations should be clear, and simple. Sometimes it helps to give the individual with autism a reference to something they already understand. For example, "Dr. B. is going to clean your cut, like Jim did last time you fell."

Orientation Some individuals with autism might need to make several short visits to the physician's office before actually being treated. Sometimes, taking the individual to the office and acquainting him or her with the staff and setting can increase the likelihood of cooperation.

Desensitization Some medical procedures might need to be gradually introduced to the individual with autism. For example, a young women with autism might not initially submit to a pelvic exam; however, by gradually introducing the procedure over several visits, cooperation might be achieved.

Maintaining Cooperation

Rituals Some people with autism will establish certain rituals, which if followed, will promote cooperation at the doctor's office. If the rituals are not allowed, then chaos could result.

Melvin's case provides an example of the reliance on rituals. During Melvin's first few visits to the doctor's office, the same events occurred. First, he was greeted by the nurse, the nurse offered him a thermometer, and then he took his temperature. This sequence of events was the same each time. Melvin came to rely on this exact sequence, and when it occurred precisely, he was cooperative and would submit to his injections. However, if the ritual was altered, for example, if he did not take his temperature, Melvin would refuse to cooperate. He would run down the hall screaming, "No needles," and the visit would have to be terminated. If certain harmless rituals develop, it is probably better to allow them than to risk total rebellion and termination of the visit.

Reinforcement Some individuals with autism might need some incentive to cooperate with medical procedures. The caregiver can often elicit cooperation by accompanying the individual on the doctor's visit and by providing verbal or more tangible rewards for cooperation. Often individuals with autism will cooperate if they can expect certain standard rewards following the visit. For example, Michelle knew that following a cooperative visit with her doctor, she would go directly to the store for hot chocolate. Alvin knew that following his cooperative visits to the doctor, he would receive ice cream.

Avoidance of Threats Physicians will need to be careful to avoid threatening tones or statements to many patients with autism. Such an approach can be disastrous. Ronald's case provides a good example of what can occur. Ronald was taken to the eye doctor. He was terrified of needles and kept saying, "No needles." The optometrist explained the procedures and assured Ronald that there would be no needles. Ronald was fairly cooperative, but continued to protest by saying, "No needles." Finally, the doctor said, "You better sit there quietly or I'm going to get 22 needles." Ronald ran off screaming and that was the end of the eye exam.

Avoidance of Third Person Conversations The caregiver might accompany the individual with autism to the physician's office; however, the caregiver and the physician should avoid speaking of the individual in the third person as if he or she was not present. Any conversation about procedures or recommendations should be directed to the individual as much as possible.

Difficult Procedures Occasionally, it will not be possible to obtain the individual's cooperation with a medical procedure, and drastic steps might need to be taken. For example, some women with autism refuse to submit to pelvic exams. If there is a compelling reason to do a procedure and the individual does not cooperate, it might be necessary to do the procedure under some form of anesthesia.

In some cases, cooperation can be obtained by prescription of an anxiety-reducing or psychotropic medication prior to the visit. In other cases, general anesthesia might be required. The physician will need to provide justification for psychotropic medication or anesthesia, as well as an explanation of risks and benefits. Then, the parents, advocates, or others in a decision-making capacity for the patient with autism can make the decision along with the physician. Many agencies will require human rights committee approval for such procedures.

DENTAL SERVICE

Providing dental services can be a challenging task. Many people with autism, particularly those with good language skills, will be cooperative and have no problem receiving dental care. However, for those individuals with no language, dental services can be difficult to explain and provide. Dentists can take certain measures to maximize cooperation of patients with severe autism who have difficulty cooperating. These measures are similar to those taken by physicians.

Establishing Cooperation

Short Waits   Waiting in a crowded office can be quite difficult for some individuals with autism. The waiting problem was solved in one case by allowing the patient with autism and the caregiver to wait outside of the building until the dentist was ready.

Home-Like Office Setting   One dentist was able to successfully see a number of individuals with autism who were initially resistant to dental services. One favorable factor seemed to be that the dentist's office was in a home. Since the setting was home-like, and appeared less like an office than most, the individuals with autism were more willing to enter and cooperate. An added bonus was that the furniture in the dentist's office was identical to furniture in the group home. Although this is not a necessary feature, it did seem to have some benefits.

Scheduling Considerations   Individuals with no speech often make loud sounds, such as hoots, shrieks, and screams. These sounds may increase under stressful conditions, such as visiting a dental office. Scheduling patients with autism toward the end of the day when there are no additional patients in the waiting room has its advantages. This scheduling ensures that other patients, who may be undergoing difficult procedures themselves, will not be alarmed by the unusual noises. The patients with autism can make as much noise as they like. The dentist can also take his or her time in acclimating the patient with autism, without having to worry about falling behind schedule.

Conditioning Some people with autism are very frightened by dental offices. Allowing the individual to become acclimated to the office requires time and patience, but can result in cooperation. Burt's case with Dr. D. provides a good example. Burt is a 30-year-old man with autism. He has no speech and has a history of severe self-injury. On Burt's first visit, he refused to allow the dentist to work on him. He took one look at the dental instruments and decided that they were not for him. Dr. D. simply brushed Burt's teeth with a regular toothbrush, and the visit ended. For 6 consecutive weeks, Burt came to the office, had his teeth brushed, and left. Each visit was about 10 minutes. Eventually, Dr. D. used the polishing machine and allowed Burt to use it as well. After 6 weeks of visits that included regular toothbrushing and polishing, Burt was cooperative for routine dental care with standard instruments.

Allowing the caregiver to acquaint an individual with autism to the equipment and procedures can also be helpful. Some individuals will not allow a dentist to approach them, much less put his or her fingers in their mouths. However, they usually allow the caregiver to do so, so, for several visits, the caregiver can put the bib on, rinse out the individual's mouth, and even operate some of the dental equipment. This procedure allows the patient with autism to become familiar with the dental equipment and procedures, and eventually allow the dentist to work with him or her.

Maintaining Cooperation

Rewards Some people with autism gladly cooperate in the dental office when provided with sufficiently powerful rewards. These rewards may need to be given throughout the procedures. One limitation is that food cannot be used conveniently as a reward during dental procedures; however, promises of food and favorite activities for cooperative behavior can be effective.

Cooperation has been achieved with individuals with autism who have no verbal language by promising them favorite foods, drinks, and activities when the visit is over. The promises are made throughout the dental visit, when the patient is cooperating. For example, as Burt allows the dentist to brush his teeth, his caregiver would say, "Burt, you're sitting so still. That's great. When we're done here, we'll go right to the swimming pool." Again, certain standard rewards that reliably follow the visit to the dentist can help increase cooperation.

Minimize Pain People with autism are similar in many ways to people without autism. If they go to the dentist and have a painful experience, they will not want to return. Dentists often insure that the actual visit is relatively painless by ample use of anesthesia. However, if the patient goes home, and then experiences pain, it will be obvious that the pain is associated with the dentist. Such an awareness could discourage cooperation on later visits.

Therefore, it is important that the dentist not only seek to eliminate pain during the actual visit, but that pain be managed following the visit.

Anesthesia   In some cases, as with medical procedures, psychotropic medication or anesthesia might be necessary to perform procedures. The same risk-benefit analysis and approval procedures should be followed with dental cases as discussed in the medical section.

SPECIAL CARE PROVIDERS

As the child with autism becomes an adult with autism, primary care and supervision might need to continue. Even people with the severest forms of autism can work and live in group homes in the community. However, they might require special support personnel in order to do so.

Job Coaches

As illustrated throughout this book, adults with autism can work; however, in many cases they cannot go to work by themselves. Job coaches supervise small groups of workers with autism by helping them obtain and maintain suitable jobs. A person with autism might work in a factory, a stockroom, or a variety of other places. A job coach accompanies the worker to work and, as the liaison between the worker with autism and the employer, is responsible for teaching the worker the duties of the job. The job coach should also carry out strategies recommended by other support personnel. For example, the job coach might implement a behavior plan, promote speech and language goals, and follow-through on suggestions made by the occupational therapist. In some cases, the job coach can eventually be faded. For others, the job coach will be needed indefinitely for months or years.

A person with autism who has some verbal language and problem solving skills but who does not have serious behavior problems might be able to work independently or with drop-in supervision. However, if the individual has severe autism, profound retardation, no verbal skills, and a history of severe behavior problems, long-term coaching will most likely be a necessity.

Job coaches can enter the field with little or no experience, provided they receive intensive training in autism and behavior management once hired. Training needs to be didactic as well as on-site. With good initial training, follow-up at the job site, and ongoing monitoring, paraprofessionals can become competent job coaches who are expert in providing on-the-job support to workers with autism.

Residential Counselors

Historically, people with autism were most likely living either with their parents or in institutional settings. Only very mildly affected individuals were integrated independently into the mainstream of society. People with autism have been given increasing opportunities to live in apartments and houses in the community. However, in order to do so, they often need support services in the form of residential counselors.

Some individuals with autism might only need occasional or drop-in supervision while others need around-the-clock supervision for help with behavior management, self-care, and home care tasks. Residential counselors can teach these individuals the skills needed for activities of daily living. They can also implement recommendations made by consultants, such as the behavior management consultant, the speech and language therapist, and the occupational therapist.

Training of group home counselors is similar to the training of job coaches. Again, paraprofessionals with little or no experience, given proper training and follow-up support and monitoring, can become expert at providing residential care and supervision to individuals with autism.

COORDINATION

Any one individual might require several support services. These services need to be coordinated to prevent overlap and contradiction. Well coordinated support services can be vital in promoting adaptation to school, home, and work. Without coordination, contradictions, overlap, and lack of follow-through can inhibit rather than promote adjustment. Coordination has several important elements.

Communication

Support service providers with overlapping concerns need to be aware of each other's goals and plans. This communication can be done by telephone, by mail, or through a liaison such as a case manager. The mechanism for providing for this communication is not fixed and can vary from agency to agency. What is essential is that communication exists.

Consistency

It is also essential that approaches and services be consistently provided to the individual. For example, if the psychotherapist is attempting to teach the individual to reveal problems, but the behavioral consultant is trying to decrease complaints, then these two approaches could be in conflict. Consistent goals and approaches must prevail.

Follow-Through

It is one matter for support professionals to make recommendations and develop programs, and it is quite another matter for follow-through to take place. When the caregiver is the family, follow-through is relatively simple. The family decides whether or not to accept the recommendations, and if accepted, the services are provided.

When agencies serve as caregivers, follow-through becomes more complex. The recommendations of support service professionals often must be carried out by direct care staff. However, these people usually need training, supervision, and monitoring in this role. The agency must work with the consulting professional to provide direct care staff with the necessary support and monitoring to achieve follow-through. Unless people in supervisory positions provide sufficient training, support, and monitoring to direct caregivers, follow-through may not occur.

SUMMARY

People with autism can adapt to the community. They can live and work in integrated community settings with the help of support services. In many cases, the support services must be tailored to meet the needs of the individual with autism.

Possibly the most critical support service for a person with autism is the behavior management service, provided by a behavioral consultant who is knowledgeable about autism and expert in the principles of behavior. A well developed behavior management plan can be an essential component of school, home, and job adjustment. Some individuals with autism might also benefit from therapy. Psychotherapy, art therapy, music therapy, and/or occupational therapy all can contribute to good adjustment. These services must respect the principles of behavior and work in concert with the individual's care provider and behavior management plan.

Speech and language services are often necessary. Since autism is a disorder of language and communication, speech and language services can be critical. These services should be geared to meet the individual needs of each person and should be functional and integrated throughout his or her life.

Many individuals with autism can receive dental and medical care as easily as people without autism; however, some will need to have these services adapted to meet their special needs. Finding cooperative physicians and dentists who are willing to make adaptations and take the extra time can allow people with autism to have their medical and dental needs met with the least intrusive procedures possible.

Therapists from the variety of specialties can do much to enhance community adjustment. However, many people with autism will need ongoing daily support throughout their lives from parents or other caregivers such as instructors, teachers, residential counselors, or job coaches. These people must provide ongoing supervision and instruction at the level necessary to ensure safety and adaptation. There is no compensation for lack of support in this area since failure to provide such support can result in failure at home, school, and work. People with autism can be good students, workers, neighbors, and friends as long as they have a little (expert) help from others.

Chapter Fourteen

KEEPING A JOB DESPITE BEHAVIOR PROBLEMS

Severe behavior problems associated with autism, such as self-injury, aggression, pica, property destruction, and self-stimulation, although not universal, can present adjustment problems for people with autism. Less serious problems such as social skills deficits are also common.

Dramatic improvements in the severity and frequency of behavior problems are possible; for example, life threatening head banging can be reduced to mere taps. The same results can be achieved with other severe behavior problems as well as social skills problems. People with autism can learn social amenities, conversation skills, and cooperation skills necessary for home and job adjustment.

However, as there is no cure for autism, there is no guarantee that severe behavior problems can be eliminated in any given individual, and although severity and frequency can be greatly reduced, permanent elimination cannot be assured. Therefore, people with autism might continue to display serious behavior problems despite conscientious and competent intervention. Even if the problems are eventually eliminated, there is still an interim period of learning when the problems are present, although decreasing.

People with autism can retain jobs despite the continuing occurrence of behavior problems. Behaviors that are considered job threatening might continue at some level despite all efforts to teach new, more acceptable behaviors. However, failure to totally eliminate such behaviors does not necessarily mean that the individual must lose the job. By maintaining good relationships with employers, and by providing adequate support, it can be possible for the worker to have a successful job experience despite the continuing presence of "job threatening" behaviors. This chapter explores methods for achieving and maintaining employment despite continued behavior problems.

I would like to recognize Susan Naylor for her contributions to this chapter.

IT HAS BEEN DONE

People with severe autism have been able to work despite continued behavior problems. These people have been able to find and maintain employment through the assistance of supported employment. Jobs are found by the agency providing the services. The workers with autism are supervised at work by job coaches (provided by the supported employment program) and are paid by the employer. The job coaches are paid by the supported employment agency.

Table 14.1 provides a list of workers with autism, along with a description of their behavior problems and the type of jobs they have been able to maintain. Workers with autism are typically employed in pairs, with each pair supervised by one job coach. Supervision by job coaches is continual for workers with severe behavior problems. Workers with simple social skills deficits have in some cases been able to work independently of a job coach.

The list provided in Table 14.1 is not inclusive of all cases of employment held by people with severe behavior problems. Sample cases have been reported as representative of what can be achieved.

CRITICAL ELEMENTS OF SUPPORT

Maintaining a successful job experience despite the continuing presence of job threatening behaviors generally requires a number of efforts on the part of the supporting agency. The overall theme of these efforts is the provision of adequate support. The employer must feel confident that, should an emergency occur, the supporting agency will deal with it quickly and efficiently, with a minimum of disruption to the worksite. The following elements are essential.

Adequate Supervision

Adequate supervision is essential for workers with serious behavior problems. People with self-injurious, aggressive, and destructive behaviors can hold a job and might even be able to work as quickly as their nonhandicapped co-workers. However, they might need significantly more supervision if safety and decorum at the worksite are to be maintained. Individuals with severe self-injurious, aggressive, and destructive behavior have been able to maintain competitive employment when supervised in ratios of one job coach to two workers with autism.

Emergency back-up procedures must be available for individuals who have serious problems with aggression or property destruction. The job coach must have easy access to help from the supervising agency should a behavioral emergency occur. In some cases, it might be helpful to make a list of warning signs that usually precede serious behavior problems. Should those signs be present, then back-up help can be assigned, or be on call if assistance is necessary.

Table 14.1 Jobs held by individuals with autism and severe behavior problems

Worker	Behavior problems	IQ level	Language	Company	Tasks
Milton	Severe social skills deficits, stereotypic behaviors	Moderate MR	Short phrases	Printing company	Collating, binding books, covering books, sorting books
Saul	Aggression, self-injury, screaming, crying, property destruction, stereotypic behaviors	Moderate MR	Some speech, abnormal melody	Department store stockroom	Pricing items, preparing items for sale
Kelly	Head banging, property destruction, screaming	Profound MR	No speech	Women's clothing store stockroom	Hanging clothes, preparing clothes for sale
Michael	Pica, aggression, property destruction, stereotypic behaviors	Profound MR	No speech	Department store stockroom	Removing items from boxes, pricing items, preparing items for sale
Aaron	Aggression, screaming, verbal threats, stereotypic behaviors	Moderate MR	Speech with abnormal melody	Printing company	Binding books, separating books, covering books
Stuart	Severe self-injury, toileting problems, stereotypic behaviors	Profound MR	No speech	Department store stockroom	Hanging clothes, pulling plastic from clothes

(continued)

257

Table 14.1. *(continued)*

Worker	Behavior problems	IQ level	Language	Company	Tasks
Bert	Self-injury, aggression, occasional noncompliance, stereotypic behaviors	Moderate MR		Clothing outlet stockroom	Pricing clothes, putting sensor on clothes, hanging clothes, preparing items for sale
Velma	Loud shrieking, stereotypic behaviors	Profound MR	No speech	Rental company	Folding napkins and tablecloths
Elvis	Severe head banging, stereotypic behaviors	Moderate MR	Short phrases, mostly demands	Restaurant	Cleaning before restaurant opens
Jonathon	Severe self-injury, screaming, stereotypic behaviors	Profound MR	Two-word phrases	County department of transportation	Tearing unused bus tickets
Carl	Tantrums (jumping, hand flapping, screaming)	Average intelligence	Fluent speech	T-shirt factory	Removing newly printed clothing from machinery and stacks
Bart	Self-injury, stereotypic behaviors	Above-average intelligence	Mute, but can write	Library	Sorting books

Art	Self-injury, aggression, stereotypic behaviors	Profound MR	No speech	Restaurant	Cleaning before restaurant opens
Allen	Loud echolalia, crying, stereotypic behaviors	Profound MR	Echolalia	Department store stockroom	Unpacking items, pricing items, preparing items for sale
Martha	Screaming, crying, self-injury, property destruction, aggression	Low-average intelligence	Fluent speech	Manufacturing firm	Making electronic parts
Jake	Tantrums (jumping, arm flailing, screaming)	Low-average intelligence	Fluent speech	Printing company	Sorting books, covering books, binding books
Tom	Aggression, self-injury, crying, property destruction, stereotypic behaviors	Moderate MR	Limited speech	Warehouse	Sorting, cleaning, repacking damaged goods

Note: IQ levels were estimated from standard measures of intelligence. Since it is difficult to measure intelligence levels in persons with severe autism, reported levels might be invalid.
Stereotypic behavior refers to repetitive, ritualistic behaviors such as rocking, pacing, hand flapping, and finger flicking.

Job Matching

The first step in maintaining a job despite severe behavior problems is to choose jobs that are compatible with the present problems. Although a behavior intervention plan might reduce or even eliminate the problem, one can never be sure of the rate of decrease. It is best to find the individual a job that would minimize the effects of serious behavior problems. Job/behavior problem compatibility can be assessed across several factors.

Job Tasks Tasks should be chosen that do not magnify the behavior problem. Some rather obvious suggestions are provided:

1. Individuals who tear clothes should not be placed in a job hanging clothes for a clothing store.
2. Individuals who do a lot of pacing should not be given a job that requires seat work, but should be given a job that involves walking. Likewise, workers who prefer to sit or remain in one place should not be given jobs that involve a lot of moving around.
3. Individuals with food stealing behaviors should not work in a restaurant, nor should people with problems such as spitting or rectal digging.
4. Individuals who destroy property should have jobs in which they are not working with or near items of the sort that they destroy.

Location of Work Area Location of the work area can be a valuable means of minimizing the effects of behavior problems. Workers with autism who have a history of darting or running away should not work near exits. Individuals with autism who scream, shriek, or hoot should work in areas in which they will not disturb others, or they should work in environments that are already noisy so that they cannot be heard above the din.

Individuals with aggressive or self-injurious behaviors also might need to work in locations that are somewhat distant from others to prevent inadvertent injury to co-workers. Although this might not be necessary in all cases, in some it might make the difference between employability and unemployment.

Proximity to Other Workers Ideally, workers with autism will work right alongside workers without autism. However, some workers might display behaviors that prove distracting to co-workers, or the behaviors might be considered unacceptable by the employer in certain locations. For example, an individual who grabs at someone else's materials and possessions might need to work some distance from co-workers, or an individual who screams or hoots might need to be kept slightly away from other workers.

Behavior Management Plan

A behavior management plan must be developed to attempt to teach the worker more acceptable behaviors and to specify exactly how job threatening behaviors are to be handled should they occur. This plan must include preventive measures as well.

Involvement of Employer and Co-workers

The amount of information to give to employers and co-workers is always debatable. Too much information can be stigmatizing, too little information can prevent others from understanding what they might see. In cases where behavior problems are obvious and serious, it might be necessary to provide the employer with a description of the behaviors that might occur, and an explanation of how the behaviors will be handled by the job coach. In cases where the behavior may affect or be witnessed by co-workers, such as food stealing or tantrumming, then the co-workers might also need an explanation of how the behavior will be handled. Furthermore, they may be asked to cooperate, generally by inaction. For example, they may be told that Jennifer may occasionally head bang, and since the job coach is trained to respond in a certain way, they do not need to provide assistance.

Training of Job Coaches

Job coaches must be thoroughly trained on the intervention plan. Untrained job coaches can lose a worker's job more quickly than the worker can lose his or her own job. In cases that involve a history of aggression, self-injury, property destruction, or other behaviors that could cause damage, injury, or disruption at work, the job coach needs thorough training on how to intervene in such crises in order to prevent injury or property destruction. Job coaches must be capable of managing such situations in a calm, efficient manner, to minimize disruption to co-workers.

Familiarity with Setting

Job coaches must be totally familiar with the work setting. In cases where an individual needs to be removed to prevent property destruction or injury, the job coach needs to move quickly and calmly with as little disruption to the worksite as possible.

WORKING WITH BEHAVIOR PROBLEMS

Following are several examples illustrating how individuals with autism who continue to have typically job threatening behaviors have been able to maintain employment despite the continuing presence of these behaviors.

Aggression

Two individuals have histories of severe aggression and property destruction. They have been employed at a department store in the stockroom where they assist in preparing stock for display and sale. One of the workers has occasional aggressive outbursts of hitting, kicking, and head butting others as well as destroying property such as furniture, windows, and toilet seats. The other worker has a history of breaking windows, as well as biting and hitting others.

These workers are accompanied to work by a job coach who is trained and physically capable of preventing injury to persons and property. Furthermore, the following steps have been taken to maintain a successful job experience for these two workers:

1. A behavior management plan was put into place (see samples in Chapter Ten) that provides rewards for acceptable behavior to prevent aggression and property destruction.
2. The employer was made aware of the nature of the possible problems and was also told that down time (nonworking time) was most difficult for these individuals. The job coach taught the workers how to obtain the next set of work materials once a task was finished, as a way of eliminating down time.
3. The employer rearranged the stockroom so that the workers could work in a relatively quiet area and would not be disrupted by equipment and boxes moving through.
4. If one of the workers started to become aggressive or destructive, the job coach would escort the individual outside until the behavior was under control and the individual responsive to verbal instructions. This quick, calm response on the part of the job coach allowed the co-workers to continue work without disruption.

Co-workers and supervisors quickly learned that although these workers might occasionally have serious behavior problems, the problems were handled quickly, safely, and without disruption to the worksite. The employer was pleased with the workers' productivity, and both workers were given a raise within their first year on the job. Additionally, the workers were featured in the company's newsletter.

Stealing Food

A young man with autism who had a history of snatching other people's food was employed as a book sorter at a public library. The following steps were taken, in addition to the individual's behavioral intervention plan:

1. The library staff was given an explanation of extinction, and the importance of not overreacting to the behavior should it occur.
2. Co-workers were encouraged not to leave food out.

A decrease in food stealing occurred, and co-workers and supervisors were very pleased with the individual's progress. The supervisor occasionally praised the individual for eating his own food and for leaving co-workers' foods on their desks. Occasionally, co-workers would buy the worker special snacks from the vending machine.

Pica

A young man with severe autism and a high frequency of pica was employed in the stockroom of a department store. Department store staff were enlisted to cooperate in behavior management and preventive procedures. The following steps were taken:

1. The job coach explained pica to co-workers, and the need to minimize social attention to the behavior.
2. The work area was frequently vacuumed—to eliminate items that might be eaten, such as scraps of paper.
3. The behavior program was explained to co-workers.

Co-workers were cooperative in ignoring the pica behavior. The worker was given a raise for his increased productivity. Although pica is no longer a problem, vigilance on the part of the job coach and cooperation by co-workers enabled this young man to maintain his job despite this aberrant behavior.

Property Destruction

Jeanette is employed at a manufacturing firm where she assembles electronic components. She has a history of property destruction and aggression that has been fairly successfully managed by a behavior management program. However, despite decreases in the frequency of these behaviors, Jeanette had sporadic incidents of yelling and property destruction at work. Approximately every 2 months she would throw a tool or destroy property in her work setting. Jeanette has maintained her job at the company for almost 7 years, despite the occasional occurrence of property destruction. The following steps have encouraged employer cooperation:

1. The supervisor attends Jeanette's annual meeting during which goals are set for the year. The supervisor can then provide input and can receive information on Jeanette's progress and plans.
2. The supervisor is contacted by the vocational program director whenever major changes occur in Jeanette's life (such as a residential counselor resigning), since major changes are often accompanied by property destruction or aggression.
3. Back-up assistance is made available to the job coach in the event of difficulties at work.
4. Should Jeanette become disruptive at work, she is escorted from the building until she is calm and responds to verbal instructions. The reason for escorting her from the work area is to prevent disruption to co-workers.

Jeanette has been able to maintain her employment, despite these periodic problems, for almost 7 years. The supervisor cooperates by calling the vocational director if back-up assistance is needed; assistance is provided immediately. The employer does suspend Jeanette from work for the day if property destruction or throwing of tools occurs. This suspension is not part of Jeanette's behavior program; rather, it is a consequence that is imposed by the employer.

Refusal to Work

Under ordinary circumstances, refusal to work would be a job-threatening behavior. Mitchell, a young man with autism, occasionally refuses to work. Although behavior management plans have resulted in some improvement in his willingness to attend work and perform his duties, the problem remains on an intermittent basis. The following steps were taken to assist Mitchell in maintaining employment despite his occasional refusal to work:

1. Mitchell's behavior was explained to the employer and co-workers prior to his commencing employment.
2. If Mitchell refuses to work, his job coach completes his work so that the employer does not suffer the consequences of his work refusal.
3. If Mitchell does not work, he does not get paid.

Following these procedures, Mitchell has been able to keep his job despite occasional instances of refusal to work. Continued attempts are made to motivate Mitchell to work through behavior management programs. In those situations, the work gets done with the assistance of the job coach, and Mitchell is able to remain employed.

Self-Injury

Elvis has a history of high rates of self-injurious behavior, including arm banging, head banging, self-kicking, self-scratching, and ear banging. Behavior management strategies resulted in dramatic decreases in self-injury, but not in elimination of the problem. Rates of self-injurious behaviors decreased from over 100 occurrences per day to approximately 15 occurrences. The following steps have allowed Elvis to remain employed at a manufacturing firm despite self-injurious behavior:

1. The self-injury was described to the employer before Elvis started work.
2. The job coach assists Elvis in doing the job.
3. An adaptation to the task was suggested by the employer that resulted in significant increases in Elvis's productivity.
4. Severe incidents of self-injury are managed by the job coach, without co-workers needing to assist or being disturbed in their routines.

The employer is pleased with Elvis's productivity, despite the fact that he is self-injurious. The employer has expressed interest in hiring two other workers with autism.

Tantrumming

Individuals with behavior problems that include crying, kicking, screaming, and work refusal can learn more acceptable ways of behaving at work. Although improvement can be realized through structured behavior management programs, it may not be possible to completely eliminate tantrumming.

Case 1 Anita's case is an example where dramatic improvement in tantrumming behavior was achieved, but a low incidence of the behavior remained. Anita occasionally sulks, cries, kicks over boxes, and refuses to work at her job in the warehouse of a toy supply company. The following measures were taken, along with consistent implementation of a behavior management program that stressed positive reinforcement for productivity:

1. Anita's tantrum behavior was described to the employer and co-workers.
2. Anita's intervention plan, including the rationale for positive reinforcement and extinction, was explained to the employer and co-workers.
3. If Anita begins to kick boxes, she is escorted outside by her job coach to prevent property destruction and disruption of the work setting. As soon as she becomes calm and responds to verbal instruction, she is redirected to her work area and her tasks.
4. If tantrumming is lengthy and severe, Anita and her counselor leave the worksite for the day. Although leaving the job is not the ideal response to this behavior, it is necessary in order to prevent disruption of the worksite.

The employer and co-workers have accepted Anita's occasional outbursts, confident that her job coach will handle the situation in such a way that disruption of the work environment does not occur. She has maintained her job for over a year, and is considered a valued employee because of her reliable attendance and her productivity.

Case 2 Arthur has occasional tantrums at the electronics firm where he works. His tantrums include yelling, cursing, and kicking. The frequency of this behavior markedly decreased over time, but the problem remained at a low, infrequent level. The same procedures outlined for Anita were implemented for Arthur at his worksite. Additionally, the supervisor meets with Arthur monthly to review the work rules with him. Arthur has been able to keep his job despite the presence of these tantrum behaviors. He has received several raises based on his high productivity. He participates in company picnics and other social events, and frequently goes out to lunch with co-workers.

Social Skills Deficit

Workers with autism may have social skills deficits that interfere with work. Such deficits can be ameliorated through intervention. However, problems can still occur. Procedures must be in place that dictate how such problems will be handled.

Case 1   Claude is a young man with autism whose supervision at work by a trained counselor was gradually eliminated because of his successful, independent adjustment to work. Although Claude could do his job well, his deficits in social skills were fairly obvious, and at times were considered job threatening because of his rudeness to co-workers. The following measures were taken to assist in Claude's continued success at work, despite occasional incidents of rudeness to co-workers:

1. Co-workers and the employer are aware that Claude has difficulty establishing and maintaining relationships with others. They have come to expect that occasionally Claude will display behavior that is generally considered rude or unacceptable at work.
2. When a problem arises, the supervisor contacts the supported employment agency, and a job coach will go in daily for several hours to teach, through role play and practice, more acceptable social behaviors, and to monitor the behavior. Once Claude has mastered the target social skills, the job coach stops coming on a daily basis, but remains available should a new problem arise.

Claude has been able to work independently for several years, after being supervised by a job coach for 4 years. The employer remains alert to new training needs, and support is provided as needed.

Case 2   Gilbert was an 18-year-old man with autism with fluent speech and no history of aggression toward others. Gilbert was hired by a retail store to do stocking on the floor. He worked with one other young man with autism under the supervision of a job coach. Customers would occasionally approach Gilbert and ask him for assistance. Gilbert was given social skills training to teach him to say, "Ask at the front." When the job coach was nearby, Gilbert would respond politely to customers; however, when the job coach was not in sight, Gilbert would respond with great exasperation. On one occasion he hit a customer who was persistent in asking him for assistance. The following measures were taken to assist Gilbert's adjustment to work:

1. Co-workers and the employer were aware that Gilbert has difficulty relating to people. They have come to expect that Gilbert will keep to himself.
2. Gilbert had been wearing a store uniform that attracted customers to him. The uniform was removed so Gilbert now dresses only in his street

clothes. Since he is not wearing the uniform, customers are less likely to ask him for assistance.

3. The job coach remains much closer to Gilbert while he works out on the floor of the store. Should a customer ask Gilbert for assistance, the job coach remains nearby, ready to intervene and provide assistance if necessary.

4. A behavior management plan was devised and implemented. The program includes a rating system that has an item stating, ''Kind to customers.'' Gilbert receives daily training on the meaning of this item, and daily positive reinforcement for compliance and daily social skills training on responding to customers.

Gilbert has maintained his employment despite his rude behavior toward customers. The manager considers him a valued employee and has sought to hire several more workers with autism. It is hoped that increased supervision will prevent further instances of aggression toward customers.

Case 3   George is a young man with autism who avoids eye contact with others. The employer complained to the job coach that he found this behavior to be rude and requested that George be taught to make eye contact with him.

Although lack of eye contact is not as serious as other behaviors that have been known to occur at work, in this case it was taken seriously because of the employer's complaint. The following steps were taken to assure George's continued employment, and also to try to meet the demands of the employers:

1. The job coach explained the nature of autism to the employer and the difficulties that people with autism often have in making eye contact.

2. A social skills training package was implemented to teach George to make eye contact.

Toileting Problems

Matthew was a young man with autism with no speech and with problems of occasional severe self-injury. He was employed in the stockroom of a major department store where he worked alongside a young woman with autism under the supervision of a female job coach.

Matthew had toileting problems that began to affect his adjustment to work. On several occasions, co-workers who used the bathroom following Matthew were overheard to comment about finding feces in the sink. Since the job coach was a female, she could not enter the men's room with Matthew to observe or supervise him. Matthew's job coach gave him a sponge and told him to wipe the sink after using the bathroom. He was given the sponge each time he went into the bathroom. After several months, a supervisor approached the job coach and said that feces had been found in the bathroom sink. The supervisor handled the situation with tact by stating that a cashier also used that bathroom, so it was not possible to say for sure whether the feces was from the cashier or from the worker with autism. Nonetheless, the supervisor wanted the job coach to be aware of the possibility. Despite the supervisor's tact, the problem was clear and steps would need to be implemented to teach Matthew toileting skills. The following measures were taken:

1. The job coach was a female and could not accompany Matthew to the bathroom. She also could not be replaced because the female worker with autism also needed assistance in the bathroom. Therefore, a male assistant job coach was temporarily assigned to the workplace.
2. The male assistant job coach had only one duty: to observe Matthew in the bathroom, determine what toileting skills he needed, then teach those skills to him.
3. Once several observations had been made, a task analysis of toileting skills that Matthew lacked was developed.
4. The male assistant job coach remained on duty for about 4 months. He accompanied Matthew on all his trips to the bathroom and taught Matthew how to toilet correctly.
5. After Matthew was able to toilet independently with good hygiene, the male job coach was removed from the worksite.

The temporary addition of a male job coach allowed Matthew to continue to work despite problems with toileting. Fortunately, Matthew was able to learn toileting skills and became independent in the bathroom.

Shrieking

Shrieking would typically be considered a job-threatening behavior, but despite careful implementation of behavior management plans, it might not be totally eliminated. Workers with shrieking behavior can successfully maintain employment under certain conditions. The case of Danielle, a stockroom worker in a department store, described in Chapter Nine, illustrates the significant reduction of shrieking following positive reinforcement for more appropriate behavior. However, shrieking still persisted, but at a reduced level. In order to assist Danielle with maintaining employment despite this behavior, the following steps were taken:

1. The job coach described the behavior to co-workers (shrieking, hand flapping) and explained Danielle's behavior program. The principles of positive reinforcement and extinction were explained, as well as their application to Danielle's shrieking.
2. Co-workers were encouraged to talk with Danielle on work breaks.

3. Co-workers were encouraged to comment to Danielle on her good work when she was working steadily and quietly and to ignore shrieking and flapping.

Danielle has been able to maintain her job despite her shrieking. She received a raise within her first year on the job, and co-workers have given her a birthday party and have included her in many activities at work.

SUMMARY

Problems associated with autism might seem overwhelming in nonsheltered settings. However, caregivers should expect that job-threatening behaviors or circumstances might develop. A support system with an optimistic problem solving process needs to be in place to efficiently solve these problems and maintain employment.

If the standard reaction to an apparently job-threatening problem is to terminate employment or change worksites, then in time one might find that there are no worksites left to move to. However, if a problem solving process exists that systematically identifies the problem, designs a solution, and implements solutions, then the individual might ultimately make an adjustment to the work setting. Failure to attempt to solve problems in the setting as they arise limits the employment options of the individual both in that setting and in the job market in general. The supported employment program must recognize that although behavior problems might persist, so can employability.

Epilogue

Helen is a 30-year-old women with autism. She was placed in a mental institution by her parents at 3 years of age. Helen was originally diagnosed as a schizophrenic with mental retardation, and given a poor prognosis. Helen is self-abusive. At times, she scratches herself and creates sores by picking her skin. Occasionally, she also has aggressive and destructive behavior. Helen will strike out at others by hitting, kicking, or pulling hair, and she destroys property, both her own and that of others. Clothes tearing is a particular problem. Helen's social skills are very poor, she has few if any meaningful relationships, and her conversations are considered bizarre.

Helen remained in the institution until age 23. A social worker noticed that she was not like the other patients and suspected that Helen was not mentally ill, but that perhaps had autism. Helen was diagnosed as having autism and was accepted into an integrated community program for persons with autism.

APARTMENT LIVING

Helen left the institution and moved into an apartment with two other adults with autism. This apartment was the first real home that Helen knew. She had her own address, room, and possessions for the first time since early childhood. A residential counselor is on duty at all times to assist and provide training in self-care, home-care, and recreational activities. The counselor provides the necessary supervision, as well as initial evaluation on a variety of skill areas, including home-care, self-care, language, social relationships, money skills, and travel skills.

LANDING A JOB

Upon acceptance into her new program, Helen was given a psychological evaluation and an initial vocational evaluation. The purpose was to determine her strengths, deficits, and interests. Shortly after entering the program, supported employment staff began to look for a job for Helen.

271

Despite the fact that Helen has autism, the vocational director was able to obtain employment for her by selling the employer on Helen's skills and strengths. Furthermore, since on-the-job training is provided by the job coach, and the employer only has to compensate Helen based on her productivity level, the employer could view Helen's employment as a low-risk situation. The employer was made aware of the benefits of hiring Helen: she would be reliable and would learn to perform the task accurately. The employer agreed to hire and pay Helen for her work, with the job coach providing the training and immediate supervision. Helen took a job at an electronics assembly firm working Monday through Friday, 40 hours per week.

The job coach's function is to train Helen on vocational skills and social skills necessary for job success. Helen is paid wages by the employer commensurate with her productivity rate. Since the employer agreed to hire both Helen and another person with autism, the job coach provides training and supervision to two workers at the job site.

INDIVIDUALIZED PROGRAM PLAN

Within 30 days of entering the program, an interdisciplinary team met to establish goals for Helen for the coming year. The team consisted of Helen, her residential counselor, her job coach, supervisors from the agency, her case manager, a psychologist, and a speech and language specialist. The product of this team meeting was a set of goals, entitled the Individualized Program Plan (IPP).

Residential Goals

Helen's target behaviors in her residence, based on initial evaluations done by residential counselors, the psychologist, and a speech and language specialist were as follows: brushing teeth and cooking frozen vegetables.

Vocational Goals

The interdisciplinary team also targeted vocational goals for Helen. The team choose the following work goals for Helen: asking the supervisor for assistance, performing the necessary assembly tasks, and increasing productivity.

Behavioral Goals

Helen needed to learn specific job, home-care, and self-care skills. However, her more pressing needs were in behavioral areas, so several behavioral goals were targeted. The self-disclosure goal was designated as a primary goal. Helen had a tendency to say, "Fine" when anyone attempted to elicit information from her, even if it seemed obvious from her behavior that things were in fact not fine at all. Helen might cry, tear her clothes, or scratch her skin, but when asked what was wrong, she would state, "Everything is fine." Helen clearly needed skills in revealing her problems. A self-disclosure goal was targeted that stated whenever Helen had a problem, she would tell her job coach or residential counselor.

Since Helen had a history of aggression, the team chose respecting others as a goal. Behaviorally defined, this goal meant keeping her hands and feet to herself. Helen's team also targeted correct use of property as a goal. Helen had a history of throwing objects, destroying property, and tearing her clothes. A final goal involved maintaining her skin in a healthy manner. This goal referred to Helen's problem of scratching and picking at her skin, often leaving sores that required medical attention.

Note that Helen's behavior problems (reluctance to discuss problems, aggression, property destruction, and self-scratching) were translated into positive goal statements such as self-disclosure and maintaining skin in a healthy manner. The positive goals provide a basis for an intervention plan that can teach her alternatives to her problem behaviors.

Written Training Plans

The goals chosen were considered essential for her adjustment to her new home and job. These goals were considered priority one goals and as such, each goal had a written training plan. Training plans were designed specifically for Helen to meet her chosen goals. Furthermore, data were taken, on a schedule determined by the team, on Helen's performance on each goal.

Additional Activities

In addition to determining priority one goals, the team also chose activities that Helen would participate in during the year. These activities included travel training on public transportation, attending church, eating in restaurants, shopping, and participating in recreational and leisure activities both in her home and out of the residence. The team agreed that Helen would receive instruction in home-care and self-care skills other than the ones designated as priority one, the difference being that staff would not take data on progress.

In conclusion, the team agreed that Helen would be taught to be a full participant in the chores needed to maintain herself and her home and to hold a job in an integrated nonsheltered setting. Since Helen was a member of the team, she was able to contribute to her own plan, and state her own preferences for leisure and recreational activities.

CHOOSING INTERVENTION STRATEGIES

Once the goals were designated, it was necessary to determine effective training/intervention strategies. These strategies were designed by professionals working in cooperation with team members. Direct care staff, including residential counselors and job coaches, were full participants in plan development. The strategy for each goal follows.

Brushing Teeth

A toothbrushing training strategy was used to teach Helen to brush her teeth. After Helen was able to carry out the steps following initial modeling, demonstration, and physical assistance, the staff reverted to a graduated schedule of prompts to encourage independence.

Cooking Frozen Vegetables

Helen was taught to cook frozen vegetables according to the same instructional strategy used for brushing teeth. A task analysis was constructed that listed the steps involved in cooking frozen vegetables. Helen was given demonstrations and explanations for each of the steps, then staff reverted to the graduated schedule of prompts to encourage independence.

Asking For Assistance

In order to become integrated into her work environment, Helen needed to learn to ask for assistance. The asking for assistance program (Chapter Seven) was implemented on a daily basis. Training focused on asking for assistance when having difficulty with a task or when a tool was broken. It was hoped that this skill would help reduce Helen's self-scratching, since she was known to self-scratch when she was having difficulty with a task or when a tool was broken.

Specifying Vocational Tasks

Tasks analyses were constructed, and Helen was given ample demonstration and physical guidance where necessary.

Increasing Productivity

Once Helen could independently perform the vocational tasks, a production program was implemented as described Chapter Five, Case 1. She was given praise and feedback for working quickly, and a record was kept of her productivity. Increases in productivity were rewarded with praise from her counselor. Additionally, since her wages were based on productivity, as her productivity increased, so did her earnings.

Self-Disclosing

Helen seemed most likely to self-scratch, become aggressive, or destroy property when she was having some type of difficulty dealing with her environment. Teaching her to self-disclose about her difficulties would enable her to obtain assistance, and learn effective ways of handling those difficulties. These more effective responses would hopefully decrease the likelihood of self-scratching. The self-disclosure program described in Chapter Seven was chosen to help Helen learn to make truthful self-disclosures to her counselors. This program was implemented in her residence as well as at her job site.

Respecting Others and Property

Helen was put on a daily report card system. Each morning, each afternoon, and each evening she received checks for respecting others and respecting property. These terms were behaviorally defined so that she knew exactly what they meant. After 2 years of counselor ratings, Helen began rating herself.

Maintaining Skin in a Healthy Manner

It was recognized that gains in self-disclosure would not necessarily preclude all self-scratching. In order to teach Helen to interrupt the scratching behavior herself, stop training (described in Chapter Seven) was implemented to teach her to stop herself from scratching. Additionally, Helen's job coach and residential counselors complemented her several times a day if her skin was clear, and frequently gave her hand lotion to rub on her clear skin.

INDIVIDUAL THERAPY

Helen left the institution with severe social problems and had extreme difficulty relating to others. She was also very fearful of people and had a great deal of trouble relating to men. Some of her difficulties went beyond autism, and apparently stemmed from abuse toward her by others. Therefore, individual counseling by a social worker knowledgeable about autism was instituted. Many of the benefits described in Chapter Thirteen on individual psychological therapy applied to Helen.

TRAINING HELEN'S COUNSELORS

Helen's residential counselors and job coach were trained to implement each of Helen's programs. First, they were given specific verbal and written instructions on these programs. The trainer went over the written programs, and the procedures were role played. Then, the trainer went to the home and job sites and demonstrated for staff. Staff then implemented the procedures under supervision to ensure accuracy. Finally, staff implemented the programs at both home and work. The staff's supervisors periodically rated their performance to ensure continued compliance with the written program.

HELEN'S DAY

The following schedule provides an overview of how the training strategies were integrated into Helen's day:

7:00 A.M. Wake up.

7:20 Counselor runs brushing teeth program with Helen as she brushes her teeth.

7:30 Helen prepares for work, eats breakfast.

8:00 Clear skin checks are done in accordance with self-control program.

8:15 Helen leaves for work.

9:00 Helen arrives at work, and asking for assistance training program is run.

9:15 Helen begins work. Any necessary skill training programs are run, as well as the productivity program. As Helen works she will occasionally be praised for working quickly, and systematic feedback will be given throughout the day.

10:00 Helen takes a scheduled break.

10:15 Helen returns to work.

12:00 P.M. Helen has lunch with co-workers in lunch room. Ratings are done on behavioral checklist.

12:45 Self-disclosure training program is run.

12:55 Helen returns to work.

4:45 Ratings are done on behavioral checklist.

5:00 Helen leaves work. She is taken to the bank by her job coach and assisted with making a deposit. She then takes the public bus home.

6:00 Helen arrives home. She assists in preparing dinner and the cooking frozen vegetables program is run.

6:30 Helen, her housemates, and the counselor eat dinner.

7:15 Dinner is over and Helen assists in cleanup.

7:30 Helen, her housemates, and her counselor go out for ice cream for dessert. They also do some personal shopping.

8:30 Helen returns home. The self-disclosure program is run.

9:15 The clear skin check is done as designated by self-control program.

9:30 Helen makes her lunch for the next day, prepares her clothes for the next day, and prepares for bed. Ratings are done on behavioral checklist.

10:00 Brushing teeth program is run with Helen as she brushes her teeth before bed.

Note: Between 8:30 P.M. and 10:00 P.M. when not engaged in scheduled activities, Helen is free to watch television, look at magazines, or participate in other leisure activities around her apartment.

EVALUATING PROGRESS

The data from Helen's programs were evaluated systematically to determine the effectiveness of the programs. Data were taken daily, or in some cases weekly, by her counselors, and were summarized on graphs. Monthly progress reports were produced by both the residential counselor and the vocational counselor.

OUTCOME

Helen made progress on all goals designated on her Individual Program Plan. In cases where she met her goals, such as brushing teeth, cooking frozen vegetables, and specific vocational tasks, instruction could be terminated and new goals designated and trained.

Progress was made on behavioral goals. Helen became willing to tell counselors when she had difficulty or when something bothered her, and the counselors could then assist her in finding a solution. Self-scratching markedly diminished. Prior to intervention, she continually had sores on her hands. During the course of the intervention plan, Helen would go almost 2 months with no new marks. Since self-scratching continued to occur from time to time, her team decided not to attempt to fade the program, but to leave it in effect. Self-disclosure training also remains in effect because several attempts to fade the program resulted in Helen reverting back to her old response of, "Everything's fine," when in fact things were not fine. Helen continues to see her therapist weekly. Her therapist has remained a stable force in her life, given the continual turnover of group home staff.

At work, Helen achieved work rates commensurate with the rates achieved by nonhandicapped co-workers. She has received several raises over the years. She continues to require training and supervision by a job coach, but this supervision has been gradually decreased. Helen is now able to ride the bus alone to work and is able to go shopping without supervision. She goes to restaurants, banks, movies, and participates in recreational activities outside her home. Although she still lives in a group home with a counselor in attendance, she is able to be unsupervised up to 5 hours per day.

INDEX

Assistance—*continued*
self-management and, 105–108
verbalizations and, 151–152
Attention
as purpose of destructive
behaviors, 216–217
as purpose of self-injury, 195
as purpose of self-stimulation,
130–131
as purpose of verbalizations, 151
Authority figures, speaking with, 88
Autism
causes of, 6–7
characteristics of, 1–6
ability to perform special
skills, 6
abnormal sensory responses,
4–5
behavior problems, 5–6
dependence on routine, 4
impairment in communication,
2–3
impairment in social
relationships, 2
mental retardation and learning
disabilities, 6
perseveration on interests and
activities, 3–4
incidence of, 6
Avoidance response, punishment
and, 22

Behavior(s)
antecedents to, *see* Antecedents
consequences of, 36, 44–45
desirable, purpose of, 45
destructive, *see* Destructive
behaviors
duration of, 38
environmental opportunities for,
ratio of responses to, 38–40
extinction of, *see* Extinction

purpose of, 31
target, 30–31, 33
verbal, 149–150
Behavior change, strategies for,
52–61
choice making, 56
combinations of, 61
extinction, 60–61
instructional training, 54
physical setting and, 53
picture schedules, 55
positive reinforcement, 56–60
provision of goal of behavior,
53–54
scheduling, 54–55
self-management procedures, 60
social skills training, 54
supervision, 52–53
written schedules, 55
see also Behavior management
strategies; *specific behaviors*
Behavior management consultation,
236–237
Behavior management principles
application to art and music
therapy, 242
application to psychotherapy,
240–241
Behavior management strategies,
13–26
behavior modification, early
history of, 14–16
effectiveness of, 31–32
employment and, 261
functional analysis and, 16–19
occupational therapy coordination
with, 247–248
punishment, 19–26
early studies of, 19–20
history with autism of, 20–21
justifications for, 21
problems with, 21–26
varieties of punishers and, 20

Discontent, signs of, 125
Discrimination training,
    verbalizations and, 155, 165
Disruptive behavior, in
    communication, 3
    see also Verbalizations,
    inappropriate
DRH schedule, 57
    vocational skills and, 78
Drugs, psychiatric therapy and,
    242–243
*DSM-IIIR (Diagnostic and
    Statistical Manual of Mental
    Disorders-III* [Revised]), 1, 6
Durational events, 37
Duration measurements, in
    behavioral assessment, 38

Educational services, 8
    history of, 7
Education and training
    behavior change and, 54
    behavior problems and, 5–6
    communication and, 3
    of job coaches, 70, 261, 275
    mental retardation/learning
        disabilities and, 6
    perseverations and, 4
    routine versus change and, 4
    sensory patterns and, 5
    social functioning and, 2
    of staff, 275
        for intervention plan, 63–64
    see also specific areas, e.g.,
        Social skills development
Electric shock, 20
Emergency procedures
    for aggression management,
        179–180
    psychiatric, 243
Emotional responses to punishment,
    22

Employer, involvement of, 261
Employment, 255–269, 271–272
    aggression and, 261–262
    appropriate, occupational therapy
        and, 246
    despite behavior problems, 256,
        257–259
    food stealing and, 262–263
    job matching and, 260
    job site adaptations and, 247
    pica and, 263
    property destruction and,
        263–264
    refusal to work and, 264
    self-injury and, 264–265
    shrieking and, 268–269
    social skills deficit and, 266–267
    supervision and, 256
    tantrums and, 265
    toileting problems and, 267–268
    see also Co-workers; Supported
        employment; Vocational
        entries
Employment status, in behavioral
    assessment, 42
Environment
    aggression and, 173–174
    behavior change and, 53
Environmental enrichment, self-
    stimulation and, 130
Environmental opportunity,
    behaviors dependent on,
    38–40
    inappropriate verbalizations, 150
Escape
    as purpose of destructive
        behaviors, 217
    as purpose of self-injury, 195
    as purpose of self-stimulation,
        130
    as purpose of verbalizations, 151
    as response to punishment, 22
Etiology of autism, 6–7